*New York à la Carte*

# New York à la Carte

BY

## Jay Jacobs

## Drawings by Dora

McGraw-Hill Book Company

NEW YORK • ST. LOUIS • SAN FRANCISCO
DÜSSELDORF • MEXICO • TORONTO

## Permissions and Acknowledgments

Recipes on pages 207–210 were adapted by permission from *The Chinese Menu Cookbook*, by Joanne Hush and Peter Wong, © copyright 1976 by Joanne Hush and Peter Wong; Holt, Rinehart and Winston, New York, 1976.

Recipes on pages 314–317 were adapted by permission from *Lüchow's German Cookbook*, by Jan Mitchell, © copyright 1952 by Jan Mitchell; Doubleday and Co., Garden City, New York, and from *Lüchow's German Festival Cookbook*, by Gene and Fran Schoor, © copyright 1976 by Gene and Fran Schoor; Doubleday and Co., Garden City, New York, 1976.

Recipes on pages 305–309 were adapted by permission from *The Grand Central Oyster Bar & Restaurant Seafood Cookbook*, by Jerome Brody, © 1977 by Jerome Brody; Crown Publishers, Inc., New York, 1977.

Recipes on pages 290–293 were adapted by permission from *"21": The Life and Times of New York's Favorite Club*, by Marilyn Kator, © 1975 by the "21" Club; The Viking Press, New York, 1975.

1 2 3 4 5 6 7 8 9 0   DO DO   7 8 3 2 1 0 9 8

Library of Congress Cataloging in Publication Data

Jacobs, Jay.
New York à la carte.
Bibliography
Includes index.
1.  New York (City)—Restaurants.   2.  Cookery,
International.      I.  Title.
TX909.J33      647'.95747'1      78-6515
ISBN 0-07-032151-5

*For Nancy*

**WHO PLUCKS THE OLIVES**
**FROM MY MARTINIS**
**AND EATS THEM**

# Contents

# Hors d'Oeuvre

*T*he life of a restaurant critic can't be said to be fraught with peril but it has its minor occupational hazards. Sauces and gravies spangle the necktie, and an offended waiter's umbrage may easily dissolve the marrow in one's bones. The threat of gout—or, worse, perceptible flatulence—lurks within every *cassoulet* and *confit d'oie,* and even the digestive system of a billy goat is no guarantee against the occasional disruption of one's plumbing. Add to this the critic's gnawing awareness that his readers stand to lose their time, money, and tempers should his judgment be faulty, and it can be seen that his life is no bed of roses.

Not much, it isn't.

For some years now, I have covered New York restaurants for a national magazine devoted to the care and feeding of the most pampered percentile of the species *Homo sapiens americanus.* The odd bout of dyspepsia notwithstanding, the gig has been an enviable one, and I can well understand the incredulous cries of casual acquaintances who, on learning that I eke out my daily bread by gorging on truffled *foie gras,* exclaim, "Don't tell me you're *paid* to live it up like that!" I am indeed, but that doesn't make the job any less a labor of love.

My love affair with the restaurants of New York City began half a lifetime ago, when, fresh out of uniform and still very wet behind the ears, I wandered into a scruffy Eighth Avenue bar and was latched onto by a well-endowed and apparently unattached young woman. After a very brief conversation (which, as I remember it, had to do neither with Shelley nor Schopenhauer), the lady let it be known that she'd had enough of slumming for one evening. If I craved more of her company, she added, I could escort her to a higher-class joint around the corner. I followed her to a little French bistro on Fifty-first Street, dispersed half my severance pay for the privilege of looking on while she marinated herself in Chivas Regal, and then was abruptly informed that she had urgent business elsewhere but would meet me at the same restaurant the next night.

Needless to say, my inamorata didn't show, and, without the distractions of the previous evening, I was able to have a leisurely look at my surroundings. I liked what I saw. So much so that I remained in more or less permanent residence for the next half-dozen years.

In those days Tout Va Bien—the restaurant in question and the curriculum vitae for the prime of my life—seemed to me the most worldly place imaginable. Owned by a marvelously earthy Marseillaise, a stout, putty-complexioned woman of middle years who was reputed to have been a great beauty in her day and was known to all and sundry simply as Irès, it attracted a wildly disparate gang of transients and regulars. French and Algerian whores (and one from Pottstown, Pennsylvania) rubbed shoulders—at least, when nothing else was doing—with ranking diplomats. Import-export nabobs drowned their doxies in champagne at discreetly located tables, while postmen from New Jersey and sailors from Toulon drank beer at the bar. Pacifistic European middleweights, purple-eyed and fat-lipped from lopsided wars at the then-nearby Madison Square Garden, brooded over Perrier or *pastis* on man's inhumanity to man before limping off to their hotel rooms. A crazed French architect with the catfish mustachios and impenetrable enunciation of a Salvador Dalí would concuss himself nightly on red wine and then hold forth, interminably and hilariously, on abstruse theories of staircase design, seduction, and life in general. Small- and big-time hoodlums came in occasionally for good homely Provençal cooking, as did Vivien Leigh, James Baldwin, Charles Addams, and Marcel Cerdan; rodeo performers and bicycle racers, soccer players and pool hustlers, an Irish pharmacist from the Bronx, and a self-styled philologist from Andorra.

Cheap as a full dinner was in those days, I was rarely able to afford one but seldom went hungry. A platter of *hors d'oeuvre variés*—which, if memory serves, cost seventy-five cents—made an adequate meal in itself, and, since it consisted in large part of whatever kitchen scraps and leftovers came to hand, was never quite the same on any two nights. Moreover, Irès, giving the lie (as most Provençaux do) to generalizations about Gallic parsimony, often would take it into her head to lock the front door once the transient customers had cleared out, announce that all further guzzling was on the house, and proceed to cook up a huge pot of spaghetti. At other times, when even the hors d'oeuvres were more than I could afford, I'd be hustled off to the kitchen once the chef had called it a night, with instructions—despite my transparent protestations that I wasn't really hungry—to make a meal of whatever I found there.

In flush moments I'd sit down with the paying customers to a real tuck-in: *escargots de bourgogne,* onion soup, *coq au vin*—what I then considered to be the works—and, if I had a woman in tow, a salad from which the usual overdose of garlic ("the vanilla of Provence") tactfully was omitted. But it was at those times when I was invited—commanded, I should say—to forage for myself in the kitchen that I was happiest at the restaurant. Then I could cut myself a thick slab of country-style pâté, heat up some leftover soup on the first professional range I'd ever seen, or even try to make myself an omelet.

There is an ineffable odor about restaurant kitchens when they have been closed down for the night, a muted commingling of disparate aromas—iced fish, refrigerated meats, cold sauces, congealed stews; *cornichons,* radishes, chilled white beans and beets and salami; hard-boiled eggs, anchovies, sardines, vestigial traces of garlic and oil, cut parsley (in one of the most poignant lines he ever wrote, Dylan Thomas has one of his drowned sailors ask, "What's the smell of parsley?"). It was on this heady stuff, spiced with the slightly clandestine nature of my culinary efforts, that I really fed.

All that was a long time ago, and I've since been made privy to the inner workings of hundreds of restaurants, growing, I hope, a bit less naïve in the process and perhaps a bit more understanding of the confraternity of dedicated professionals who are at pains to see to it that New York, battered as it may be, remains the greatest all-around restaurant town on the planet.

The purpose of this book is to share with its readers the richly rewarding experience of dining out in New York with some frequency. Insofar as was possible in the circumstances, I've tried to make that experience apprehensible in its totality. For some, the experience will be retrospective; for others, anticipatory. For what I hope will be a very few, it will be purely vicarious; an opportunity not otherwise available to spend an occasional night on the town at home, so to speak. As I see it, the book represents a three-way collaboration. I've tried to set the stage, the city's great chefs have written the script, and the acting out of our little fantasy is up to you, the reader.

It was a precept of the showman Mike Todd that the audience never be permitted to see what goes on backstage. Perhaps it's a valid theatrical theory, but I've always believed that the appreciation of most experiences deepens with one's understanding of them. Several sections of this book are devoted to aspects of restaurant and culinary history and restaurant operation with which the casual diner-out may not be familiar. Some years ago a reader of my magazine reviews wrote to ask why a piece of sole that might have cost him ninety-five cents at a fishmonger's cost him ten times that much in one of the city's better restaurants. This book is in part a direct outgrowth of his question.

In response to that question I've examined three restaurants— each representative of one of the three cuisines that have had the greatest impact on international gastronomy—in considerably more detail than the others I have chosen for inclusion in the book. Although each of the three is an outstanding example of its kind, my choices were determined by practical, not qualitative, considerations, not least of which were the availability of physical layouts that enabled me to hang about busy kitchens for extended periods of time without getting hopelessly underfoot.

The conversational icebreaker "What do you do?" is a gambit I tend to decline whenever I can get away with it. My usual response is calculatedly evasive, if not downright perjurious. It's not that I'm particularly ashamed of my calling; it's just that I've learned that a direct answer unfailingly will elicit two further questions for which I really have no answers: "Which is the best restaurant in the city?" and "All right then, which restaurant do *you* like best?" The best or one's favorite *when,* and for what purpose? One doesn't dance the hustle to Debussy or ride a skateboard to a funeral. One can't find *sushi* at Lutèce or *foie gras* at Saito. One doesn't compare apples and oranges.

One of the great things about New York is the diversity of its restaurants, the almost limitlessly nuanced range of options available at every price level and every stratum of gastronomic pretension. If one is in the mood to honor the traditions of Carême and Escoffier, superlative temples of *haute cuisine* can be found by the dozen. A simple little bistro where good bourgeois cooking and casual camaraderie can be found? There are scores of them around town. If nothing suits your mood of the moment as much as an expertly prepared black bean soup or *paella a la valenciana,* at least half a dozen places turn out superior versions of both dishes. Chinese food? First decide whether it's Cantonese, Mandarin, Shanghai, Pekingese, Hunanese, or Szechwanese food you want, and in what sort of surroundings you want to enjoy it, and then choose from among hundreds of possibilities. *La cucina Italiana?* After you've figured out which type of *cucina Italiana* you prefer for the nonce—Neapolitan, Sicilian, Tuscan, Lombard, Roman, Abruzzese, or whatever—*then* try to narrow your choice of restaurants down to one.

Indian, Japanese, Thai, or Filipino food? Hungarian, Czech, Greek, Yugoslav, Mexican, Brazilian, Cuban, Puerto Rican? Lebanese, Syrian, Turkish, Persian, English, Irish? Jamaican food? Soul food?—you name it. It's all there. Do you want to dine in the splendorous surroundings of the Four Seasons or Windows on the World? Blow a king's ransom at the Palace? Rub elbows with the internationally celebrated at P. J. Clarke's or Sardi's or "21," or find a discreet corner table at some obscure little hideaway? Whatever it is, you've got it.

The restaurants represented in this book are *all* favorites of mine. Many of them generally are considered to rank with the world's finest and some are relatively little known—informal establishments that I frequent when the delights of *haute cuisine,* and all its attendant ceremony and expense, begin to pall. In all cases they are superior restaurants of their particular genres, and I hope they will become your favorites at home as they have become mine *in situ.*

Here, then, is dining out in New York. Enjoy your dinner!

—J. J.

## PART ONE

# A Scrupulous Attention to Dinner

*T*he cuisines of nations are shaped by necessity, not choice; not by aesthetic preference, but early adaptation to contingencies over which men have little or no control. Indigenous cultural groups don't eat what they like. Rather, they like what they eat. And once they have learned to like it, they don't much like what other people eat. Even within national boundaries, regional culinary chauvinism persists. If the southern French prefer oil to butter and their northern countrymen butter to oil, it's because neither group had much choice in the matter to begin with. The husbandry of dairy cattle would have been as difficult a business under the Provençal sun as the cultivation of olives would have been in Normandy.

From classical times onward, the cuisines of the great Western metropolises, unlike those of larger cultural entities, have been shaped in large part by a combination of acculturation and aesthetic preference. Nowhere else on earth has this been truer than in New York, a city populated since its founding by non-indigenous peoples. For the first couple of centuries of the city's existence—a time when it produced most of its own food—its citizens didn't particularly like what they ate. Since then, they have tended increasingly to eat what they like. Today the New Yorker pampers the most eclectic belly in the known universe. However exotic the cuisine he fancies at a particular moment may be, some restaurateur is there to feed it to him.

It wasn't ever thus.

It was Jean-Anthelme Brillat-Savarin, sometime musician, sometime magistrate, and lifelong gastronome, who devised perhaps the earliest and certainly most durable definition of a restaurateur. "A restaurateur," he wrote in *La Physiologie du goût,* "is a person whose trade consists in offering to the public an ever-ready feast, the dishes of which are served in separate portions, at fixed prices, at the request of each consumer."

By Brillat-Savarin's definition—and by general consent—the first American restaurateurs of any consequence were a pair of Swiss-born brothers, John and Peter Delmonico (né Giovanni and Pietro Del-Monico), a sailor-turned-wineseller and a pastry cook, respectively. In 1827, the year after Brillat-Savarin's death, they launched a dynasty and a revolution by opening a modest café in lower Manhattan. Their unpromising venture, housed in a single small room and furnished with half a dozen plain deal tables, was to play a role in the history of American gastronomy roughly comparable to that played by the abbey church of St. Denis in the history of Gothic architecture.

It is difficult today, when a restaurant in West Lafayette, Indiana, advertises *cailles aux cognac* as a house specialty and another in Hancock, Maine, prides itself on its *brandade de morue* and *lapin aux pruneaux,* to grasp the sorry state of cookery that obtained in pre-Delmonican America or to assess the magnitude of the Delmonican impact, not only on nineteenth-century gastronomy but all subsequent *gourmandise* in the United States. Of that impact, a journalist of the 1880s, hardly overstating his case, wrote:

> Many persons who had been in the habit of regarding their dinners as a mere means of sustaining nature, and a scrupulous attention to dinner as unworthy of an earnest mind, learned for the first time at Delmonico's that dinner was not merely an ingestion,

but an observance. . . . When we compare the commensalities of our country before the Delmonico period . . . with our condition in respect of dinner now, and think how large a share of the difference is due to Delmonico's, we shall not think it extravagant to call Delmonico's an agency of civilization.

To appreciate the magnitude of the revolution wrought by that particular agency of civilization, it should be remembered that although the term "restaurant" was coined in 1765 (by the grandiloquent keeper of a shabby Paris soup kitchen), no restaurant worth the name existed—even in Paris, let alone New York—until around 1782, when the Grande Taverne de Londres was opened in rue de Richelieu by an erstwhile courtier named Beauvilliers, who, according to Brillat-Savarin, was the first "to combine an elegant dining room, smart waiters, and a choice cellar with superior cooking."

With or without restaurants, the French had a tradition of good eating that went back at least as far as the arrival in their midst of Catherine de Médicis. The Americans had nothing of the sort. Before the advent of the Delmonicos, a population with access to a cornucopia of raw materials undreamed of elsewhere on earth fed itself wretchedly, ignoring most vegetables and subsisting on a monotonous cuisine that led James Fenimore Cooper, after educating his palate during an extended sojourn in Europe, to call his countrymen "the grossest feeders of any civilized nation known." Their victuals, he added dyspeptically, were "heavy, coarse, and indigestible, taken in the least artificial [i.e. artful] forms that cookery will allow." (Cooper's contemporary, Captain Frederick Marryat, who toured the United States in 1837–38, begged to differ, characterizing the American cuisine somewhat ambiguously as being "in ratio with the degree and refinement of the population," but concluding that good cooking was to be found in the homes of the principal cities. Marryat's credentials as a *bec fin* are open to question, however; the man was nurtured on an English cuisine described by one of his more enlightened compatriots, Sydney Smith, as nothing much more than "barbarian Stonehenge masses of meat.")

A somewhat earlier and perhaps better qualified observer

than either novelist was the Frenchman Constantin François Chasseboeuf, Comte de Volney. After sampling turn-of-the-century American fare, Volney delivered himself of these animadversions in 1803:

> I will venture to say that if a prize were proposed for the scheme of a regimen most calculated to injure the stomach, the teeth, and the health in general, no better could be invented than that of the Americans. . . . At dinner they have boiled pastes under the name of puddings, and the fattest are deemed the most delicious . . . their turnips and potatoes swim in hog's lard, butter or fat; under the name of pie or pumpkin, their pastry is nothing but a greasy paste, never sufficiently baked.' . . . As Chastellux says, the whole day passes in heaping indigestions on one another. . . .

Curiously, the otherwise demanding Brillat-Savarin, who had waited out much of the Terror in New York, took a far less severe view of the American table than his countryman Volney. It might be noted, however, that almost any combination of food and pretty women had a catnip effect on the man, and that the single American meal he describes in any detail was prepared and served by a Connecticut farmer's "four buxom daughters"— a quartet of charmers on whom he lavishes considerably more description than he does on the viands and who may have thrown his critical faculties slightly out of whack.

As one historian of Delmonican Manhattan, Robert Shaplen, wrote in *The New Yorker* some years ago, "The table around which the Dutch settlers of the city practiced the commensality was in the home, and the food planked down on it had but one purpose: to satisfy hunger. Meals were as flat as they were functional—three of them a day, washed down with cold water. As a rule, fish, fowl, and roasts were thoroughly overdone, and the idea of improving them with sauces seldom crossed a *huisvrouw's* mind; gravy was for fops. Fruits and vegetables were so little in demand that the local farmers scarcely bothered to grow them."

Conditions hardly improved with the onset of British rule in 1664, although, as Shaplen goes on to say, the British "managed, bit by bit, to cut loose from the old Dutch custom of eating exclusively at home." The coffeehouse, which had made its first appearance in England in 1650, became a popular fixture in New York soon after the British take-over. Another eighty-odd years were to pass, however, before the city was to be graced by anything even remotely resembling a true restaurant. This—hardly a gastronomic watershed—took the form of the "ordinary" introduced by a tavernkeeper named Thomas Lepper.

The ordinary, an institution that had originated in Jacobean England, was a fixed meal, served at a fixed hour for a fixed price. By all accounts, its sole virtue was that it enabled harried businessmen and hungry workers to ingest enough sustenance to get them through an afternoon's work without having to go home for the midday meal.

The quantities of food demolished at the traditional ordinary never failed to astonish foreigners. The quality was something else again, and any resemblance between feeding at a tavern, an eating house, or a hotel and dining in a modern restaurant would be superficial in the extreme. Even as late as 1834, seven years after the opening of Delmonico's, an English visitor, Robert Burford, remarked that in a typical hotel public room "fifty to one hundred persons sit down at the same time. A vast number of dishes covers the table, and the dispatch with which they are cleaned is almost incredible. From five to ten minutes for breakfast [i.e., for a meal that might include griddle cakes, sausages, ham, eggs, fish, chicken, beefsteak, roast or pickled pork, oysters, and a complete assortment of breads], fifteen to twenty for dinner [the main, midday meal] and ten for supper is usually sufficient. Each person, as soon as satisfied, leaves the table without regard to his neighbors; no social conversation follows."

Clearly, New Yorkers of the first third of the nineteenth century, like the Dutch settlers two centuries before them, were people who viewed eating much as they did any other bodily function—as a necessary evil to be dispensed with as briefly, as privately, and with as little overt relish as circumstances permitted.

Such, by and large, was the state of gastronomy in New York when the Delmonicos opened for business. A few tavernkeepers and hoteliers, to be sure, served meals a cut or two above the general run and in more gracious surroundings than might be found at the average ordinary. Samuel Fraunces (né Francis), for one, the proprietor of the Queen's Head at Broad and Pearl streets, was West Indian–born mulatto whose fierce loyalty to the Revolutionary cause had impelled the Redcoats to drop one of their first artillery rounds "thru the roof of Black Sam." Black Sam (whose skin, if one contemporaneous portraitist can be credited, was hardly darker than his powdered wig) prided himself on the quality of his food but was better known in his time for the fine Madeiras he stocked. Today he is remembered for neither, of course, but for the tavern where George Washington bade farewell to his officers. (Although much restored, Fraunces Tavern still exists and is the city's oldest restaurant.) Fraunces and one or two others notwithstanding, New Yorkers were not eating very high off the hog in 1826.

In his book *Delmonico's: A Century of Splendor,* Lately Thomas quotes the nineteenth-century historian James Ford Rhodes. "Any person who considers the difference between the cooking and service of a dinner at a hotel or restaurant before the Civil War and now," Rhodes wrote, "will appreciate what a practical apostle of health and decent living has been Delmonico, who deserves canonization in the American calendar." Rhodes, it might be noted, was not a mere culinary historian descrying an Everest among the molehills of a narrowly specialized interest, but was engaged in a serious study of what he took to be the movers, shakers, and pivotal events of the period 1850–77. The Delmonico to whom he referred was Lorenzo, nephew of John and Peter and ruler of the Delmonico dynasty during the years of its finest flowering. Had Rhodes been writing a generation earlier, he might well have had the same to say of Lorenzo's uncle John, the dynasty's founder and, all things considered, perhaps the most farsighted restaurateur who ever lived.

John Delmonico, the youngest of Siro and Giuseppa Del-Monico's three sons, was born in the farming village of Mairengo in the southern, Italianate Swiss canton of Ticino in 1788, but grew up speaking French (family tradition had it that the Del-

Monicos originally were Monegasque and related to Monaco's ruling Grimaldis). Although the landlocked Swiss haven't been notable producers of sailors, John went to sea and had risen to the command of a three-masted schooner, *Fidelity,* by the age of thirty, steering a triangular course from Havana to Cadiz and thence to New York and successively trading Yankee lumber for tobacco, tobacco for wine, and wine for cash at his three ports of call. Just why he eventually abandoned the maritime life is as unclear as why he went to sea in the first place. Whatever the reason, he had settled in New York by around 1824 and set up as a bulk importer of French and Spanish wines, which he bottled and sold at retail from a small shop near the Battery.

At that time the city, fed by highly navigable inland waterways, had already assumed a position of ascendancy over the ports of Boston and Philadelphia. Then, with the opening of the Erie Canal in 1825, it suddenly gained trade access to the American heartland and, with it, the potential for seemingly limitless economic growth. The opportunities for his own economic growth weren't lost on the perspicacious ex-sailor. He closed his wine shop the following year, returned to Switzerland, and persuaded his brother Peter, by then a prosperous forty-three-year-old confectioner in Berne, to pull up stakes and resettle in New York. Early in 1827 the brothers opened a wine and pastry shop at 23 William Street, near the heart of the city's burgeoning business district. Whether by accident or design, the hyphen was dropped from their surname when their signboard went up over the door.

New York was then a community of 160,000 inhabitants, the vast majority of whom were clustered together on a small stretch of lower Manhattan that extended from Battery Park, at the island's southernmost tip, only as far north as what is now City Hall Park—an area about six city blocks long and two-thirds as wide. While there was no dearth of grogshops (their estimated number works out to something like one per 120 inhabitants of all ages and both sexes) and taverns, there was little to appeal to a sizable contingent of expatriated Europeans; export agents for the most part, who were ill at ease amidst the hurly-burly and questionable company of the city's primitive eating houses and who would have much preferred the gentler pace, the more palatable fare, and the more civilized atmosphere they had known in the coffeehouses and cafés that had been fixtures in their homelands since the seventeenth century. It was these deracinated foreigners who at first made up the bulk of the Delmonicos' clientele. Their lead was soon followed by native sons, probably drawn to the little shop on William Street less by the prospect of bibbing fine wines or nibbling on Frenchified dainties than by the fast-spreading word that a woman—Peter's wife, as it happened—actually presided at the cash drawer, in full view of a houseful of males.

The brothers prospered from the start despite stiff competition from a miserly Frenchman named François Guerin, whose dingy premises were more advantageously located on Broadway, opposite the City Hotel. Before their venture was a year old, a nephew, Francesco Delmonico, was brought over from Mairengo to lighten the work load. Not long after that the enterprising John convinced his cautious, somewhat stolid brother that, profitable as the sale of wines, coffee, and cakes might be, expanding the operation to include a full-fledged restaurant would be even more so. Their "Restaurant Français" opened in the adjoining building, 25 William Street, in 1831. By September of that year it was doing so well that a second nephew, the Lorenzo Delmonico mentioned earlier, was sent for by his overburdened kinfolk.

Delmonico's may not by the broadest of definitions have been the city's first restaurant or even, by slightly narrower definition, the first French restaurant in New York. In December of 1827, the year the brothers opened their original café, one Joseph Collet had awarded himself "the honor to inform citizens of the City of New York, strangers, and transient customers, that his *French Restaurant* will be opened on the 11th instant." In his advertisement in the *Evening Post,* Collet went on to enumerate several of the dishes he proposed to serve, of which only one, beef à la mode, sounded even vaguely Gallic. Then, too, there was the flamboyant William Niblo, a self-styled gourmet and culinary showman who operated the Old Bank Coffee House and specialized in such more or less edible exotica as hawk, owl, eagle, and bear, the last-named of which he somehow contrived to roast whole and serve forth standing, as it had in life, on all fours.

What immediately set Delmonico's apart from the welter of catch-as-catch-can eating houses that had sprung up in the 1820s was its seriousness of purpose and its dedication to classical, orderly culinary principles. At its tables New Yorkers were introduced to concepts utterly new to them. For the first time, they realized that sauces were not mere foppish affectations but, in proper liaison with their meats and vegetables, might enhance a meal immeasurably. For the first time they saw that a near-infinitude of previously ignored raw materials, coupled with a far wider range of culinary techniques than they had dreamed existed, could be combined to produce a cuisine of endless variety and consummate subtlety. At long last they began to entertain the notion "that dinner was not merely an ingestion, but an observance"; to realize that an intelligently orchestrated meal could be as fulfilling as any other aesthetic experience and more pleasurable than most.

At this remove it is impossible, of course, to gauge the caliber of the food served at the original Delmonico restaurant. No menus survive, but neither John nor Peter was a trained chef and it's unlikely that the establishment would have made much of an impression on the more knowledgeable diners of the present day. But its impact on the unsophisticated New Yorkers who visited it for the first time was seismic and was perhaps best summed up by the banker Samuel Ward, the product of a Puritanical upbringing and typically American diet, who recalled his first impressions almost forty years after the fact:

> I remember entering the café with something of awe, accompanied by a fellow student from Columbia. The dim, religious light soothed the eye, its tranquil atmosphere the ear. . . . I was struck by the prompt and deferential attendance, unlike the democratic nonchalance of the service at Holt's Ordinary, in Fulton Street, at Clark and Brown's, in Maiden Lane, and at George W. Brown's, in Water Street. . . . The Burgundy disappointed us and did not prove comparable to the March & Benson Madeira of those days. But we rose from the table with a sigh of regret that our next visit

would have to be postponed until our next pocket-money day. We dined perfectly for half a dollar apiece, if not less.

Ward, who with maturity became one of the century's more celebrated epicures, presumably realized the futility of comparing Burgundy and Madeira somewhere along the line. That he was naïve enough to compare them in the 1830s may be taken as an indication of the low state of American connoisseurship when Delmonico's appeared on the scene.

Despite some resistance from the older generation, the restaurant flourished; so much so that a second establishment was opened at 76 Broad Street in 1832, in premises until then occupied by Joseph Collet, whose vaunted beef à la mode had drawn more flies than paying customers before he converted his restaurant to a ·lodging house.

The Delmonicos had intended to finance the remodeling of the three-story Broad Street building with the income from their original venture. Their plan literally went up in smoke— along with the William Street operation and a substantial portion of the city's business district—during the night of December 16, 1835, as fire raged uncontrolled over lower Manhattan. Between the conflagration and attempts to limit its spread by blowing up buildings in its path, eighteen million dollars of damage was done, and every insurance company in the city went bankrupt. In his survey of the devastation, a reporter for the *Daily Express* made it quite clear that New Yorkers viewed the destruction of the restaurant on William Street as far from least among the city's losses.

The setback proved to be a blessing in disguise. The young Lorenzo Delmonico convinced his uncles that if a phoenix were to rise from the ashes, it would need more wingspread than the original William Street site afforded. Accordingly, they invested in a much larger plot of ground at the corner of South William and Beaver Streets and, by 1837, had opened the doors to an opulent three-story structure, complete with a portico supported by a pair of massive pillars dug out of the ruins of Pompeii.

The new restaurant was far and away the most ambitious the city had seen until then, and the ten-page menu that went into effect the following year, with upwards of 370 separate dishes listed in both French and English (with prices given in shillings and pence), documented a quantum leap forward for American gastronomy. A scant decade earlier, as has been noted, New Yorkers had subsisted for the most part on an unedifying diet of mercilessly overcooked beef and pork, served chokingly dry, all but devoid of vegetable accompaniments, and wolfed down amidst the same sort of conviviality that obtains in a Trappist refectory. Suddenly they found themselves with twelve soups from which to choose (a contemporaneous menu from the Astor House, then the city's most prestigious hotel, lists just one), no fewer than thirty-one hors d'oeuvres and a like number of beef dishes; forty-odd poultry options; veal prepared forty-six ways; 20 mutton offerings; 22 game selections; 48 fish and seafood entrées; and a bewildering array of thirty-nine vegetables, including such innovations as *salsifis au jus, champignons à la Provençale,* sautéed truffles with champagne sauce, *chicorée à la crème,* stuffed baked eggplant, and *artichaux* (sic) *Barigoule* (i.e., braised, with a filling of mushrooms, bacon, ham, and parsley). Some sixty wines also were listed, with twelve-year-old bottles from some of the greatest vineyards of Bordeaux priced at three dollars or less. Clearly, New Yorkers, mired for two centuries in the gastronomical Dark Ages, had crossed the threshold of the Age of Enlightenment.

Delmonico's was more than a menu of mind-boggling prolixity. It hadn't taken long for word to spread abroad that the family was willing to pay top dollar for outstanding chefs and to supply them with the finest, freshest ingredients to be had. (Lorenzo never outgrew the habit of personally showing up at the Washington Market each day at the crack of dawn, to pick over the choicest meats, fish, poultry, and produce, and was instrumental in the establishment of a twenty-acre family farm in then-rural Brooklyn, where vegetables that met his rigorous standards could be grown.) Moreover, the elegant private dining rooms on the restaurant's second floor brought the socially prominent flocking to South William Street *en famille,* thus breaking down both the long-standing tradition of supping at home and the tacit taboo against dining out in mixed company. Finally, the service, by all accounts, was far better than any that

Americans had encountered in the past. As one such account had it, "The waiters have been regularly trained to their profession, and, without seeming to observe you, are always at your elbow just at the moment when you are beginning to think about ordering something. They listen to you with a grave attention which assures you that you are to receive exactly what you have ordered, and in the shortest possible time."

If John Delmonico had been the great pioneer among American restaurateurs, his nephew Lorenzo was the genius of their golden age. When John died in 1842—"widely and justly lamented," in the words of Sam Ward—while hunting deer on Long Island, he left an aging, unenthusiastic Peter as titular head of the family enterprises. It was then that Lorenzo came into his own. He was made a full partner the following year, bought out his surviving uncle in 1848, and was to reign supreme over the firm until his own death in 1881.

Moving steadily northward as the city's population increased almost geometrically, Lorenzo opened one restaurant after another, each more glittering than the last. While denizens of the financial district continued to throng through the Pompeian entrance at South William and Beaver streets for lunch, another establishment at Broadway and Chambers Street, opposite City Hall, catered to a mixed bag of regulars and transients during the day and, in the evening, to residents of the smart new "uptown" quarter nearby. "Thus by the spacious conveniences of their new location," Sam Ward recalled in his memoirs, "a more varied and brilliant career was opened to the second generation of the [Delmonico] family." More varied and brilliant opportunities also seem to have opened to a couple of generations *outside* the family. "Young bloods from the New York Club," Ward wrote, "and old stagers from the Union revelled, the one in truffles and Burgundy, the others in simpler viands and less gouty wines; while the merry laugh of well-matronized maidens musically thrilled the air."

It had not taken long for the success of the Delmonicos to inspire competition. Their most formidable rival of the period by far was one Martinez, who had opened a very highly regarded restaurant called Maison Dorée in 1861, while Lorenzo was negotiating for the nearby Grinnell mansion at Fifth Avenue and Fourteenth Street. If some partisans found Martinez's food even better than that served at the various Delmonico establishments, it was little wonder; his chef was Charles Ranhofer, a justifiably imperious perfectionist who during his lifetime had no peers in this country and very few in his native France. Although it was obvious that the area around Fourteenth Street was to be one of the city's more fashionable enclaves for years to come, Lorenzo's decision to settle his new enterprise there probably was motivated at least in part by the prospect of swatting down a challenger on the upstart's own turf. It was certainly not by mere happenstance that Ranhofer appeared in Lorenzo's office not long thereafter. With Ranhofer's engagement as *chef de cuisine,* Lorenzo solidified a Delmonican supremacy that wasn't again to be seriously challenged for another two decades or eclipsed until well into the twentieth century.

Ranhofer, a third-generation chef, was one of those culinary prodigies that French soil produces as effortlessly as it produces truffles. Born in St. Denis in 1836, he was appointed *chef de cuisine* to Prince Henin of Alsace while still in his teens, and was looking for new worlds to conquer by the time he was twenty. In the heyday of his extended tenure at Delmonico's, he ruled no fewer than forty-two *sous chefs* with an iron hand, letting both his employers and underlings know in no uncertain terms that "things must be done as I direct."

Today Ranhofer is remembered chiefly as the architect of two classics of the American cuisine: baked Alaska and lobster Newburg. As it happens, he was the author of neither dish. The invention of baked Alaska, which he supposedly originated in 1867, in commemoration of the territorial acquisition that quickly became known as "Seward's Folly," variously had been credited to Thomas Jefferson, Count Rumford, and an anonymous pastry chef attached to the Chinese mission in Paris before the dish made its first appearance at Delmonico's. The recipe for lobster Newburg was given to Ranhofer in 1876 by a shipping executive named Ben Wenberg, who claimed to have discovered it in South America. The dish, received with great enthusiasm by Ranhofer and listed on the menu as lobster

Wenberg, underwent an anagrammatical change of sorts when the eponymous donor got into a brawl at the restaurant and was banished from its decorous premises. Ranhofer's only discernible contribution to it was the addition of more egg yolk to a formula that hardly needed further enrichment.

Dubious as his credentials as a culinary innovator may have been, Ranhofer was probably the greatest executive chef this country has ever seen, and a caterer whose abilities to rise to an occasion left observers awestruck. "It was not unusual," Lately Thomas has noted, "for him to supervise the preparation of half a dozen dinners to be served in private houses in different parts of the city, dispatch refreshments for two or three hundred spectators at a horse or yacht race, and watch over the regular restaurant service, all in one day." In an age of easily come-by wealth and outrageously conspicuous consumption, he was a veritable chameleon of adaptability, ever ready, in his own words, to "set before [clients] dishes which fill the sensitive chef's heart with despair" or to produce banquets whose sole purpose was to set the tongues of the envious wagging. His only proviso, as he himself put it, was that his client's purse dance "in close attendance upon his whimsicalities of taste." A day-long four-meal tuck-in, to be served to three hundred guests aboard the steamship *City of Peking?* But of course! Truffled ice cream for Leonard Jerome, who was striving to one-up August Belmont and William Travers in a round-robin, hang-the-cost dinner-throwing tournament? Why not? A thirty-foot lake, complete with landscaping, waterfalls, and live swans, as the centerpiece for a modest dinner to be given by the import tycoon Edward Luckmeyer? No problem—hadn't Luckmeyer decided to blow a $10,000 tax windfall in one go at the restaurant?

But if Ranhofer was all too willing to dance attendance upon the whimsicalities of other men's taste, at least when the price was right, he remained steadfast to classical French notions of harmony, order, and logic on less flamboyant occasions and in his day-to-day operations.

When the young Charles Dickens toured the United States for the first time in 1841–42 he was tendered a banquet at the City Hotel by a group of New York's most distinguished personages. At that time, a decade and a half after the opening of the original Delmonico café, the hotel's dining room enjoyed quasi-official recognition as *the* site for civic blowouts. Moreover many New Yorkers who remained unconverted to the rich new gravy faith still considered its kitchens to be the finest in the nation. On the occasion in question, the assembled company was regaled with a stupefying farrago of culinary redundancies; a medieval array that might have given pause to a Henry VIII, let alone the author of *Oliver Twist*. Aside from fruits and nuts, no fewer than sixty-five separate offerings were served forth in a formless gamut that included seven boiled dishes, ten roasts, at least five stews (among which terrapin and pigeon appeared twice), four macaronis, and, among the notably banal desserts, jelly puffs, French puffs, plum puffs, and apple puffs.

A gouty Dickens returned to New York a quarter of a century later, by then, it would seem, in improved odor among the aborigines he had so mercilessly savaged in *Martin Chuzzlewit* and *American Notes*. Once again a banquet was given in his honor—this time at Delmonico's Fourteenth Street restaurant. Although New Yorkers of 1868 were still redoubtable trenchermen by present-day standards, the meal he was served— made up of half as many offerings as the City Hotel affair had comprised—seems a model of variety, symmetry, and restraint when compared with the earlier shindig. It consisted of oysters on the half shell, one thick and one thin soup, a single hot hors d'oeuvre, two fish selections, two meat dishes, a couple of dainty game preparations, two roasted birds, and two cold meats, along with a few green vegetables, veal sweetbreads in pastry, and an infinitely more sophisticated choice of desserts than the visiting lion had encountered on the earlier go-round.

At one time or another various Delmonicos operated eleven different establishments under the family name and numbered everyone who was anyone, including every American president from James Monroe to Franklin Roosevelt, among their guests. By 1868, when the first American dining car was christened Delmonico, the adjective "Delmonican" had become a part of the American language and a scrupulous attention to dinner part of the American way of life.

Despite the loss to Delmonico's of Charles Ranhofer, the Maison Dorée continued to attract its own adherents, including a few who previously had been Delmonico regulars. Opened in 1861, even as hostilities between the North and South were getting under way, and immediately acclaimed for the excellence of both its cuisine and cellar, it was a success from the outset. Then, as the war progressed and New Yorkers increasingly fell into factional disputes about how it should be waged, a number of influential Republicans, led by George Templeton Strong, a power in the Union League and longtime Delmonico regular, switched their base of operations from the Beaver Street Delmonico's (a nest, as the Strong forces saw it, of Democratic moderatism) to Martinez's fledgling operation on the south side of Union Square. Martinez and the Delmonicos contended for patronage throughout the war, but neither side actually incurred losses. Both in fact prospered apace as new money swelled the coffers of various war profiteers, who were not in the least averse to redistributing their pelf almost as quickly as it flowed in. Indeed, with the war's end, Martinez was well enough off, after less than five years of operation, to close the Maison Dorée and retire in comfortable circumstances.

Gradually the Delmonican approach was adopted by the city's better hotels, among them the Astor House, where Charles Roux, an imported master chef, presided over the kitchens. Along with the half ton of beef and some eight thousand oysters consumed there weekly, one of the house specialties was an iced custard "served in a tall glass as slim as a Greek vase" and so delectable that one sweet-toothed chronicler of the period "had six of them for dessert the first time—and stopped then only as one should always arise from the table a little bit hungry."

It would seem that Adah Isaacs Menken arose from the table a little bit hungry one June evening in 1861, just before electrifying New York by appearing for the first time in *Mazeppa,* a melodrama in which she not only played the female lead but co-starred, however unconvincingly, as the leading man; a role which required that she ride a galloping horse while strapped, naked and supine, onto its back. The little lady prefaced her performance with dinner at Pfaff's, a raffish cellar restaurant at Broadway and Bleecker Street in what was then the theater district, where she casually destroyed a large platter of oysters, a tureen of soup, an outsize steak, and a whole fruit pie before leaving for the theater with a turkey sandwich clutched to her bosom as a hedge against starvation.

Pfaff's, it hardly need be added, was a popular bohemian hangout of the day. Frequented by Walt Whitman and other, lesser members of the literati, and operated (around the clock) by a German immigrant, the restaurant didn't precisely conform to the Delmonican mold, but offered simple, substantial German-American fare at reasonable prices and in a nondescript setting, playing a role in its time much like that played today by Sardi's, where theater people turn up as a matter of course after a premier performance. (After *her* opening-night exertions, Miss Menken savored the first moments of her escape from obscurity by putting away three copious helpings of gumbo and a pleasant sufficiency of roast beef. Thus fortified, she reportedly took on the poet and novelist Charles Edmond Burke in an under-the-table wrestling match, subdued him with little difficulty, and dragged the carcass home to her bed.) The DeSoto, located just a few doors down the street from Pfaff's and fitted out along the lines of a steamship's saloon, was the most stylish and one of the most popular theatrical restaurants of the period, but the district's countless oyster saloons did a lively business of their own.

Today, with the once seemingly inexhaustible oyster beds of New England, Long Island, and Chesapeake Bay either drastically depleted or unusably contaminated, oysters are considered a luxury food. They were anything but that during most of the nineteenth century, when they could be had cheaply by the barrel, even in the American hinterland; when the annual consumption, although restricted to eight months of the year, sometimes ran as high as 150 million pounds of shucked meat; and when many of the city's oyster saloons offered as many of the mollusks as one could eat for a flat six cents. (The offer wasn't quite as magnanimous as it may sound. For the most part, the oyster saloons were lurid basement establishments where the possibility always existed that one's consumption of the *spécialité de la maison* might be impeded somewhat by the unforeseen ingestion of a knuckle sandwich or even by a cut throat. Besides, their proprietors weren't above slipping tainted bivalves onto the plates of customers who took the advertising too literally.)

Oyster eating was by no means restricted to the theatrical district or to the seedy haunts of bellicose roughnecks. Canal Street was honeycombed with oyster saloons, many of them reasonably presentable, as was the neighborhood of the Fulton Fish Market on the East River. In the market itself some fifty thousand oysters a day were consumed on the spot and off the half shell during the 1870s, while at Downing's, an elegantly appointed establishment in the financial district, the absorption of *Ostrea virginica* was elevated to something like a fine art, with oyster sauces, oyster pies, scalloped oysters, and oyster-stuffed turkey available for the delectation of connoisseurs.

One such connoisseur, the same Captain Marryat whose view of American cookery of the late 1830s contrasted so sharply with James Fenimore Cooper's, was not quite so charitable where American oysters were concerned. They were, he found, "very plentiful, very large, and, to an English palate, rather insipid." Marryat went on to concede that English and French oysters might indeed taste coppery, as some American travelers charged, but patriotically concluded that a flavor of copper was "better than no flavor at all." Marryat's compatriot Thackeray, who sampled American oysters in the 1850s (in all likelihood at Delmonico's, where he was a frequent guest), was far too put off by the size of the critters to concern himself with fine distinctions of flavor. Eating one, he wrote, was like swallowing a baby.

Whatever visiting Europeans may have thought of the oysters of the Eastern Seaboard, New Yorkers loved them and consumed them in such prodigious quantities that the six-cent saloons were little more than a happy memory by the early 1880s. By that time oysters were indeed a luxury food—which didn't deter Diamond Jim Brady, the most flamboyant of American feeders, from downing close to a thousand of them a week, all taken care of by a liberal expense account. (At one of Brady's wonted haunts, Rector's, on what is now Times Square, the largest Lynnhaven oysters procurable were reserved for him.)

Elsewhere around the expanding city, "ethnic" restaurants, operated by (and chiefly for) the political refugees and hope-filled immigrants who were arriving in successive waves, had begun to initiate those New Yorkers venturesome enough to investigate them into the mysteries of Italian, bourgeois French, Middle European, and even Chinese cookery. Expatriated German brewers and wine importers opened beer halls and *Weinstuben* as showcases for their lagers and Rhine wines, weaning native-born Americans away from such time-honored libations as grog, port, sherry, and Madeira and, in the process, popularizing such accompaniments as cheese, wurst, dark bread, pretzels, and sauerkraut.

By 1880, when the city's population was nearly two million, the area around Union Square, previously the more or less exclusive domain of the Maison Dorée and Delmonico's, teemed with German, Austrian, and Hungarian drinking halls where the purchase of a nickel beer or a glass of wine entitled patrons to play fast and loose with the free buffet. At that time, Union Square was one of the city's most stylish enclaves, a tranquil, fountained park shaded by stately trees and bordered on its west side by such smart shops as Tiffany's, Brentano's, Vantine's, and Macy's. Lovers of music and the drama were lured to the area by Tony Pastor's theater, Steinway Hall, and the Academy of Music; aficionados of carnage by the spectacular streetcar accidents that occurred with almost predictable regularity along the notorious Dead Man's Curve. To the east of the park along Fourteenth Street lay an almost unbroken stretch of *Gemüt-lichkeit* that included Lienau's beer hall, Brubacher's Wine Garden, the Alhambra Gardens, the Café Hungaria, Munchen-heim's Arena, and a modest drinking establishment run by one Baron von Mehlbach, where a young Hanoverian, August Lüchow, waited tables and tended bar.

Lüchow had arrived in New York in 1879 and immediately found employment at Stewart's Saloon, a rather pretentious watering hole on Duane Street, near City Hall. Within a year he was working for Mehlbach and two years later bought his boss out with the financial backing of the piano manufacturer and impresario William Steinway. Steinway provided more than just working capital. He soon made Lüchow's the haunt of the leading composers and performers of the day. Moreover, neither the appointment of Lüchow as the exclusive American agent for Würzburger beer (an agency he later consolidated by gaining a lock on the importation of Pilsener, too) nor the restaurant's location on Irving Place, a five-block thoroughfare intensively populated by literary and artistic celebrities, in any way impeded Lüchow's rush to a position of ascendancy.

Physically and gastronomically, the restaurant was not precisely Delmonican but in some ways harked back to the pleasure gardens that had flourished in the city a half-century earlier. Decorated with a schmaltzy exuberance that drew little distinction between the handiwork of journeyman taxidermists and Flemish and German little masters, it was a place where heavy, hearty Teutonic food was consumed in prodigious quantities and washed down with German beers or wines while an eight-piece Viennese orchestra, led by no lesser a personage than Victor Herbert, played in the background. It was a boisterous, rollicking place where physical behemoths drank like whales, coming up for air only long enough to wipe the suds from their handlebar mustachios before plunging into another seidel of brew. It was in honor of Lüchow's that Harry von Tilzer wrote the music, and Vincent Bryan the lyrics, for a 1902 drinking song, "Down Where the Würzburger Flows"; a ditty that enjoyed immense popularity, not only at the restaurant but in the beer halls of Cincinnati, St. Louis, and Milwaukee and led Lüchow to remark that he felt like "a beer Columbus." During the restaurant's heyday, the Würzburger flowed at a torrential pace as twenty-four thousand seidels of imported beer were knocked back daily and one titled customer, Baron Ferdinand Sinzig, set an individual house record by sponging up thirty-six seidels—thirty-one-and-one-half quarts—without rising from his seat to off-load any of the intake.

As he prospered, Lüchow enlarged the restaurant, buying up properties adjacent to Mehlbach's original establishment one by one and incorporating them into his grand, if somewhat improvisatory, design. One such building housed Hubert's Museum, a waxworks-*cum*-menagerie, and was in the process of being vacated when a geriatric lion got loose and followed the scent of *Bratwurst* and *Kassler Rippchen* into Lüchow's main dining room. The volume of squeals emitted by the ladies as they climbed onto the tables may or may not have exceeded that produced some years later when the redoubtable Jim Brady brought twenty chorus girls in for dinner after first arranging to have their places set with five-hundred-dollar bills and diamond sunbursts. Andrew Carnegie, Jules Bache, and J. P. Morgan also dispensed scandalous sums on a fairly regular basis, but other regulars, including Steinway, weren't so incautious. When in the face of rising costs Lüchow reduced the number of oysters served with the forty-five-cent set lunch from a dozen to six, his benefactor stormed off the premises, vowing not to return. To Lüchow's immense relief, Steinway reappeared a few days later, having found the competition wanting, and made do from then on with half a dozen bluepoints each noon.

Despite the success of Lüchow's and of various hotel restaurants (notably those of the Gilsey Hotel, the Hoffman House, the St. James Hotel, and in particular the Hotel Brunswick, which stood at Fifth Avenue and Twenty-sixth Street and which not a few New Yorkers considered the ne plus ultra of epicureanism), the several Delmonico enterprises, although by then bereft of the most brilliant Delmonicos, faced no serious challengers of their own class and style as the century drew toward its close. Then, Louis Sherry arrived on the scene.

Sherry, a Vermonter of French extraction, had started in business for himself in 1881, much as John and Peter Delmonico had more than half a century before him, with a modest confectionery-restaurant. Unlike the founding Delmonicos, though, he was well connected and not altogether inexperienced, having worked in the dining rooms of the Brunswick and a fashionable resort hotel on the Jersey shore.

From the outset, Sherry saw himself as a potential peer of the Delmonicos. Few other New Yorkers did and after a couple of lackluster years he betook himself to Paris to bone up on his chosen métier. Then his luck turned in 1883. Having wangled a commission to cater a kermis at the new Metropolitan Opera House, he brought off the job brilliantly, garnered a good deal of press coverage as a result, and soon was handling some of the town's poshest bashes.

Once fairly launched, Sherry's rise was meteoric. When the Goelet mansion at Fifth Avenue and Thirty-seventh Street was put up for sale, Sherry, who had been operating in undistinguished quarters at Sixth Avenue and Thirty-eighth Street, pounced on it. But, grand as the building was, he soon outgrew it and, deciding to mount a direct challenge to Delmonican supremacy, commissioned no lesser an architect than Stanford White to design a new twelve-story base of operations for him. The battle was joined on October 10, 1898, at Fifth Avenue and Forty-fourth Street, where by a curious coincidence the last and most stately of all the Delmonico restaurants had opened, in a building designed by James Brown Lord, less than a year earlier. Delmonico's occupied the northeast corner of the intersection, Sherry's the southwest.

As the weekly *Illustrated American* observed, "It will be a fight to the death, with the odds in favor of Delmonico." And a fight to the death it turned out to be, with first one restaurant and then the other holding the upper hand while what one chronicler of the period, the hotelier Frank Case, described as a "fickle and uncertain" public "would shift for no apparent reason back and forth across the avenue. One year, Sherry's would have the advantage, until suddenly everyone would begin going to Delmonico's, and continue for a year or so before they suddenly shifted back."

While it was generally conceded that the food served at Delmonico's was still the city's best, the cuisine at Sherry's was more than good enough for a clientele that increasingly was concerning itself less with gastronomic niceties than with sensationalism. Louis Sherry earlier had demonstrated his willingness to go along with the latter when he cheerfully allowed the sinuous Little Egypt, a belly dancer who had scandalized the nation during the Chicago World's Fair of 1893, to put her talented navel through its paces during the course of a raucous dinner party held at his first establishment.

Attitudes and mores were changing. Smoking was permitted in the dining rooms at Delmonico's and, as Robert Shaplen was to write long after the fact, the Little Egypt affair "was merely the forerunner of a series of dinners at which the amenities of sharing good food and drink were almost wholly subordinated to antic and generally heavy-handed forms of diversion." Evidence that Sherry's was far more hospitable to such forms of diversion than its more straitlaced rival across the street soon materialized. Indeed, it was made spectacularly manifest in the first year of the new century, when a well-heeled sportsman named Billings disbursed fifty thousand dollars at the restaurant on a quaint conceit designed to provide an evening's surcease from boredom for a small troop of cronies. This took the form of a fourteen-course Horse Banquet for which the assembled company, fetchingly got up in hunting pinks, forgathered in a temporarily bosky Sherry ballroom. There, Billings' cavalry siphoned champagne through rubber tubes from their saddlebags and dined from trays attached to the withers of their steeds.

The questionable taste of some of the affairs he catered notwithstanding, Sherry succeeded in attracting some very prestigious patrons to his opulently appointed premises. The formidable Mrs. William B. Astor (sans horse) put her imprimatur—in the form of a grand ball—on the place soon after it opened, and J. P. Morgan took up more or less permanent residence there at about the same time. The young Ethel Barrymore dined there regularly, as did Richard Harding Davis, while such luminaries as the newspaper publisher Frank Munsey and the social arbiter Harry Lehr occupied private apartments above the restaurant.

While Delmonico's and Sherry's slugged it out on Forty-fourth Street, other establishments catered to an emergent clientele that took a-plague-on-both-their-houses view of the rivalry. It was still possible to regale a party of six with a fine dinner at Delmonico's for a total cost of twelve dollars, a perfectly drinkable *vin ordinaire* included. It was also possible, however, to dine regally for *nothing* almost next door, where Richard Canfield operated a gambling house and where such delicacies as terrapin, canvasback duck, and pheasant under glass, all excellently prepared by a French master chef, were served to the city's high rollers without charge.

The age of the lobster palaces—glittering, luxurious establishments like Churchill's, Shanley's, the Knickerbocker Grill, Bustanoby's, and Rector's, in the burgeoning theater district around Forty-second Street, and the Café Martin and Cavanaugh's farther downtown—had dawned with the emergence of a new breed of flamboyant self-made spenders and showy, convention-flouting women, the forerunners of the café society of a later period. Ostentation was the order of the day, as the high-living likes of Jim Brady, "Bet-a-million" Gates, Stanford White, Lillie Langtry, Anna Held, and Lillian Russell sallied forth each evening to conquer the city anew, sweeping grandly into one or another of the lobster palaces for an after-theater supper, carousing the night away, and winding up in the small hours with muttonchops and champagne at Jack Dunstan's or Harry Hill's. It was Brady who summed up the ethos of an era when, standing arm-in-well-upholstered-arm with Lillian Russell at the end of one of their innumerable nights on the town, he regarded the glittering city with a bleary gaze and exclaimed, "God, Nell, ain't it grand!"

The Café Martin, one of the best and most popular of the newer ventures, opened in 1899 on Twenty-sixth Street and Fifth Avenue (in quarters previously occupied by what many old-timers considered to be the finest and most agreeably located of the Delmonico establishments, which the *Pall Mall Gazette* of London had called one of America's two greatest wonders, the other being Yosemite Valley). Its owner, Louis Martin, a sometime hotelier who took the precaution of checking out European innovations before opening the place, was the first New York restaurateur of any consequence to fit out his premises with banquettes (which made for more intimacy than a good many observers deemed proper) and an alfresco dining terrace. He also installed a cycle of murals that might be considered no more than mildly erotic by today's standards but were described in their time as of interest to "art lovers, food lovers, and plain lovers." His food, by all accounts, was superb, with a *prix fixe* eight-course dinner incurring a tab of $1.25— unimaginable today but moderately steep at the turn of the century—on weekdays. For such an outlay, his customers were offered dinner music, multiple hors d'oeuvres, soup, a choice of lobster or fish, an entrée of generously garnished beef or game, asparagus or spaghetti, a roast, dessert, and demitasse.

The most scintillating of the lobster palaces, though, was Rector's, which stood on Broadway between Forty-third and Forty-fourth streets, its electrified façade aglitter, its habitués even more so. With one hundred seventy-five tables (not including those in the restaurant's four private dining rooms) and almost as many employees, it too had opened in the last year of the 1890s, with first-night arrivals literally in a whirl as the first revolving door they had ever seen went into operation.

Charles Rector, the son of an upstate tavernkeeper, had begun his career rather inauspiciously as a New York City horsecar conductor. Then, after relocating in Chicago, he parlayed an inherited talent for kitchen organization and his minimal experience in mass transit into a position of some importance as a supervisor of dining-car operations for George Pullman. He left Pullman in 1884 to open what would soon become known throughout the country as Chicago's finest restaurant. Nine years later, he was awarded a singular plum: the license to operate the only restaurant at the World's Fair. Thus accredited, he reintroduced himself to New York and took the city by storm.

Rector's success was no fluke. Rather it was the result of meticulous planning, a fine eye for detail, a piratical disregard for the prior claims of competitors that allowed him to snatch several key staff members from Delmonican employ, a willingness to pay premium prices for custom appointments and handpicked personnel, and a disposition to indulge the whims of his patrons that might have given pause even to a Louis Sherry. When Diamond Jim Brady expressed a salivary interest in sole Marguery, a dish served exclusively at its Parisian birthplace, the Café Marguery, Rector didn't hesitate to yank his son George out of law school and pack him off to France. His mission: to worm his way into the kitchen and confidence of Monsieur Marguery himself and not return until he had the recipe, a zealously guarded secret, in his possession. (If Marguery took the eminently successful exercise in plagiarism with better grace than anyone might have expected, it may have been because he realized that the end of a distinguished career was at hand and it isn't given to every man to achieve immortality by poaching a flatfish. Once his recipe was made public, the dish became a classic of the French repertory. As Julian Street, an American observer of the gustatory scene, put it several years after the chef's demise, "His sole goes marching on.")

Once Brady got into the habit of coming to Rector's, he

foraged there twice nightly, before and after the theater, dismantling three dozen of the largest Lynnhaven oysters obtainable in the course of his first visit along with a septet or so of boiled blue crabs and a like number of four-pound lobsters. Warming to his task, Big Jim would then put himself on the outside of a small lake of green turtle soup, a couple of portions of terrapin, a brace of canvasback ducks, a veritable landscape of assorted vegetables, and a beefsteak of modest dimensions—modest, at least, in comparison with the square mileage of Rhode Island—before polishing off the pastry tray in its entirety and calling for a two-pound box of chocolates.

Rector described Brady as his "best twenty-five customers," but those of his regular clients who ate their way through one life at a time weren't doing the restaurant any harm, either. While a party of four could dine copiously there for twenty dollars, two bottles of bubbly included, few of Rector's steady customers confined themselves to such a Spartan approach. Some idea of their collective expenditure may be gathered from the fact that the income from the maître d'hôtel's Christmas tips alone often ran as high as twenty-five thousand dollars. During the early years of the century Rector's was *the* place to be seen, preferably in the process of disbursing lucre in carload lots, and if most of the restaurant's habitués seldom were seen in the same company two nights running, so much the better for unpaid advertising. Or so the Rector's, *père* and *fils,* discovered when the hit song of Florenz Ziegfeld's *Follies* of 1907 turned out to be "If a Table at Rector's Could Talk."

As mixed doubles eating partnerships go, Brady's and Lillian Russell's may not have affected the general run of humankind quite as profoundly as the teaming up of Adam and Eve, but its effect on New York restaurant life and the lives of professional restaurant people was incalculable. It was the voluptuous Diamond Lil, for example, who by merely transporting her embonpoint from the doorway of Delmonico's to a waiting carriage one evening in 1887 unwittingly launched the career of the legendary Oscar of the Waldorf.

Oscar Tshirky was a young Swiss who had gone to work as a busboy at the Hoffman House upon his arrival in New York in 1883. Still clearing tables four years later and with no discernible prospect of one day becoming a celebrity in his own right, he spent his little free time gaping at notabilities as they entered and left Delmonico's Madison Square restaurant, a block from the Hoffman House. On the fateful evening in question, he had taken up his usual stand outside the restaurant when La Russell emerged and undulated across a short stretch of pavement. The effect was galvanic. "I was captivated by this fleeting glimpse," Tshirky recalled years later. "She was the loveliest woman I had ever seen." Resolving to feast his eyes on a more regular basis, he applied for a job at Delmonico's the next morning and was taken on a few weeks later as a waiter— in the men's café. Deliverance came not long thereafter, however, when he was transferred to the private dining rooms, and unalloyed triumph (or so he thought) sometime after that, when he was put in complete charge of those facilities and assigned himself to the table reserved for Miss Russell and Jim Brady. Again, victory turned to ashes, as Tshirky's vision of loveliness vied with her escort to see who could put on the most tonnage. For the star-struck headwaiter the spectacle was "the surprise and disillusionment of [a] lifetime. Lillian Russell ate more than Diamond Jim."

Thus disillusioned, Tshirky composed a testimonial to himself, persuaded most of Delmonico's better-known patrons to sign it (the endorsements covered eight pages of foolscap), and submitted the document to the manager-designate of the Waldorf Hotel, which was then being readied for its 1893 opening. He was hired as headwaiter of the hotel's Palm Garden restaurant.

"The Waldorf," quipped Oliver Herford, "brought exclusiveness to the masses." His epigram was somewhat hyperbolic. True, any reasonably presentable citizen could gawk at the ornate lobby or loiter about as the swells preened themselves in the corridor that soon came to be known as Peacock Alley. But the restaurant was another story; with reservations and formal dress *de rigueur* and with the beady-eyed Oscar—whose hauteur could be withering when the occasion demanded— freezing out undesirables, its hothouse precincts soon became the haunt of both the blue blood and the *nouveau riche*. It was an excellent restaurant in its heyday, with one of the finest cellars in the city. For better or worse, though, the contribution to American gastronomy for which it is best remembered is one of the most forgettable dishes ever devised: Waldorf salad, an invention not of any of the restaurant's chefs, but of the striver who became known throughout the Western world as "Oscar of the Waldorf."

Literally and figuratively, life in New York was getting faster. The horseless carriage was no longer a novelty by 1908, when a fleet of seven hundred motor cabs whisked those who could afford them from one to another of the smart gathering places. Unescorted women were permitted in the dining rooms of the merged Waldorf and Astoria hotels, and Mrs. Patrick Campbell calmly puffed a cigarette in a public room of the newly opened Plaza Hotel. (It was at the Plaza that the resident chef, Louis Diat, was to concoct a gussied-up, born-again version of a staple of French bourgeois cookery, leek-and-potato soup, and dub it vichyssoise. Today, his brainchild is as inescapable a feature of French menus from coast to coast as onion soup *gratinée, escargots de bourgogne* and celery root *rémoulade.*)

Quick to co-opt an accelerating trend, the socially impeccable Mrs. Stuyvesant Fish branded as hopelessly déclassé the meal that ran through eight or ten interminable courses, decreed three courses to be a sufficiency, and set a fifty-minute limit on dinner. Her dicta may in no way have fazed either Jim Brady or his edacious consort Lillian Russell but were instrumental in reorienting a society that until then had striven to model itself on those partners in gluttony. Serious eating was in fact destined to suffer a succession of setbacks, not least among which would be the emergence of the motion picture—a medium inherently inhospitable to corpulence as the stuff of anything but low comedy—as the art form to which a nation would turn for its new concept of ideal beauty.

Inexorably, the Delmonican standard of *gourmandise*—a standard that had prevailed for half a century—was eroding under a many-pronged assault. In 1898 the brothers William and Samuel Childs, whose nine antiseptically tidy chain eateries had already captured as many as twenty thousand customers a day from the independent restaurateurs, opened the city's first cafeteria. Four years later, a couple of ingenious Philadelphians

named Horn and Hardart went the Childs brothers one better—
or worse, depending on who was evaluating the innovation—
by opening an automated cafeteria at Broadway and Thirteenth
Street. Increasingly restrictive game laws wrought havoc on a
cuisine that had been distinguished above all else by the
magnificence of its wildfowl and venison. A new vogue for
cocktails (which complemented no known dish) and Champagne
(which supposedly could be drunk with anything edible),
spawned in the trendy lobster palaces and immensely popular
new rooftop cabarets, made a meaningless charade of the
orchestration of a meal. "The young folk nowadays are not
epicures," observed the musician and critic James Gibbons
Huneker. "Wine palates they have not; cocktails and the
common consumption of spirits have banished all sense of taste
values." The same young folk, unencumbered by the bay
windows of their Apician forebears, took to dancing cheek to
cheek while their food congealed, forgotten, on their plates.

With the United States' entry into World War I, the already
parlous state of American gastronomy worsened apace. The
sale of alcohol, on which most of the luxury restaurants
depended for their survival, was prohibited within a five-mile
radius of any military installation; a prohibition that had the
incidental effect of eliminating various wine- and brandy-laced
dishes—most notably, terrapin, a delicacy that couldn't be
prepared properly without fortified wine—from the nation's
culinary repertory. Another mainstay of American epicureanism, the canvasback duck, became perhaps the most lamented
of the wartime casualties when its principal feeding area, a
35,000-acre tract in the marshy upper reaches of Chesapeake
Bay, became the Aberdeen Proving Ground. Deprived of the
wild celery that had imbued generations of canvasbacks with
their inimitable flavor, "one of the noblest institutions of the
republic" was reduced to ordinary duckhood. Today, when only
a handful of surviving gaffers can savor the true canvasback in
retrospect, it is hard to appreciate the magnitude of the loss.
At the time, however, it was an occasion for nationwide
crepehanging. As one San Francisco weekly keened, "An afflicted
world must bear with such fortitude as it may a truly grievous
calamity." Mercifully, James Buchanan Brady was by then dead.

It was the Volstead Act of 1919 that sounded the last knell

for the Golden Age of dining out in New York. With ratification of the Eighteenth Amendment, most of the great hotels and restaurants one by one closed their doors. Sherry's was among the first to go, to be followed by Shanley's, Churchill's, the Café Martin, Chez Moquin—just about every epicurean landmark save Rector's, which had already succumbed to changing tastes, and Lüchow's, which somehow was to struggle through thirteen years of aridity before Repeal got the Würzburger flowing again.

The last of the Delmonico establishments still in family hands, the restaurant at Fifth Avenue and Forty-fourth Street, had clung to its existence in relative disarray as conditions worsened, then went bankrupt and was sold to an incurable optimist named Edward Robins, who closed the deal on the very day that Prohibition went into effect. By 1923, Robins had in turn lost his shirt and a lugubrious last supper was served to a small gathering of invited guests on the evening of May 21. The era of *grand luxe* restaurants, with their rain forests of potted palms, their sybaritic appointments, magnificent service, marvelous food, and superb wines, had come to an end. Its epitaph was written by Arthur Nies, a longtime Delmonico factotum and avocational versifier:

> No more the grape with fire divine
>   Shall light the torch of pleasure gay,
> And where the gourmand paused to dine,
>   Hot dog and fudge shops have their day.

Not every New Yorker craved fudge. For those with a taste for something more stimulating a plethora of speakeasies mushroomed virtually overnight to engender a social mix undreamed of even in the days when upstart denizens of the lobster palaces occasionally were nodded to by their betters across a crowded room. It was a mix made up in more or less equal parts of the bluebloods, bohemians, and bootleggers that collectively came to be known as café society. At one time or another, café society forgathered at any of the hundreds of ephemeral establishments that operated, a step ahead of the law and in varying degrees of presentability, all over the city and on West

Fifty-second Street in particular. Of these ventures, the most elaborate—and, as it turned out, most durable—was Jack Kriendler's and Charlie Berns's "21" Club, a many-chambered mansion that not only was to survive the Volstead era, but survives today as the city's most impenetrable bastion of exclusivity, a few privately chartered clubs excepted.

By and large, the speakeasies in no way advanced the cause of American gastronomy. But if the food was bad the booze, for the most part, was worse, and few of the survivors were in any condition to recognize, let alone evaluate, whatever it was that they were washing down with their libations. For those who failed to find adequate sustenance in bathtub gin or watered Scotch smuggled over the Canadian border, the ethnic restaurants were a godsend. Although located mostly in such ghettos as Chinatown, Little Italy, and the Middle European enclaves of the upper and lower East Side, they were no longer too far off the beaten track for a generation of Anglo-Saxons accustomed to getting its kicks wherever it could find them; a generation that had made "slumming" chic and was altogether at home in the cabarets and eating houses of black Harlem. Moreover, with prices geared to the means of financially marginal immigrants, the ethnic ventures attracted the city's proverbially impecunious artists as the grand restaurants of a bygone era never could have. And, the traditional disdain of the wellborn moneyed for the scruffy bohemian notwithstanding, the former can always be counted on to trail the latter to his haunts. (The syndrome is abundantly evident today in the lower Manhattan district called SoHo. The refuge of a handful of illegally ensconced painters and sculptors in the late 1960s, it has since launched a number of apparently durable enterprises that would have been laughed out of existence just a few years ago.)

What Prohibition had begun the Great Depression consolidated. The small ethnic restaurant, typically a family-operated hole-in-the-wall whose minimal amenities produced a minimal tab at meal's end, was far better equipped for survival than the more presentable establishment in one of the city's high-rent districts. If both the Chinese and Italian restaurants at first served a bastardized cuisine tailored to what Americans supposedly were prepared to swallow, few Americans were either knowledgeable or solvent enough to complain that nobody in Canton would have recognized chop suey as part of his culinary heritage or that nowhere in Italy were spaghetti and meatballs eaten as components of a single dish.

The overwhelming preponderance of Italian immigrants had come from the impoverished, overcrowded south of Italy, and it was their exuberant regional cuisine—with its heavy emphasis on garlic, oil, tomatoes, oregano, and eggless machine-made pasta—that a couple of generations of New Yorkers (and Americans all over the country) were to mistake for Italian cooking in its richly diversified entirety. Similarly, the vast majority of Chinese who reached the city, at least until very recent times, came from the overpopulated port of Canton and its environs. As a consequence, the prevailing notion of "Chinese food" was formed by a relatively bland regional cuisine that conveyed little idea of Chinese cookery in all *its* manifold variations.

As it became increasingly obvious that prosperity might not lie just around the corner for the general run of Americans, the more enterprising of the ethnic restaurateurs were finding that the road to relative solvency might lie somewhere outside their immediate purlieus. At first one by one and later in droves, they sallied forth from their own neighborhoods to make themselves more accessible to a clientele that might be capable of scratching up the price of a meal, but not carfare to boot. The sidestreets of midtown Manhattan were clotted during the 1930s with cozy cellar, street-level, and walkup restaurants where five-course Neapolitan or bourgeois French meals were served for less than a dollar and often as little as sixty-five cents. In Greenwich Village, candlelighted Italian establishments predominated. On the Upper West Side, good, cheap Hungarian restaurants—presided over by grandmotherly types in paprika-dusted aprons and largely patronized by the weekend family trade—occupied the parlor floors of innumerable brownstone dwellings. Other Hungarian ventures, less homelike but more apt to serve schmaltzy violin music with the chicken *paprikás,* sprouted in the Yorkville section of the Upper East Side, cheek by jowl with Czech and Polish places where the best duck in the city, if not anywhere between Rouen and Peking, was to be found. The German restaurateurs, following the migratory pattern of their upwardly mobile fellow expatriates, took over East Eighty-sixth Street, while maintaining outposts as far-flung as the downtown financial district and the west Forties. The Greeks could be found on Eighth and Ninth avenues, the Lebanese and Armenians in the east Twenties and Thirties. And while the Yiddish-speaking kosher restaurateurs from Middle Europe were slow to export their *gefilte* fish, kasha, and *schmalz* from the Lower East Side, the Chinese were everywhere, ensconced in some cases in elaborately decorated jazz palaces, but usually in walkup premises where carved teak room dividers provided a measure of camouflage for the resident cockroaches.

All this acculturation gradually transformed the New Yorker into the most eclectic feeder on earth. But while Prohibition and the Depression combined to widen his gustatory range, he was simultaneously cut off from the deepening experiences that the now-defunct temples of *haute cuisine* had provided in a happier time. Without fine, intelligently selected wines—first unobtainable, then unaffordable—gastronomy could be only half an art. Moreover, the modest French bistro, with its inescapable *coq au vin, boeuf bourguignonne,* and *blanquette de veau,* wasn't exactly the center of higher learning, delectable as its limited range of dishes might be, that a restaurant such as Delmonico's, Sherry's, Rector's, or the Café Martin had been. And tasty as the standard antipasto plate, minestrone, red-sauced pasta, and chicken *cacciatore* were in themselves, a steady diet of such dishes didn't make for a very cultivated palate. Nor did a combination dinner of egg roll, fried rice, and subgum chow mein, washed down with tannic acid and followed by one or another of such ubiquitous (and utterly incongruous) desserts as "Jell-O, ice cream, pineapple, almond cake, or fortune cookie" (to parrot the waiter's inevitable litany). With Repeal, most of the Italian restaurants were quaintly festooned with Chianti bottles, but little else changed. The city and nation were still in the grip of the Depression and were steadily unlearning what a near-century of dining in the Delmonican manner had taught them. From a gastronomical standpoint it would require a global war, its aftermath, and the onset of accessible jet travel to get us back on the right track.

One institution that managed to sail through the hard times with all flags flying was the Algonquin Hotel on West Forty-fourth Street. Owned since 1907 (its fifth year of operation) by Frank Case, it was already a haunt of theatrical personalities in 1918, when a little-known journalist and quasi-gourmet named Alexander Woollcott came home from the wars to discover that "a little, unpretentious hotel, tucked away on a side street" served the sort of apple pie he had lusted for while in uniform. Woollcott persuaded a pair of colleagues, Franklin P. Adams and Heywood Broun, to make a regular Saturday ritual of lunching there with him. Before long, various acquaintances joined them, Case took to seating the group regularly in the same corner of the dining room, and the fabled Round Table was spawned.

Recalling its origins a couple of decades after the fact and some years after the group had disbanded, Case had this to say:

> The real Round Table flourished when none of the boys or girls had yet done anything in particular; they were the hopefuls of the future. . . . They were just a crowd of unusually agreeable folk, none of whom had any money (there was more than one guest in the Algonquin whose single account would total more in a week than the whole table together), but they were more welcome, more appreciated than any of the big money guests.

Not everyone found the knights and ladies of the Round Table as agreeable as Case did, but the innkeeper's retrospective appreciation is understandable enough; the group's puns, quips, and epigrams—supposedly ad-libbed but often the result of laborious advance work—unfailingly were relayed by the journalists in its midst to the world at large, usually with due mention of their point of origin. If Case's boys and girls pumped little cash into his coffers, the free publicity he derived from their capers more than made up for their pecuniary deficiencies. They made a landmark of his hotel.

Was the Round Table the endlessly plashing fountain of wit it is supposed to have been? Probably not. The handful of one-liners remembered today seems a rather scant output for ten years of manic effort by a sizable clutch of what were supposed to be the most scintillating conversationalists of their generation. Be that as it may, the hotel prospered while many others were going under, and its restaurant is still frequented by the spiritual inheritors of the Round Table. Some swear by the food, others at it. As George S. Kaufman remarked under the same ceiling a couple of generations ago, "One man's Mede is another man's Persian."

With—or perhaps despite—the legitimacy conferred on it by Repeal, "21" also weathered the Depression, as did several other establishments that suddenly found themselves on the right side of the law. The Palm, a popular newspapermen's hangout on the East Side, for example, continued (and still continues) to draw a crowd of dedicated carnivores to its sawdust-strewn dining rooms, there to wreak devastation upon some of the most heroically proportioned steaks and lobsters in captivity. A great many other places, though, just couldn't function as licit operations and quietly folded up.

To say that New York was utterly devoid of *haute cuisine* during the Depression would be to overstate the case. Voisin, named for one of the epicurean landmarks of Paris (with the concurrence of the latter establishment's ownership), had opened on upper Park Avenue before the outbreak of the first World War and was probably the city's finest French restaurant, if only by default, during the years before Recovery. The Colony Club, originally a rather furtive enterprise at Madison Avenue and Sixty-first Street, had been taken over in 1922 by an ambitious young waiter named Gene Cavallero, in partnership with a longtime colleague, Ernest Cerutti, and the restaurant's chef. Cavallero—whose ups and downs since his birth near Mantua had included a captaincy at the Savoy Hotel in London, another in Berlin (which ended when he accidentally doused the future King Paul of Greece with writing ink), and the operation of a Westchester hot dog stand—had little reason to rejoice over his investment until Mrs. William K. Vanderbilt, somewhat disoriented from her wonted rounds, wandered in for dinner one evening, found the underpopulated dining room to her liking, and passed the word along to a few friends through whose hardening arteries pumped blood of the purest cerulean. During the 1930s, the restaurant's seafood crêpes, lobster *à la Cardinal,* and *poire belle Hélène,* not to mention its liberal credit policy, sustained the august likes of Archduke Otto, Bernard Baruch, the Duke and Duchess of Windsor, and Eleanor Roosevelt, and to be seated at a favored table in the bar was as good as a listing in Debrett's.

The problem was that no more than an infinitesimal fraction of the populace could afford to go to such places—including perhaps a majority of the people who did; not a few restaurants and nightclubs that appeared to be going concerns regularly packed the house by picking up the tabs of decorative but indigent socialites whose presence, it was hoped, would encourage the patronage of honest-to-God paying customers. Thanks to an emergent species, the gossip columnist, the hoi polloi knew which places were in or out almost before their proprietors did. The intelligence was of little practical use; what negligible dining out was being indulged in by the common run of the citizenry took place in the city's chain restaurants, its dessert-oriented tearooms (usually operated by genteel ladies of reduced means), and the ethnic establishments discussed earlier. Moreover, at a time when the man who pleaded "Brother, can you spare a dime?" might have done so in the hope of feeding his family on eight cents' worth of bologna and two cents' worth of crackers, people simply got out of the habit of eating well. By the time the economy began to perk up, the nation was conditioned to junk food and Americans were little more sophisticated gastronomically than they had been two centuries earlier, when John and Peter Delmonico first set up shop at 23 William Street.

What the Delmonicos had done for the nineteenth century, Henri Soulé did for the twentieth. Following a pattern that has shaped the careers of great chefs and restaurateurs since the time of Antonin Carême, Soulé, who was born near Bayonne in 1903, began his professional career while still in his early teens. After an apprenticeship as a busboy in Biarritz, he rapidly worked his way up the pecking order and at twenty-three was the youngest waiter captain in Paris. Thirteen years later he was put in charge of what may have been the single most edifying showcase at the New York World's Fair of 1939, the restaurant of the French Pavilion. For Americans who had suffered through two decades of gustatory privation, the installation became a sort of gastronomic Lourdes. Inspired by its success, Soulé opened a restaurant of his own, Le Pavillon, on East Fifty-fifth Street two years later.

It would be an absurd exaggeration to say that Le Pavillon changed the city's dining habits overnight. Soulé, a perfectionist who let no detail escape his notice, was perspicacious enough to realize that to turn a quick profit by overcrowding his classically appointed, flower-bedecked dining room would ultimately work to his detriment. He restricted his dinner capacity to seventy-five well spaced places, of which the majority were preempted by the cream of international society. Most New Yorkers knew only by hearsay the restaurant's exquisite *potage Germiny aux paillettes, quenelles de brochet Nantua,* and *sole Archiduc;* its truffled pheasant, *rocher hericart,* and *boules de neige;* its luxurious damask upholstery, dazzling chandeliers, and mirrored splendor. And in any event, few New Yorkers were yet either sophisticated or affluent enough to have dined comfortably at Le Pavillon even had its impenetrable precincts been much more accessible than they were.

The real importance of Le Pavillon was that it served as a training ground for the small army of chefs, waiters, and maîtres d'hôtel who, after rigorous drilling by the Napoleonic Soulé, were to open great restaurants of their own when circumstances became more propitious. Such establishments as La Caravelle, Le Cygne, La Grenouille, La Côte Basque, Café Argenteuil, Le Périgord, and Le Périgord-Park, to mention just a few strongholds of *haute cuisine* that have survived the attrition of recent years, are all direct or collateral descendants of Le Pavillon. And, although Soulé himself died in 1966 and his restaurant expired a few years thereafter, scores of restaurateurs around town—the keepers of the flame, as it were—still speak of having worked under "Monsieur Soulé" in tones that might have been used years after the event by those who partook of the Last Supper.

The sort of dining Le Pavillon had come to symbolize was not to become relatively common currency until after World War II. The war itself and its immediate aftermath, during which American forces were scattered all over the globe, had introduced a new generation to a whole spectrum of previously unknown cuisines. Not long thereafter, post-war affluence enabled significant numbers of Americans to indulge tastes that grew increasingly sophisticated and increasingly eclectic as jet travel became commonplace. With Paris the target of much of that travel, New York's French restaurateurs were the chief beneficiaries at first. Later, as casual travelers expanded their itineraries, the Neapolitan cookery that generations of Americans had taken to be the be-all and end-all of Italian cuisine became hopelessly déclassé. New Yorkers, always in the vanguard of gastronomic progress, suddenly craved nothing but "northern Italian" food and a batallion of restaurateurs materialized to oblige them. All at once, black olives and red sauces were out; white truffles and green *pesto* were in. Mamma no longer served forth spaghetti from the kitchen. Instead, waiters in black tie hovered at tableside over chafing dishes of creamed *tortellini*.

As memories of Pearl Harbor, Bataan, Iwo Jima, and Hiroshima faded, Japanese restaurants proliferated like fruit flies. And if New Yorkers at first cringed at the thought of ingesting raw fish, restricting their exploration of still another "new" cuisine to such innocuous options as tempura and sukiyaki, not many years would pass before they were swallowing *sushi* and *sashimi* with the equanimity of pelicans. Spanish food, long erroneously considered to be identical to the Mexican fare it in no way resembled and served only in a handful of restaurants in Greenwich Village, along Fourteenth Street, and in a couple of uptown outposts, Fornos and Chateau Madrid, in turn enjoyed a considerable vogue after the World's Fair of 1965 and the establishment in chic quarters on Park Avenue of an outgrowth of the restaurant maintained by the Spanish Pavilion. Later on in the 1960s, Cantonese cooking, like Neapolitan cooking before it, was relegated to the epicurean attic as the fiery cuisines of Szechwan and Hunan all but engulfed the city.

Traditionally, the overriding appeal of New York's Chinese restaurants had been credited to the extremely low prices most of them charged. This was made possible, at least in theory, by paying low rents and near-slave wages (for the most part to illegal aliens who understandably weren't inclined to air their grievances outside the kitchen), by providing minimal amenities, and by padding out a few slivers of meat with disproportionate amounts of fodder. All quite tasty when laced with the monosodium glutamate that tended to induce a vague malaise known as the "Chinese restaurant syndrome," but only fleetingly filling, in the opinion of most Caucasians. By the mid-1970s, however, Chinese dining had become so chic that the original missionary of Szechwan food in New York, an audacious restaurateur named David Keh, confidently opened a splendiferous establishment on the fashionable upper East Side, stocked it with a creditable wine cellar, installed Hugh Shannon, the Pied Piper of the Southampton country club set, at a piano in the sleek Aquarium Lounge, and was incurring an annual florist's bill that ran to five figures. If dinner for two was no more expensive than at, say, Lutèce or La Caravelle, it was hardly less so.

Keh, who opens restaurants with the frequency of a W.C. Fields opening bank accounts, belongs to a line of impresario-restaurateurs that began in the 1820s with William Niblo of the Old Bank Coffee House and includes the proprietors of the pleasure gardens, lobster palaces, and roof gardens of later times. Loosely defined, their mission has been to add a dimension to dining out that transcends the mere service of food in an agreeable atmosphere but stops short of regarding the ingestion of a meal as ancillary to the evening's entertainment. Present-day exemplars of the breed include Rocky Aoki, in whose Benihana chain of Japanese restaurants the preparation of the meal, performed in full view of the diner, combines Samurai swordsmanship with Kabuki theater; Larry Ellman, the proprietor of a couple of gastronomic horse operas called The Cattleman and Cattleman West, along with a chain of ubiquitous clones called Steak and Brew; the flamboyant, blindingly haberdashed Warner LeRoy, an erstwhile theatrical producer who operates both the showy Tavern on the Green in Central Park and Maxwell's Plum, a stupefyingly decorated three-ring circus of a restaurant-*cum*-café-*cum*-singles bar on upper First Avenue; and Frank Valenza, who, by the simple expedient of charging four times as much as any other restaurateur in the city, invests patrons of the Palace with the sort of cachet normally associated with people named Rockefeller. And then there is Joseph Baum, who is *sui generis*.

As presiding genius of Restaurant Associates, Baum, who

grew up in the hotel business in upstate New York, radically altered dining styles in the city during the 1950s and '60s. As the man in charge of all restaurant facilities at the World Trade Center, he continues to do so today. Stamped from the same mold that produced Lorenzo Delmonico and Henri Soulé, Baum is a martinet, a visionary and a stickler for detail (at one of his restaurants the chef was compelled to cook the same chicken dish day after day for weeks before Baum, having tasted every version, would allow it to be put on the menu). He also might be said to have made an art form of gimmickry and something like a philosophy of sheer panache. At his now-defunct Forum of the Twelve Caesars, a team of resident pyromaniacs set everything ablaze but milady's beehive hairdo in a continuous display of pyrotechnics that often came close to scorching an unusually high ceiling but, according to Baum, "didn't really hurt the food much." The menu, a compendium of mock-historical anachronisms and slyly erudite gags (a featured pastry, tart Messalina, for example, was named for Claudius's promiscuous third wife), listed such sybaritic offerings as ash-baked truffle-stuffed quail wrapped in vine leaves, deviled cutlet of wild boar, and pheasant in full gilded plumage. Even for the few Forum customers who weren't dining on expense accounts, it little mattered that the cost of dinner might obviate the possibility of taking in a postprandial show. Dinner itself was theater enough for one night.

During the halcyon days of his tenure with Restaurant Associates, Baum simultaneously was responsible for more restaurants than a significant number of New Yorkers visited in a year: the Hawaiian Room at the Hotel Lexington, which in season monopolized the senior prom trade; Brasserie, a round-the-clock operation just off Park Avenue; a Mexican hat dance called Fonda del Sol; the button-down Tower Suite; a Teutonic wurst mill dubbed Zum Zum, where the sturdy German serving wenches were sometimes indistinguishable from the pendant sausages, of which there were twenty-nine varieties; Trattoria, where a menu depiction of Sophia Loren's toothsome cleavage had little to do with the matter at hand but may have whetted some appetites for the restaurant's *torta rustica* and *spiedini alla romana*; Charley O's, where shellfish could be picked up at a specially designated bar, and women almost anywhere on the premises, in any quantity from one up; the bosky Tavern on the Green; the Fountain Café, which converted one of Central Park's seediest cruising grounds into a Watteausque *fête champêtre*; Mamma Leone's, which had been a mecca for visiting firemen and assorted squares since about the time of Piero della Francesca; Charlie Brown's, in the Pan Am Building over Grand Central Station, where the stately mating dance of junior executives and nubile secretaries was performed nightly between quitting time and the departure of the last commuter train for the suburbs and less transitory alliances; Paul Revere's Chop House, a hangout for the hotel trade on Lexington Avenue; and The Four Seasons.

Each of Baum's handsomely packaged ventures had a clearly defined style, theme, and function. Some represented serious, if somewhat spotty, attempts to divest *haute cuisine* of its traditional religiosity, others were more casual. Zum Zum, which eventually spawned a sub-chain of its own, was simply a fast-food operation, albeit distinguished by quality and imagination. The Four Seasons, though, was an altogether different story.

The restaurant had (and still has) a soaring grandeur about it that even Lorenzo Delmonico and Louis Sherry might not have envisioned in their wildest dreams. Located on the ground floor of the Seagram Building and swathed in a ceaseless ripple of metallic curtain (a serendipitous effect that wasn't foreseen when the place was designed), it boasted ceilings lofty enough to dwarf the full-grown trees that, along with impeccably manicured flower beds and shrubbery, table appointments, menus, and even waiters' uniforms, were changed four times a year to reflect the mood of each season. A pool that might have been the envy of the curator of cetaceans at the Coney Island Aquarium occupied the center of the main dining room; a king's ransom in contemporary art softened the austere planes and masses of Philip Johnson's architecture.

The menu Baum devised flouted a century and a quarter of tradition by anglicizing conventional French nomenclature, shook up the city's classical chefs by combining seemingly anomalous ingredients to startlingly satisfactory effect, and left its readers grappling with a two-foot-long document on which no fewer than one hundred separate dishes were listed, not counting desserts. Iced oysters were served with hot *chipolata* sausages, beets and lobster combined to produce a marvelously refreshing madrilène. A brace of grilled quail was garnished with chestnut *gnocchi*, and spit-roasted pigeon with candied figs. *Bouillabaisse* was converted from a soup to a salad, broccoli blossoms and nasturtium leaves were served as side dishes, sherbets were made from pomegranates. It may have been the most revolutionary bill of fare seen in the city since 1838, when the oldest surviving Delmonico menu was printed. Moreover, the food was superbly prepared and presented, and the cellars excellently stocked.

By overextending and indiscriminately diversifying its operations, Restaurant Associates ultimately was dragged down like a dinosaur in a tar pit. Those of its ventures that survive today are mostly in other hands, and those that failed to survive the disintegration of Restaurant Associates were probably doomed anyway; the period from the late 1960s onward hasn't been propitious for restaurants conceived and operated in the grand manner. One by one, seemingly indestructible institutions have gone down the drain, adding their names to a doleful, open-ended litany: Le Pavillon, the Colony, Baroque, La Seine, Café St. Denis, Le Voisin, Café Chauveron, Chambord, Maud Chez Elle, L'Armorique, Au Canari d'Or, l'Étoile, Lafayette, Passy, and Le Mistral, to mention a few of the more ambitious French restaurants. Keen's English Chop House, an institution since the time of Mark Twain and Teddy Roosevelt, is gone. The Lobster, the Blue Ribbon, and Jaeger House, all venerable landmarks, are gone. So are the Spanish Pavilion, the Castilian, and Alicante. Le Champlain, possibly the most authentic bistro the city has ever known, is gone. The Oyster Bar at Grand Central Station went, but has risen again. The Forum of the Twelve Caesars went. Le Colisée, a spectacularly unlucky French seafood house of some pretension, went almost before anyone knew it existed. Ratner's, a mecca (if that's the word one wants in the circumstances) for generations of kosher food mavens, is as defunct as the pterodactyl.

The reasons for all this attrition are many and varied. Runaway costs, previously nonexistent operating expenses, unionization, and restrictive immigration laws that made it almost impossible to replace aging chefs and waiters with trained European personnel, all have something to do with the plight du jour. So has the deterioration of some neighborhoods (and, paradoxically, the upgrading of others). A parlous economy and concomitant shrinkage of expense-account entertaining haven't helped, and neither has organized and street crime. It is probably a radical adjustment in the American lifestyle, though, that has had the most devastating effect of all. The rituals and protocols of the traditional restaurant simply have no place in the lives of today's Beautiful People and their imitators. When a society's superstars take to wearing their shirts open to the navel, the old-line restaurant, with its decorous ceremonial, ceases to be a viable institution.

And yet scores of fine new restaurants have cropped up all over town during the middle 1970s. If few of them were laid out, appointed, stocked, or staffed in the grand manner, many were little jewels that offered more imaginative cuisine than had the old red-plush palaces, with their interchangeable menus, décor, and personnel. Minuscule establishments such as Box Tree, Chez Pascal, and Da Silvano, usually owned by their chefs and headwaiters, with meals served in two shifts nightly to a handful of customers, have recharged the city's gastronomic batteries, each by concentrating on a few innovative dishes prepared with a degree of attention that the large-scale operations of the past were never capable of lavishing on the crowds they served.

The glaring exception to the trend toward smaller, simpler restaurants is another brain-child of Joseph Baum's. After a period of eclipse following the Restaurant Associates debacle, Baum reappeared in 1976 to present New Yorkers with the most splendorous bauble of them all: Windows on the World, an extraterrestrial pleasure dome that overlooks city and hinterland from atop the 1,350-foot-tall, 107-story north tower of the World Trade Center. A city-within-a-city-within-a-city, it may not be the equal, from a purely culinary point of view, of the Four Seasons, Le Pavillon, Sherry's, or Delmonico's. Still, it is the most stunning restaurant the world has ever seen and, even without terrapin and canvasbacks, leaves one grieving for Diamond Jim and Diamond Lil, who are not around to gaze down from its dazzling promenade upon a bejeweled Manhattan, knowing that what lies beneath them for the taking is still the greatest restaurant city there is, exclaiming, "God, ain't it grand!"

# A Word about the Recipes

$\mathscr{T}$he recipes that appear in the following sections are either unique to, or unusually well prepared at, the restaurants that supplied them. Insofar as has been practicable, every attempt has been made to avoid the inclusion of dishes that appear in substantially the same form in the standard cookbooks. In a very few cases this hasn't been possible. Not every fine restaurant is a startlingly innovative restaurant. One doesn't go to a typical bistro, for example, in search of *la nouvelle cuisine,* but because it prepares and serves the dependable classics of bourgeois cookery precisely as one expects them to be prepared and served.

In most cases, the menu for a complete meal is given, salads and some side dishes excepted to avoid endless repetition. In the relatively few cases where the menu is incomplete (usually because the restaurant in question had nothing of great originality to contribute), it would not be amiss, when preparing the meal at home, to plug the gap by appropriating a compatible recipe from a comparable establishment.

To a certain extent, an effort has been made to standardize the format and style of the recipes, but without getting hidebound about it. Professional chefs are neither home economists, pharmacists, nor Julia Children, and tend to boggle at any attempt to pin them down to precise measurements, temperatures, and the like. (Among measurements received: "some chickens"; "a coffee cup [demitasse or breakfast coffee unspecified] of sauce"; "a rice bowl of oil"; "a pluck of salt"; "garlic a lot"; "onions"; "carrots"; "green"; and "You know, about this much"—that last illustrated with a cupped palm.)

Nor, for the sake of brevity, has much of an attempt been made to avoid such syntactical ambiguities of standard cookbook parlance as "Sauté, stirring constantly, until hot and brown." (Let the hot brown cook jump on the lazy writer's back.)

Finally, while cooking, like genius, may be ninety per cent perspiration and only ten per cent inspiration, the smaller part of the equation shouldn't be discounted. Probably no chef represented in this book would insist that his recipes be followed slavishly down to the last half-teaspoonful of this or that. Stay loose, improvise when your instincts so dictate, and enjoy what you're doing. After all, if you can't have a good time in the kitchen, well . . . you can always go to a restaurant.

---

Recipes for all compound ingredients starred with asterisks are included in the appendix that follows the last section.

The more exotic ingredients specified in several Greek, Middle Eastern, and Oriental recipes can be found in most well-stocked specialty shops.

Regretfully, one type of restaurant, the traditional American steak house, has been omitted from this book. New York has its share of superior steak houses—Christ Cella, Al Cooper's, the Palm, and Broadway Joe's, to mention a few. I haven't included them simply because the average home cook can't begin to approximate real steak-house cooking with the meats and equipment at his or her disposal. In any case, the recipes—however succulent the finished products may be—are simplistic to the point of banality.

PART TWO

## A la Française

Unquestionably, the three cuisines that have had the greatest impact on world gastronomy are the French, Italian, and Chinese. It is no coincidence that these also happen to be the most distinctive of the major styles of cookery and the most notable for the variety and subtlety of their sauces. Their underlying approaches to the saucing of foods, however, hardly could be more dissimilar. As Waverley Root, a leading authority on both French and Italian gastronomy, has remarked, "In France, a sauce is an adornment, even a disguise, added to a dish more or less as an afterthought. In Italy, it *is* the dish, its soul, its *raison d'être,* the element which gives it character and flavor." In China, he might have added, it is the unifying element without which most dishes would be disharmonious mélanges of incompatible ingredients.

Of these three great cuisines, the very eclectic French, with its emphasis on slow cooking, and the almost wholly original Chinese, with *its* stress on the quick stir-fry, might be said to represent the extremes of the culinary spectrum, with the Italian (bearing similarities to both) occupying a middle ground. Together, they account for the overwhelming majority of restaurants in New York City.

47

French cooking in its purest form is the product of two medieval contrivances: the rotating spit and hanging cauldron. Both were widely used in northern Europe, where timber abounded and long-burning log fires were both practicable and necessary for warmth; neither was much used along the Mediterranean, where both the climate and early depletion of the forests discouraged the maintenance of such fires. The cauldron, in particular, gave the French cuisine its most distinctive characteristics. Perpetually simmering, constantly replenished, emptied only at Lent, it was the prototype of the modern stockpot, the mother of French soups and sauces, the source of almost every dish that is typically and originally French.

*As has been noted earlier, three restaurants—each representative of one of the major international cuisines—have been singled out for somewhat more extensive treatment than the others represented in these pages. To repeat, the logistics of convenience played a more important role in these choices than did subjective evaluations, and any of several restaurants in each category might easily have been substituted for those examined at length.*

**58 East 65th Street**

Conventional wisdom hardly dictated the launching of a large, fully-staffed luxury French restaurant in the spring of 1975. The state of the economy was parlous in the extreme, well-established enterprises were toppling like dominoes, and even the city's most fervent boosters were forced to concede that New York was going irreversibly to pot. In the view of most old-guard observers, the *grand luxe* restaurant had had it. As they gloomily foresaw matters, the restaurant of the future would be a stripped-down hole-in-the-wall, minimally staffed and viable only so long as the public would accept "intimate" as a euphemism for "claustrophobic" and equate an absence of traditional amenities with charm.

At that unpropitious juncture, Sirio Maccione and Jean Vergnes opened Le Cirque, thereby interrupting a string of consecutive losses such as New York hadn't experienced since the days when Roger Craig and Marvelous Marv Throneberry played an approximation of baseball for the Mets. To the astonishment of their confreres, the restaurant flourished from the start and has been playing to full houses day and night ever since, unhampered by a relatively obscure location, escalating costs, and a winter of 1976 that many of the city's restaurateurs savor in retrospect with all the enthusiasm of a dogface of the Continental Army reliving Valley Forge.

Maccione, a soigné, handsome Milanese, and Vergnes, an avuncular Frenchman from Grenoble, weren't precisely a pair of fools rushing in where angels feared to tread. Both had worked at the lamented Colony—Maccione as maître d' and Vergnes as chef—where they had built a devoted following that could be counted on to get the new venture off the ground. Moreover, by locating the restaurant in the Mayfair House, one of the upper East Side's more prestigious hotels, they were more or less assured of the patronage of many of that hostelry's well-heeled guests—patronage that went a long way toward offsetting the nonpatronage of the midtown lunch crowd. Then, too, both men exude charm as effortlessly as ragweed gives off pollen—a not inconsiderable asset in their line of work. Maccioni's deeply dimpled smile, flashed from his station beside the entrance, is the stuff that wildly adulterous dreams are made of. The cherubical Vergnes, the infectious personification of well-being, although nominally the *chef de cuisine,* spends most of each mealtime cruising the dining room in his unstained kitchen attire, dispensing solicitude by the yard ("Tell me, 'ow was your dinnair? Did you henjoy the sheek-hen?"). Needless to say, the high quality of the food is in no way detrimental to the success of the operation.

A baker's dozen of ducks already have been trussed by the time I turn up in the kitchen of Le Cirque—five minutes late on a Monday morning—to observe a day's work at the restaurant. A *sous-chef* named Steve salts the birds' cavities, packs them into two large roasting pans, and drizzles oil over their breasts, while Michel, the *chef saucier,* lugs stoneware crocks, plastic containers, and stainless steel pots from a walk-in cold box. These, he explains, arranging them in the *mis-en-place*—a steel tub filled with hot water—are the sauces and stocks he made the previous Saturday afternoon. My watch reads 7:05. The kitchen here, like those of most New York restaurants, is not equipped with a woodburning fireplace. It strikes me nonetheless that the two first concerns of the day have to do with roasts and sauces—the products, so to speak, of the spit and cauldron.

The white-tiled kitchen is large, high-ceilinged, and poorly laid out—an inheritance that Jean Vergnes (who won't be in evidence until about ten o'clock) and his second-in-command,

Jean-Louis Todeschini (also not yet on the scene), occasionally grouse about but have learned to live with. Two tiers of refrigerated lockers, six to a tier, occupy the rear of the room, with the center given over to the steel shelving that bears the day's array of coffee pots, sauceboats, and trays. To the right as one enters are the gas ranges, already fired up, with their surface burners, broilers, and ovens. The bakery, tucked away behind the kitchen proper, also houses the roast oven and a huge steamer, which is drained by means of a petcock at its bottom. Much of the actual cooking equipment is antiquated; some, positively dilapidated. An oven door in the bakery has a way of falling open at inopportune moments.

By contractual agreement with the hotel Le Cirque is obligated to provide room service. The arrangement frequently results in a precipitate slide from the sublime to the ridiculous, as chefs interrupt the preparation of a *sauce grand veneur,* or some other mainstay of *haute cuisine,* to rip open boxes of Kellogg's All Bran or Special K.

*Seven twenty-five:* Some eighteen sauces and sauce bases have been arranged in the *mis-en-place.* The first room-service order—"One oatmeal!"—is called and filled. Coffee urns steam. Michel, a short, stocky, bearded Burgundian from near Dijon, tests the roast oven for readiness by thrusting a hand into it. In go the ducks, one tray upstairs, the other down below. He ties a towel to the door handle as a reminder, brings a wire basket of vegetables out of the walk-in box, hacks five Bermuda onions into rough slices, dices some carrots, rinses a bunch of celery, and tosses the vegetables into a large stockpot. "For the curry sauce," he explains. He pronounces the word as though it is spelled with only one *r.* It occurs to me that one of the earliest English cookbooks, compiled during the reign of Richard II, "the best and ryallest viander of all Christian kings," was *The Forme of Cury.* The restaurant's steward, dressed in topcoat and fedora and looking vaguely like a minor don from *The Godfather,* comes in to check the refrigerators and walk-in boxes. Supplies are arriving at the delivery entrance.

*Eight o'clock:* Jean-Louis Todeschini, in effect the executive chef, arrives, resplendent in a white-piped blue sweat suit. He congratulates himself effusively on a marvelous weekend but leaves the nature of the marvels unspecified (he is an ardent hunter but the hunting season is over), gulps a cup of coffee, and leaves for his daily workout at a nearby athletic club. Young, handsome, trim-bearded, he is built like a working linebacker.

To the average home cook, the kitchen of a major French restaurant seems a gargantuan affair. Prodigious quantities of food are flung into outsized vessels with what appears to be manic abandon. The din at peak hours approaches that of a boiler factory, and fire blazes alarmingly from ranges that laymen might mistake for blast furnaces. Everything is larger than life; the teaspoonful of cookbook recipes is more nearly the shovelful, measured by sight or heft, in a professional kitchen; a "pinch" of this or that becomes a fistful.

Using such volumes—and in some cases preparing hundreds of dinners a night—such an operation can't always compete, qualitatively, with the accomplished home cook who serves a set meal of his or her own choosing to a few friends; a meal over which he exercises complete control, taking as much time as he needs for its preparation, fussing as much as he likes over subtleties, gearing its progression to a pace he finds manageable. It is such home-cooked meals that all too often in recent years have fostered the illusion that any talented amateur can derive pleasure and profit from the operation of a restaurant. It doesn't often work out that way. What usually happens is that the amateur slaves over a hot stove for the better part of a week in order to dazzle three friends with an exquisite dinner. He has spared no expense and paid his butcher or fishmonger dearly for "waste" (i.e., the trimmings that might have made a week's soups, sauces, or cooking fat) he has failed to take home. But the meal itself, disdainfully isolated from the essential culinary chain that enables the professional to cut his costs by putting that same waste to good use, is a triumph. As he devoutly hoped he would be, he is informed that he is truly a "gourmet chef." As it happens, he is not a chef—a chief among professionals. (Moreover he has never cooked a gourmet in his life). Nonetheless, he is advised to open a restaurant. All too often, he does, finds himself hopelessly out of his depth, and resumes his former career a sadder but wiser man.

*Nine o'clock:* The kitchen is crowding up now; the volume of room-service orders increases apace. In the last hour Michel has checked his dry supplies; made out the day's requisitions; cored and quartered about five pounds of apples for the curry sauce and added them to the pot, along with spices, onions, and jellied *fond blanc;* flamed some brandy in the Newburg pot with a lighted paper twist; poured half a gallon of wine in after the brandy and sloshed another pint or so in as an afterthought; added bay leaves, thyme, pickled tarragon, salt and pepper to the mixture, and then some nine pounds of tomato paste (a full 6 lb., 15 oz. can plus the remainder of a can opened on Saturday). He has also added a fish *fumet* and "a little bit" (approximately a gallon) of water to the Newburg, skimmed and stirred all of Saturday's sauces, and made both a barbecue sauce for the day's grilled meats and a garlicky, peppery *rouille* with which to garnish some leftover fish soup. Somewhere along the line he has found time to make a *fond brun* by combining the contents of three saucepots, to add three cans of shredded coconut to the curry sauce, to knead together a considerable quantity of flour and butter, and to whisk the resultant *beurre manié* into the curry pot, where it will effect a smooth liaison. As the second hour of the day ends, he pours red wine and chicken gizzards into a simmering veal stock, grasps the Newburg pot with his left hand and yanks it laterally onto another burner, all the while stirring it vigorously with his right, using an aluminum paddle suitable for propelling a four-man life raft through heavy seas. He has earlier dumped upwards of a hundred cooked lobster carcasses into the pot, which by my reckoning contains at least eighty pounds of dead weight. It isn't hard to see why French restaurateurs are reluctant to admit women chefs to their kitchens. Few *men* could have budged that load with one hand, let alone simultaneously have stirred it with the other. The aroma of roasting ducks hangs heavy in the air.

Meanwhile other members of the *brigade* have been busy at their stations. A young redhead has taken the ducks out, drained the roasting pans of their fat (which is saved for use in pâtés), and returned the birds to the oven. Another young fellow has breaded the day's *goujonettes* of sole, rolling each between his palms to effect adhesion of the crumbs and fish before arranging them, neatly ranked on linen towels, in a large tray. The redhead has filleted, trimmed, and breaded a considerable quantity of fish, and a kid with a blond ponytail, the *garde manger,* has been preparing the cold buffet. Ponytail is the artist of the group—a miniaturist who works slowly, daintily carving lemons, trimming artichoke bottoms, twisting napkins into cornets, arranging bits of pimiento and parsley for maximum eye appeal. Just before noon his handiwork will be trolleyed into the dining room, where it will remain on display near the restaurant's entrance throughout lunch. Curiously, at a time when home kitchens are becoming increasingly mechanized and the food processor is sweeping the country, the professional kitchen is one of the last bastions of hand craftsmanship. Here, nothing is mechanically sliced, diced, or cut into julienne strips. In one corner of the room a rather quaint chain-driven contraption passes a series of metal gondolas, each bearing a breakfast egg, through boiling water. Aside from an electrically-driven mixer in the bakery and a large processor used for grinding bread crumbs and chopping spinach, it is the only mechanized device in sight.

*Nine-thirty:* Several baby lambs have arrived at the delivery entrance and, after being weighed on a scale hung in the doorway (they average twenty-one and a quarter pounds), are brought into the kitchen. The steward inspects them. "Just right. Not too fat. It's a shame to kill them. They've just had time to breathe." Jean-Louis has returned from his workout and closeted himself in his office, where he will spend the rest of the morning working on the payroll. The redhead is cooking crêpes at the range, working rhythmically with two small skillets, unerring in his ability to coerce a flipped pancake into falling precisely into a receptacle just large enough to receive it. These men have clocks in their heads; consulting no timepiece, he lays aside his skillets, moves to the roasting oven, extracts a panful of ducks, and drains it of their fat, which is boiling like mad. Before removing the second pan he poaches "one single egg—one!" for room service. Michel is everywhere at once, keeping an eye on a simmering Bolognese sauce, making a sauce for the ducks, skimming, straining, and recombining all his other sauces. The redhead has started beating a hollandaise.

Jean Vergnes arrives, all atwinkle, at 9:50. He exchanges pleasantries with all and sundry and is told his breakfast—two poached eggs—is ready. The first of the day's two fish deliveries arrives about the same time: fine, plump, bright-eyed striped bass from eastern Long Island, covered with blood and much in need of the hosing-down they promptly are given; oysters in a cardboard case ("Eat Louisiana Oysters/LOVE LONGER/ Lafourche Fish Co., Baton Rouge, Louisiana"); a crate of darkly gleaming mussels; containers of crab meat in a bushel basket; a sizable school of smoked trout, which are rerouted to the ponytailed *garde manger's* station.

In the dining room, reservations have been coming in since nine o'clock. It's a handsome room, done up for the most part in banker's gray and embellished with what the decorators are pleased to call *singerie*—anthropomorphic depictions of the smaller primates, executed in this case by an artist named Ken Stern. In a couple of hours, impeccably coiffured women will be arriving in force, their consorts shod by Gucci. Sirio Maccioni will be at the door to flash his dimples at them; Joseph, the maître d'hôtel, to tender his slyly elaborate, outrageously stylized gallantries; the cloakroom attendant, to temporarily relieve them of their minks; Joe, the barman (already checking his stock of potations) to dispense their Kirs, lemon-garnished Perriers and Scotches; the captains, to dismember their viands and toss their spaghetti primavera (for the last couple of seasons the chic-est, most publicized pasta in the city); the waiters and busmen, to play out their unnoticed roles; the cashier, also unnoticed at his high desk beside the bar, to disencumber them of their liquid assets. At the moment, however, the exterminator—as necessary and unwelcome as an undertaker—is at work, and a communal prayer goes up that the bouquet given off by his ministrations will have dissipated by noon. (To the relief of all concerned, it would.)

Down a worn steel staircase and into the basement. A woman, a colleague of Sirio's and Jean's from the old Colony days, is arranging the day's flowers while the steward checks off newly arrived cases of wines and liquors. Back in the kitchen, the redhead is still beating his hollandaise, Michel is straining soups, and Ponytail is laying out a cold poached striped bass with full military honors, with chevrons of leek, hash marks of tarragon, and decorations of pimiento and carrot. The dishwashers have begun to clean up the messes returned by the room-service attendants and the pots discarded by the chefs. Michel, having finished the soups, is busy cutting carrots in julienne strips, while Ponytail spoons half-set aspic over his bass.

*Ten o'clock:* Rudi, the Austrian-born pastry chef and a privileged character, has arrived. His handiwork won't be consumed until one o'clock, at the earliest. Therefore he has more leeway than the others. Once at his station, he works easily, efficiently; a casual one-man assembly line who appears to welcome the intrusion of a stranger. He sets and starts his oven, removes a case of strawberries from a refrigerator reserved for his use, and starts to pick over the fruit. "In this field," he says, "you have to start young. You Americans will never produce a real chef or pastrymaker or maître d' because you start them too late. In Europe, a boy with an aptitude for hotel or restaurant work is apprenticed at fourteen. It would be stupid to waste his time by keeping him in school, as you do here. Life itself will educate him, but he will never be professionally qualified if he waits too long. At twenty, it is already too late to send him someplace like the Culinary Institute. At twenty, there is not time left to learn all he must learn."

The man has a point. The American chefs one meets around town don't inspire much confidence. Their training, however professional, usually amounts to nothing more than a crash course, and, however capable of producing a few impressive dishes they may become, they remain dilettantes at bottom, all too often as ignorant of the fundamentals of their craft as the amateur mentioned earlier. (An incident that occurred a few years ago comes to mind. After scanning a menu full of truffled this and flamed that at a small "French" restaurant run by a couple of native sons, I asked about the soup du jour. "I'm afraid there's no soup at all tonight," Michael, the maître d', announced. "David's blender broke down this afternoon.") Moreover, they *aren't* as well educated in general as their European-born confreres. Most European-born restaurant people have knocked around the capitals and major resorts of two or three continents, picking up a few languages and a good deal of urbanity in the process. Humble as their origins and sketchy as their formal schooling may have been, by the time they reach maturity they are often cultured men whose range of interests considerably exceeds that of the average liberal arts major.

*Eleven o'clock:* During four hours of intensive work, much of it hard physical labor, nobody has taken a break. In the last hour, the day's bread and rolls have been delivered and stowed in the pantry; the baker's oven has been filled with the small tart shells that Rudi had made the previous Saturday; larger rectangular pastry shells have been spread with almond paste; jam has been put on a warmer to melt; strawberries have been sliced and positioned on the pastry. A case of asparagus has been peeled, trimmed, tied in bundles, steamed, and blanched with a hose. The redhead has cooked another stack of crêpes, sliced all the ham needed for lunch, laid out semi-cooked broccoli, zucchini, and pasta for the spaghetti primavera. Michel has scraped and cut into julienne strips the day's carrots, turnips and celery, diced several pounds of onions, chopped several bunches of parsley. He has also cooked a batch of saffron rice, filled a number of room-service orders, and taken care of other chores I've missed while talking to Rudi.

Potatoes have been peeled for lunch and dinner; the silver has been polished; the day's supply of shad roe (which will be served in puff pastry shells) has been received, inspected, and iced; the mussels have been bearded. Rudi has melted a potful of chocolate. As the hour draws to its close, he sets the cakes he baked last Saturday on a wire-mesh tray and pours the chocolate over them, while cream whips in the machine behind his work counter. Using a long-bladed pastry knife, he spreads the chocolate icing over the cakes, giving them the glossy, flawless finish of so many lacquered boxes.

The pace, which since seven o'clock has been anything but slack, quickens appreciably during the last hour before lunch. Bouquets of cut flowers are being placed in the dining room, where Joseph purrs into the phone as reservations are called in, and where the cashier, grim as an IRS auditor, with his gray hair cut *en brosse,* readies his desk. In the kitchen Jean Vergnes checks a delivery of rabbits and Canadian mallard breasts. The rabbits, he explains, were killed earlier this morning and will be the basis of a terrine he is preparing for a private party. The duck breasts "will be served vai-ree rahr, weeth a green peppair sauce." The redhead is sautéing spinach for chicken Gismonda, which will be featured at lunch. Ponytail, after sorting and washing a bushel of clams, is cutting melons. At the ranges, which are now clear of all sauces, broccoli and zucchini are sautéing, and the trash that eventually will be transformed into the ultimate glory of *haute cuisine*—its brown sauces—is being loaded into a stockpot.

Rudi still works easily in the bakery, getting a great deal done with no apparent effort. An unflappable veteran, he almost has me convinced he could do this work in his sleep. Not quite. We both smell something burning at the same moment. Unaccustomed to conversation on the job, he has left his tart shells in the oven too long. There must be two dozen of them, all slightly overbrowned. I apologize for the distraction, but he shrugs off an apparent disaster. "There's plenty of time to make more," he says, dumping into a waste bin what would have been a respectable morning's output for a talented amateur. He places a cheesecake on a lazy susan, which he turns steadily with one hand while troweling on whipped cream with the other. He then scores the top of the cake lightly with a toothed rowel, dusts it with sugar, and, using a heavy forcing bag, causes blossoms of whipped cream to sprout along its perimeter, somehow coming full circle with perfect uniformity. Does he ever miss? Probably not. So many puffs per pre-scored segment; a fail-safe equation—provided one works with machinelike consistency. In the next three-quarters of an hour he will finish a potful of custard picked up from the kitchen ("These French! They want cream and liquor in everything"), decorate his chocolate cakes, make the floating islands for lunch, bake another batch of tart shells, and begin work on an elaborate *gâteau Saint-Honoré* for the evening meal. By noon he will have sent a whole array of temptations to the dining room, where they will be displayed alongside the buffet. Now, as he carries one of his more fragile creations to the refrigerator, Michel playfully tries to tickle him.

*Twelve-fifteen:* Still, no one has taken a break—not so much as a cigarette (illegal in the kitchen) or quick trip to the john.

Luncheon guests have begun to drift into the dining room; habitués, for the most part, who are greeted by name at the entrance. This is not the sort of place that attracts casual passersby, and it would make little difference if it were. Tables are solidly booked for most meals, often for a nearly complete turnover, and Sirio Maccioni's biggest headache—a headache of which many a competitor would be happy to relieve him—takes the form of the irate regular who tries to make last-minute reservations and somehow must be placated.

In the kitchen, relative calm prevails before the onset of the storm. The preparatory work—at least for lunch—is largely finished, and, with most diners ordering first courses from the buffet, some minutes will pass before the *brigade* again swings into high gear. The lull is almost ominous, as though everyone were poised for battle. Jean Vergnes's eyes are everywhere. Suddenly a much more commanding presence, he moves to his post at the center of the kitchen, checking to see that each member of his crew is properly positioned and all decks are clear. The redhead is slicing apples while Michel chops spinach, and Ponytail trims sliced commercial white bread for toast.

*Twelve-twenty:* The action begins slowly as a waiter calls for two orders of eggs Benedict and the redhead moves to fill them. Another ten minutes pass before Jean Vergnes, holding a glass of coffee and showing off a postcard from a friend in Mexico, calls, "Ordering one *osso buco!*" And then all hell breaks loose.

Ordering two chicken Gismonda! . . . One order of *goujonettes! Deux omelettes*—soft! . . . One striped bass *bonne-femme!* . . . Ordering one *osso buco,* one scallops broiled, two scallops *provençale! . . . Deux asperges, deux!* . . . Ordering wan floundair! . . . *Une salade du chef!* Sauté pans come down from hooks above the *mis-en-place* like paratroopers hitting the silk; a steak begins audibly to sear as the broiler rack is slammed into position; eggs are cracked into bowls with one hand while the other jiggles a pan. The din is deafening at the ranges, where everyone is working two, three, four dishes at a time. Ordering two lobster Newburg! . . . *Un caneton et un paillard!* . . . One curry! . . . Ordering two spaghetti primavera! . . . One *moules marinière* and one broiled scallops! Jean-Louis, bitching under his breath about this goddamned disorganized kitchen, shoulders his way around the *mis-en-place,* grabs an omelet pan, and pitches in. Astonishingly, Michel will leave a sauté pan teetering on its bent bottom over an angry fire, dodge away to his cutting board, and fine-dice a pound or so of celery, returning to the range in the nick of time to finish the dish. In the heat of battle, he is already preparing for the next day's engagement. Jean Vergnes saunters off for a tour of the dining room. " 'Ow are you? Tell me, what did you 'ave? Did you henjoy it?" Minutes later, he is back in the kitchen, kneading Michel's neck muscles while giving him instructions, like a prizefighter's handler.

An hour later, the pace has slackened somewhat. The redhead is now doing most of the cooking, while Michel chops and slices vegetables for Tuesday's soup du jour. He processes his carrots, leeks, celery, turnips, and parsley at a rate of about two pounds a minute, his knife a blur as he works it in close against the bunched fingers of his left hand. The finished vegetables are arranged in a tray in ranks, their borders rule-straight. Why, I wonder, for they'll all go into the pot willy-nilly. He steps back from time to time to survey his composition with an artist's eye.

In a corridor between the bakery and the delivery entrance, scullions are polishing silver and removing waste by the drumful. Rudi, the pastry chef, is putting the finishing touches on his *gâteau Saint-Honoré* by dipping small *profiteroles* in sugar syrup and arranging them in a circle atop the cake. Jean Vergnes wanders in, samples the filling, and pats his considerable paunch. "This is a dangerous man, with his seductions," he sighs. Rudi tops each puff with half a maraschino cherry, puts the cake out of harm's way, and starts his next seduction by filling five pans with batter. His shoes are covered with flour.

*Two-twenty:* The redhead, who has been moiling like a galley slave since early morning, finally takes a cigarette break, and Jean Vergnes begins to think aloud about what we'll have for lunch. In the dining room, a few remaining patrons linger over coffee and liqueurs. The easy part of the day's work is over.

Dinner, with its expanded menu and much more elaborate dishes, is still to come.

## SEVICHE OF RED SNAPPER

*A refreshing alternative to the trite cocktail accompaniments served with monotonous regularity from coast to coast, this can be prepared a day or two ahead of time. If you can persuade your guests to drink a dry, flinty white wine with it, instead of something more potent, so much the better.*

1  4–5 lb. red snapper
salt and pepper to taste
juice of 8 lemons, 1 lime
1  small onion, very thinly sliced
2  tbsp. finely chopped fresh
    coriander

2  ripe tomatoes, peeled and
    chopped
12  green olives, pitted and sliced
1  small chili pepper, seeded and
    finely chopped
3  cups olive oil

Skin and fillet the fish or have your fishmonger do it for you. Dice fish and combine in a bowl with salt, pepper, and citrus juices. Marinate for 12 hours and add remaining ingredients. Chill and serve. Serves 10–12 as a predinner hors d'oeuvre.

## SPAGHETTI PRIMAVERA

*Edible springtime, this dish has enjoyed a tremendous vogue during the past couple of years. It requires a bit of advance preparation, but the cooking itself is quick and simple.*

1  lb. imported Italian spaghetti
1  cup thin rounds of zucchini
1½ cups sliced broccoli
1½ cups snow peas
1  cup baby peas
6  asparagus, sliced in 1"
    sections
10  mushrooms, sliced
2  ripe tomatoes, coarsely
    chopped

3  tbsp. olive oil
salt and pepper to taste
¼ cup chopped parsley
⅓ cup pine nuts
2  tsp. minced garlic
½ cup freshly grated parmesan
    cheese
⅓ cup butter
1  cup heavy cream
⅓ cup fresh basil, chopped

Cook spaghetti (Jean Vergnes recommends Di Cecco brand) in plenty of salted boiling water until *al dente* (just slightly resistant to the bite). The cooking time for various brands will vary somewhat so check package instructions. Meanwhile, briefly steam green vegetables and mushrooms and plunge them into plenty of cold water. Sauté tomatoes with 1 tbsp. of the oil, salt, pepper and parsley. In another pan sauté pine nuts in remaining oil until lightly browned, add garlic and all vegetables except tomatoes and simmer for a few minutes, taking care not to overcook. Add cooked and drained spaghetti, cheese, butter, cream, and basil. Toss with a fork. Serve piping hot with tomatoes on top. Salt and pepper to taste. Serves 6.

## CÔTE DE VEAU BELLE DES BOIS

salt and pepper to taste
4 good-sized veal chops (see note)
flour for dredging
2 tsp. Clarified Butter*
2 oz. cognac
¾ cup Veal Stock*
4 mushroom caps, fluted (see note)
1½ cups chopped chanterelles, cèpes, or morels

2 oz. heavy cream
4 puff pastry barquettes (see note)
vegetables for turnip baskets (see note)
4 stuffed turnip baskets (see note)
4 cherry tomatoes
watercress for garnish
1 oz. Madeira (optional)
1 tbsp. minced shallots

*Note Jean Vergnes recommends that the chops be* plume de veau *or, failing that, the best quality veal available. Ready-to-use puff pastry barquettes are available at most French bakeries. Fluting the mushrooms would be a pretty conceit, but the technique, albeit simple enough in practice, doesn't lend itself to simple descriptions. In any case, anyone unable to figure it out unaided shouldn't be allowed to handle the razor-sharp knife requisite to the job. Turnip baskets are simply halved turnips, cooked and scooped hollow, filled with a green vegetable such as steamed spinach and garnished with a vegetable of a contrasting color, such as decoratively carved carrot rounds.*

Salt and pepper the veal chops on both sides and dredge in flour. Cook over low heat in clarified butter. Set chops aside and deglaze pan with cognac, Madeira and veal stock, scraping all semi-solids from pan and blending with liquids. Place mushroom cap on top of each chop, pour pan juices over chops, and keep warm. Quickly sauté chanterelles in a little butter, swirl in cream, reduce slightly, and spoon into pastry barquettes. Arrange chops on serving dishes with turnip baskets, barquettes, tomatoes, and watercress and serve piping hot to 4.

## SOUFFLÉ AU GINGEMBRE

| | |
|---|---|
| 11 tbsp. butter | 8 eggs separated |
| 1 cup flour | 4 tbsp. chopped candied ginger |
| 2¼ cups milk | 1 cup sugar |
| 1 tbsp. peeled and grated fresh gingerroot | |

Preheat oven to 375°F. Rub interior of a 10-cup soufflé dish with 1 tbsp. butter and chill. Add remaining butter and flour to mixing bowl and knead thoroughly until blended. Set aside. In a saucepan bring milk and fresh gingerroot to boil, stirring. Add butter-and-flour mixture gradually, a tablespoon at a time, stirring rapidly with a wire whisk until thick and smooth. Cook, stirring often, about 5 minutes. Remove from heat and add egg yolks, stirring rapidly. Return to heat and cook, stirring, just until mixture returns to the boil. Spoon mixture into a bowl and fold in candied ginger. In another bowl beat egg whites until stiff and gradually add ¾ cup sugar, beating constantly. Add half the egg whites to the ginger mixture, stirring and blending thoroughly. Fold in remaining egg whites. Remove soufflé dish from refrigerator, add remaining sugar to it, and swirl dish to coat bottom and sides with sugar. Shake out excess sugar. Spoon soufflé mixture into soufflé dish, which it will more than fill, and smooth top of mixture into a dome. Bake soufflé 20 minutes, reduce heat to 350°F., and bake 10–15 minutes longer. Serve while hot and quite moist, or, for a firmer soufflé, bake an additional 10 minutes. Serves 6–10.

*53 East 54th Street*

One of the least intimidating of the city's *grand luxe* restaurants, Le Cygne, owned by Gerard Gallian and Michel Crouzillat, is as dependable as Rod Carew or sunup in the east. The City of Paris is the wraparound setting, thanks to a vast photographic blowup of a nineteenth-century street plan. The color scheme is the black-and-white of a copperplate engraving, set off by raspberry-red plush and splashes of hothouse flora. Service is as urbane as it can be, generosity is the watchword, and the pride of the house is its sauces—suave, mellow, lustrous. Mushroom caps are still fluted here, '59 Chateau Latour is still available, and Western Civilization is, it would seem, still in good hands.

## TOURTE AUX POIREAUX

| | |
|---|---|
| 1 7″ tart shell, unbaked, in pan | 1 pinch nutmeg |
| 2 leeks, finely sliced | salt and pepper to taste |
| ¼ lb. butter | ½ pt. heavy cream |
| 3 eggs | 6 oz. grated Swiss cheese |

Refrigerate tart shell overnight. Over very low heat cook leeks in butter 30 minutes, turning occasionally. Beat eggs well, add nutmeg, salt, and pepper, and stir. Add all other ingredients (except, needless to say, the pastry shell) to the egg mixture while oven preheats to 425°F. Bake tart shell 10 minutes, remove from oven, and fill with egg mixture. Bake 25 minutes. Serves 4.

# POTAGE MAXIMOISE

1 leek, minced
1 onion, minced
$\frac{1}{8}$ lb. ($\frac{1}{2}$ stick) butter
3 large potatoes, peeled and
   quartered

2 qts. unsalted White Stock*
1 pt. heavy cream
2 tbsp. blender-minced sorrel
salt and pepper to taste
1 tsp. butter

In a large pot cook leek and onion in butter 10 minutes without browning. Add potatoes and stock, bring to boil, and boil 45 minutes. In a saucepan, reduce cream by half. Add cream and sorrel to soup, reduce heat, swirl in 1 tsp. butter, and stir well. Serve hot or cold to 6.

# FAISAN AU POIVRE VERT

2 pheasants
salt and pepper to taste
1 lb. fatback, sliced very thin
3 oz. cognac

1 tbsp. green peppercorns
1 pt. heavy cream
1 tbsp. *Glace de Viande*
3 oz. butter

Preheat oven to 500°F. Truss and salt and pepper pheasants. Cover them completely with fatback and tie them tightly with butcher's string to keep fatback in place. Roast in an uncovered pan 40 minutes, turning occasionally. Remove pheasants from oven and remove string and fatback. Transfer birds to another pan and keep warm. While roasting pan is still hot, drain off accumulated fat. Pour in brandy, add peppercorns, and boil until brandy is reduced by $\frac{3}{4}$. Add cream and reduce by $\frac{1}{2}$. Add *glace de viande* and beat mixture with a wire whisk until smooth. Add butter, blend thoroughly, and season to taste. Split pheasants, arrange on serving plates, and pour sauce over them. Serve with Chestnut Purée to 4.

### Chestnut Purée
Shell desired amount of chestnuts, plunge briefly into boiling water, and drain. Peel off inner skins. Cook chestnuts with a

stalk of celery in white stock* to cover. When tender, drain and rub through a fine sieve or purée in a blender or processor. Before serving, warm purée in a saucepan, stirring constantly, and finish by swirling in a few bits of butter and a little heavy cream.

# CAFÉ DES SPORTS

*329 West 51st Street*

The quintessential bistro, this is where the city's French restaurant workers gather on Sunday nights. The atmosphere is typical of all Cafés des Sports, Bars des Amis and Chevals Blancs to be found in provincial France. The predominantly Breton cooking, served with few frills by sturdy Gallic waitresses, is honest, cheap, and very good, with such robust dishes as *civet de lapin,* grilled homemade *boudin, choucroute garnie,* and *tripes à la mode bretonne* featured.

*A typical bistro meal is best accompanied by nothing more pretentious than a decent, down-to-earth* vin ordinaire. *My choice for the meal that follows would be the same white wine used in the tripe dish. A tot of Calvados, knocked back immediately after the tripe, wouldn't be amiss, either.*

## RILLETTES MAISON

3 lbs. pork shoulder (with bones)
2 lbs. pork neck
2 lbs. fatback
2 medium onions, chopped fine

1 bouquet garni of bay leaves, dried sage, thyme, and peppercorns, tied in cheesecloth
salt and pepper to taste

Preheat oven to 350°F. Cut meats in 2" cubes and place them with onions, bouquet garni, salt, pepper, bones, and 1 cup water in a heavyoven proof pan. Cook in oven, turning meats every half hour or so, for about 4 hours, or until meats are quite tender but still moist. Strain and reserve rendered fat. Squeeze juices from bouquet garni back into pan and discard the bouquet garni. Discard bones and any unrendered fat. With 2 forks gently separate strands of meat until they are quite fine. Mix meat strands and reserved fat thoroughly, pour into earthenware crocks, leaving about ⅜" space at tops, and refrigerate until fat is firmly set. Serve as a spread with good crusty French bread.

*Note* Rillettes *will keep for several weeks if covered with a layer of rendered fat and refrigerated. When covering fat has set, cover crocks with rounds of white paper.*

## TRIPES À LA MODE BRETONNE

*This recipe will yield considerably more than can be consumed at a small dinner party, but it would be impractical to cook the dish in small quantities. In any case, it's even better when reheated after a day or two.*

6 lbs. honeycomb tripe
2 calf's feet, split
1 each: carrot, onion, celery
  stalk, all roughly chopped •
2 medium onions⎤
1 lb. carrots    ⎬ cut in
1 stalk celery   ⎥ ¼″ dice
2 tbsp. butter

1 qt. dry white wine
salt and pepper to taste
bouquet garni of bay leaves,
  thyme, cloves, black
  peppercorns, and 1 whole
  garlic clove, all tied together
  in cheesecloth
4 oz. Calvados

In a large pot, boil tripe in plenty of water for 1 hour. In a smaller pot cover calf's feet with water to spare, add roughly chopped vegetables, and boil about 2 hours, or until calf's feet are tender, adding water to cover as needed. Drain cooked tripe, wash in cold water, and cut into ½″ squares. When calf's feet are done, remove from pot and continue to boil cooking liquid until reduced by ¾. Reserve liquid and cut soft parts of calf's feet into small pieces, discarding bones. In a large flameproof pot sauté diced vegetables gently in butter until soft, add wine, and simmer, stirring, for 5 minutes. Add calf's feet and their reserved cooking liquid, tripe, salt, pepper, and bouquet garni. Bring to boil, add Calvados, and transfer pot to preheated 350°F. oven. Cover and cook 5 hours, stirring every half hour or so. Remove bouquet garni and serve piping hot.


### MOUSSE AU CHOCOLAT MAISON

2 oz. sweetened chocolate
1½ tbsp. water

1¼ pts. heavy cream
1 tbsp. sugar

In a saucepan cook chocolate and water over low heat, stirring until chocolate is completely melted and mixture is smooth. Allow mixture to cool. Whip the cream and fold it gently with the sugar into the chocolate, blending thoroughly. Spoon into dessert cups and chill. Serves 8.

## 212 East 53rd Street

A pleasantly informal little place that might almost pass for a bistro at first blush (and, indeed, maintains an upstairs brasserie), Le Pont Neuf is owned by Jean Jouas, a dedicated, encyclopedically knowledgeable oenophile, and Jean Dagorn, a feisty little Breton, who does the cooking. A long, narrow dining room, decorated with an altogether forgettable depiction of the Paris bridge for which the venture is named, is somewhat lacking in distinction, but the same, happily, can't be said of the food.

# CRAB FINGERS DIJONNAISE

24 fresh or frozen crab fingers, shelled
flour for dredging
1 cup milk
1 egg yolk
½ tsp. salt
¼ tsp. pepper

bread crumbs for dredging
1 cup Clarified Butter*
1 cup Velouté Sauce*
1 tsp. Dijon mustard
½ cup heavy cream
½ oz. cognac
1 tsp. chopped parsley

Dredge crab fingers in flour. Beat together milk, egg yolk, salt, and pepper. Dip crab fingers into mixture and dredge in bread crumbs, coating well. Sauté crab fingers in clarified butter until browned and set aside. Blend velouté sauce with mustard, place in a saucepan, and over moderate heat add cream and cognac. Simmer 10 minutes. Strain and serve over crab fingers. Garnish with parsley and serve to 6.

# MOULES POULETTE

*Jean Dagorn's recipe for this alternative first course doesn't precisely conform to traditional notions of how it should be made, but the finished product is excellent.*

2 lbs. mussels
2 shallots, chopped
2 tbsp. chopped parsley
1 pt. heavy cream

1 pinch salt
1 pinch pepper
1 pt. muscadet

Scrub, beard, and wash mussels. Place mussels in a good-sized pot and add all other ingredients. Bring to boil and cook until mussels open. Transfer mussels with a slotted spoon to serving dishes and keep warm. Reduce liquid for 5 minutes over high heat, strain, and pour over mussels. Serves 4.

# RIS DE VEAU GASCONNE

4 pairs veal sweetbreads
6 chestnuts
flour for dredging
1 medium onion, chopped
1 carrot, chopped
1 bay leaf

1 pinch thyme
2 sprigs parsley
3 tbsp. butter
4 oz. red wine
2 cups Veal Stock*
1 tsp. truffle peelings

Soak sweetbreads in cold water 2 hours, then trim off sinews. In a pot, cover sweetbreads with cold salted water and bring slowly to boil. Boil 5 minutes, drain, and refresh under cold running water. Meanwhile, shell and parboil chestnuts and let them cool. Slip off inner skins and boil chestnuts in water until tender. Pat blanched sweetbreads dry, dredge in flour, and shake off excess. In an flameproof pan, sauté onion, carrot, bay leaf, thyme, and parsley in butter just until vegetables begin to brown. Meanwhile preheat oven to 375°F. Add sweetbreads and brown lightly on all sides. Add wine, reduce by ½, and add veal stock. Braise uncovered in the oven for 15 minutes. Remove sweetbreads to a heated serving dish. Strain sauce and return it to boil. Add cooked chestnuts and truffle peelings to pan and cook briefly. Pour sauce over sweetbreads and serve with rice pilaf to 4.

# CRÊPES NORMANDE

2 pieces orange peel
½ cup honey
1 cup whipped cream

½ oz. Cointreau
12 Crêpes*
½ oz. Calvados

Heat a large copper-bottomed pan. Score outer sides of orange peels with a fork to release oils, twist peels, and add to pan. Add honey, whipped cream, and Cointreau and stir well. Add crêpes one at a time, folding each in half, then quarters after placing it in pan. Let simmer 2 minutes after last crêpe has been added, then flame with Calvados. Transfer 3 crêpes to each of 4 heated plates, reduce sauce to desired consistency, and pour over crêpes. Serve immediately to 4.

*A la Française* ·73

# Lutèce

**249 East 50th Street**

*Haute cuisine* at its absolute zenith. The setting, as elegant as any in the city, is a graciously appointed town house with dining rooms on two floors and a covered garden in the rear. The *pièces montées d'autrefois*—woven pastry baskets and galleons constructed of bread—are still to be found here, and to ingest *Chef-propriétaire* André Soltner's *mousseline de pigeonneau au genièvre* is to know perfect bliss. The fish pâté *en brioche* is heavenly; the crayfish in tarragon-scented, Riesling-laced cream sauce, sublime; the *mignon de veau en feuilleté,* otherworldly. Moreover, the *monde* is as *haute* as the cuisine. One of the world's great restaurants.

## CERVELAS DE FRUITS DE MER

*This, an original creation of André Soltner's, may be the most opulent sausage ever devised. The recipe given here yields ten first-course portions. My advice, if your dinner party isn't that large, would be to serve the dish on Saturday night and save what's left over for a Champagne brunch next day.*

| | |
|---|---|
| 1 lb. pike mousse (recipe below) | chopped truffles (see note) |
| ½ lb. fresh salmon ⎤ cut in | salt and pepper to taste |
| ½ lb. cooked lobster ⎬ small dice | pork sausage casing |
| meat ⎬ | |
| ½ lb. mushrooms ⎦ | |

*Note   Soltner's recipe calls for 100 grams, but your fiduciary may balk at this. Make do as best you can with whatever you can.*

Season and mix all ingredients except pork casing. Using a pastry bag, force mixture into casing, tying it with thin string at appropriate intervals. Prick each sausage in a few places with a needle before cooking. Simmer in water 30 minutes and serve hot with Nantua Sauce.*

### Pike Mousse

| | |
|---|---|
| 1 lb. pike | 1 tsp. salt |
| 3 eggs, beaten | pepper to taste |
| 2 cups heavy cream | |

Pound fish in a mortar as finely as possible, and in a bowl combine with eggs. Rub through a fine sieve and chill. Add cream a little at a time, stirring with a wooden spoon. Add seasonings and blend well.

# STRIPED BASS EN CROÛTE

*A superb dish for a large dinner party, this may also be used as the centerpiece for a cold buffet.*

1 whole 4-lb. striped bass
2 tbsp. chopped parsley
1½ tbsp. chopped tarragon

2 lbs. pike mousse (see recipe above)
2 lbs. Puff Pastry*

Have fishmonger scale and clean bass, snipping off fins but leaving tail intact. In a fish poacher, poach bass in boiling water 30 seconds. Remove to a dry cloth and peel skin from fish, starting just behind gills and ending at base of tail. With a sharp knife cut incisions at each end of skinned portion on one side of fish. Using same knife, split underside of skinned section to make a flap of one side of the fish. Lift flap and remove all bones between head and tail. Cover exposed inner half of fish successively with parsley, tarragon, and pike mousse and close flap.

Preheat oven to 350°F. Roll out puff pastry to form a thin, wide rectangle slightly longer than and slightly more than twice the width of the fish. Cut dough in half lengthwise and place fish on one half. Cover with second half of dough and seal edges, working in tight against the fish to reveal its shape and cutting around tail with the point of a sharp knife. Decorate pastry by pressing with a tilted nozzle from a pastry bag to simulate fish scales. Bake 40 minutes. Serve hot with Choron Sauce* or cold with mayonnaise. Serves 12.

# COQ SAUTÉ AU RIESLING D'ALSACE

1 4-lb. chicken
salt and pepper to taste
4 tbsp. butter
1 onion, chopped
1 garlic clove, chopped
1 bay leaf
2 whole cloves
2 cups Riesling wine
1 cup water

1 tbsp. flour
1 cup heavy cream
1 pinch nutmeg
3 egg yolks, beaten
sautéed mushroom caps for garnish
sliced truffle for garnish (optional)

Cut chicken into serving pieces and salt and pepper to taste. Over medium heat, sauté chicken in 3 tbsp. of the butter, turning occasionally, until it is golden on all sides. Add onion, garlic, bay leaf, cloves, wine, and water and simmer until chicken drumsticks are tender to the fork. Remove chicken and keep hot. Reduce pan juices 5–6 minutes and strain.

In a saucepan, melt remaining butter over low heat, blend in flour, and gradually stir in strained juices from the sauté pan. Add cream and nutmeg. Thicken sauce by adding egg yolks and heating gradually, stirring constantly with a whisk and taking care not to boil. Pour sauce over chicken, garnish, and serve to 4.

**Note**  *The traditional accompaniment is fine buttered noodles.*


## BAECKEOFFE (OR BECKENOFFE)

*Some cynic once observed that* haute cuisine *was produced by madmen for the delectation of fools. Whether practitioners of the art would agree is questionable, but it is well known that most of them prefer homely bourgeois dishes to rarefied creations when dining at home, and usually let their wives do the cooking. André Soltner is particularly partial to this hearty housewives' stew from his native Alsace and occasionally serves it at Lutèce, its humble origins notwithstanding. Traditionally, the dish was assembled early in the morning on washdays, left in the local baker's oven while the women did the laundry at the river, and picked up, ready to eat, on the way home to lunch.*


2 whole pig's feet ⎫
1 lb. lamb shoulder ⎪ cut in
1 lb. pork shoulder ⎪ 1″ cubes
1 lb. beef breast ⎭
1 pt. Alsatian white wine
½ lb. onions, thinly sliced

2 garlic cloves
1 bouquet garni of parsley, thyme, and bay leaf, all tied in cheesecloth
salt and pepper to taste
2 lbs. potatoes, thinly sliced


Marinate meats for 24 hours with the wine, onions, garlic, bouquet garni, and a few peppercorns. Line the bottom of a heavy pot with a layer of ½ the sliced potatoes. Cover potatoes with meat, then add onions, and then add a second layer of potatoes, seasoning to taste. Add wine and bouquet garni, cover and cook 2 hours in an preheated 375–400°F. oven. Remove bouquet garni and serve to 6.

## CANARD AUX FRAMBOISES

| | |
|---|---|
| 1 5-lb. duck | 2 garlic cloves, unpeeled |
| water ⎱ to cover | ½ cup raspberry vinegar |
| white wine ⎰ duck carcass | 2 fresh tomatoes, crushed |
| 1 carrot, roughly cut | 1 tbsp. tomato purée |
| 1 onion, quartered | bouquet garni |
| 2½ oz. butter | 1 cup fresh raspberries |
| 2 sugar cubes | |

Cut duck into 8 serving pieces, removing and reserving carcass, wings, and neck. In a pot, cover carcass and spare parts with equal parts of water and wine and add carrot and onion. Cover and simmer 1 hour. Strain liquid and reserve resultant *fonds blanc.*

In a cocotte or heavy pot, brown duck pieces on both sides in ½ oz. of the butter. Add sugar cubes and garlic, cover and cook at 350°F. for 20 minutes. Drain fat from cocotte and deglaze browned bits with the vinegar, loosening any particles that have stuck to the bottom. Add crushed tomatoes, tomato purée, and bouquet garni, cover, and cook 10 minutes longer. Transfer duck to an ovenproof serving dish, add reserved *fonds blanc* to pot, and boil until liquid reduces by ½. Beat in remaining butter and strain sauce back over duck through a fine sieve, pressing as much thickened matter through as possible. Sprinkle duck with raspberries and place in a hot (450°F.) oven for 5 minutes before serving. Serves 4.

## SOUFFLÉ GLACÉ

*The recipe that follows yields twelve portions, but half can be stored in the freezer for another occasion.*

2 *Fonds de Succès* (recipe below)  1 pt. raspberry purée (see note)
1 lb. sugar                          juice of 2 lemons
½ pt. water                          1 pt. whipped cream
10 egg whites, beaten stiff

**Note**  *Prepare in a blender or processor, using fresh berries.*

Prepare two 9″ earthenware soufflé dishes by cutting paper collars to encircle their exteriors. Collars should extend at least 3″ above tops of dishes. Fasten ends of collars with cellophane tape. Prepare *Fonds de Succès*. Cook sugar in ½ pt. water until temperature reaches 260°F. Slowly pour resultant syrup over beaten egg whites, beating until cooled. Gradually add raspberry purée and lemon juice, blending gently. Fold in whipped cream without overmixing. Fill each soufflé dish halfway with the mixture, smoothing tops. Lay 1 *Fond de Succès* atop each portion of soufflé mixture and cover with remainder. Freeze 3 hours and remove paper collars before serving.

*Fonds de Succès*

1½ cups almond flour            5 egg whites, beaten stiff

Blend flour and egg whites thoroughly. Using a pastry bag, squeeze mixture onto waxed paper in concentric circles, forming two disks, each slightly smaller in diameter than the soufflé dish. Bake very slowly in a 200° oven until well set.

# La Cocotte

## *147 East 60th Street*

At street level it's all intimacy whether you're seated in the bar or either of two small, simply decorated dining rooms. Descend a narrow flight of stairs, though, and you're comfortably ensconced in a spacious, tree-fringed enclosed dining garden. Set in the heart of one of the busiest shopping districts in town and steps away from innumerable cinemas, La Cocotte is one of the pleasantest and least pretentious of the city's better

French restaurants. The courtly, urbane Ernest Guzmits is your host, Guy Peuch is the chef, and, if you haven't yet tried the latter's *pannequet à la barigoule,* saddle of lamb with braised salsify, or casserole of squab with peas, you've got a lot to look forward to.

## PANNEQUETS

*Just about every Gallic establishment in town serves a seafood-filled crêpe of some sort but, to the best of my knowledge, this crackling-crisp version can be found only at La Cocotte.*

| | |
|---|---|
| 1 lb. Alaskan king crab meat | 12 Crêpes* |
| 2 cups *Court Bouillon** | 2 eggs, beaten |
| 1 tbsp. butter | 1 tsp. vegetable oil |
| 2 tbsp. chopped parsley | flour for dredging |
| 2 garlic cloves, chopped | 1 cup bread crumbs |
| salt and pepper to taste | fat for deep-frying |

Poach crab meat briefly in *court bouillon.* Drain, cool, and sauté lightly in butter with parsley, garlic, and salt and pepper to taste. Allow mixture to cool and spoon in equal portions onto centers of crêpes. Fold crêpes into rectangular packets about 2″ × 4″. Whisk eggs, oil, and salt and pepper to taste together. Dredge crêpe packets in flour, coat thoroughly with egg mixture, and roll in bread crumbs. Deep-fry in very hot fat until golden brown. Arrange on napkins, garnish with parsley sprigs, and serve immediately with Herb Butter (recipe below) on side. Serves 6.

### Herb Butter

| | | |
|---|---|---|
| 3 oz. softened butter | 47 | 1 pinch chopped chervil |
| 1 garlic clove, pressed | 48 | 1 pinch chopped tarragon |
| 1 pinch chopped parsley | | |

Knead all ingredients thoroughly and spread on *pannequets* at table.

# SALMIS DE CANARD

Salmis, *in one form or another, go back at least as far as the fourteenth century and, according to tradition, should be made with a partially roasted bird. Whether La Cocotte's version is thus a true* salmis *is debatable, but it's a very gratifying dish. The French often garnish it with croutons of butter-fried bread spread with a forcemeat of the bird's innards, insisting that the croutons be heart-shaped. Ah, those French!*

| | |
|---|---|
| 1 5–6 lb. duck, cut in 8 pieces | ⅓ cup Clarified Butter* |
| 1 carrot, roughly diced | 3 oz. flour |
| 1 onion, sliced | 2 oz. butter |
| 1 stalk celery, chopped | 1 lb. mushrooms, sautéed in |
| 1 pinch thyme | butter |
| 1 bay leaf | ½ lb. salt pork belly |
| salt and pepper to taste | 2 oz. cognac |
| 1 bottle good red wine | |

Marinate duck, carrot, onion, and celery with thyme, bay leaf, salt, and pepper in half the wine for 24 hours. Drain duck, carrot, and onion, reserving marinade, and, using a large pan, sauté the duck and vegetables in clarified butter until golden brown on all sides. Add remainder of marinade and wine and cook over low heat 45–60 minutes, until duck is tender. Strain off and reserve liquid, arrange duck and vegetables in a flameproof casserole, and keep warm. Knead flour and butter together to make *beurre manié.* In a large saucepan heat reserved liquid over medium flame, add *beurre manié,* and cook, stirring, until a liaison has been effected. Add mushrooms and salt pork and pour the mixture over the duck. Add cognac and bring slowly to boil. Remove from heat and serve immediately to 4.

# MOUSSE AU CAFÉ

| | |
|---|---|
| ½ oz. gelatin | 2 oz. Myers rum |
| ½ lb. sugar | 1 tbsp. vanilla extract |
| 6 egg yolks, beaten in a blender | 1 pt. whipped cream |
| 1 oz. Nescafé powder | |

Soak gelatin in a little cold water. Cook sugar at 240°F. until syrupy. In a bowl stir sugar into egg yolks and allow to cool. Blend together Nescafé, rum, vanilla extract, and gelatin until coffee and gelatin have dissolved thoroughly. Add to egg yolk mixture, blend well, and gently fold the mixture into the whipped cream. Pour into a bowl or individual ramekins and chill well before serving. Serves 6–8.

# La Caravelle

*33 West 55th Street*

Roger Fessaguet served his apprenticeship in Lyons, which is generally considered to be the gastronomic capital of France and, ergo, the world. Later, he cooked at l'Oustau de Baumanière when it was one of France's greatest restaurants, and, more recently, became the first chef in the United States to be awarded the French government's Ordre National du Merit. Impressive as the man's credentials may be, the dishes he turns out at La Caravelle are even more so, and to ingest (or, rather, inhale) his ethereal *quenelles de brochet à la lyonnaise,* his savory *pâté toulousaine,* or his regal *homard à l'américaine* is to know absolute bliss. Fessaguet's partners, Fred Decré and Robert Meyzen, are both alumni of that incomparable institution of higher learning, Le Pavillon, and the combined experience of the three owners is abundantly manifest in every facet of their present operation. La Caravelle, with its sprightly Dufyesque murals of a flag-bedecked Paris, its punctilious service, superb cuisine and formidable cellar, has been generally conceded to be one of the world's great restaurants almost since the day it opened its doors to the public in 1960. Its magnificent dining room scintillates now as it did then and the food, if anything, is better than ever.

## FONDS D'ARTICHAUTS CARAVELLE

8 cooked artichoke bottoms, trimmed
salt and pepper to taste
½ lb. lump crab meat
¼ green pepper, finely diced
1 tinned red pepper, finely diced

1 tbsp. chopped chives
3 tbsp. Russian dressing
1 dash cognac
Aspic*

Fresh artichoke bottoms should be used, but tinned or frozen products will do in a pinch. Salt and pepper artichoke bottoms. Mix all other ingredients except aspic, season to taste, and stuff artichoke bottoms with the mixture, rounding off the fillings with a spoon. Spoon soft aspic over stuffed artichokes and chill until glaze is set. Serves 4.

## CRÈME NOUVELLE FRANCE

*This elegant soup is an original creation of Roger Fessaguet's.*

¼ medium onion, chopped
3 tsp. butter
1½ tsp. flour
10 oz. frozen corn, thawed
1 pt. milk
1 pt. White Stock*

salt and pepper to taste
2 oz. diced lobster meat
1 oz. bourbon
4 oz. heavy cream

In a large saucepan sauté onion in half the butter over low heat until transparent; add flour and cook, stirring, 4–5 minutes (flour should not brown). Add 8 oz. thawed corn, milk, stock, salt and pepper and cook over low heat 1 hour. Purée cooked mixture in a blender or processor and strain through a fine sieve. Gently sauté diced lobster and remaining corn in remaining butter for a few minutes, remove from pan, and reserve. Add juices from sauté pan, deglazed with bourbon, to the soup. Cook soup over medium heat 10 minutes longer, then stir in cream, sautéed corn, and lobster, and serve to 4–6.

## SAUTÉ DE CANETON AUX FRUITS ET LIQUEURS

| | |
|---|---|
| 2 ducks | 4 canned half peaches |
| 1 oz. cooking oil | 4 canned half Bartlett pears |
| 6 oz. white wine | 8 lightly stewed prunes |
| ¾ cup sugar ⎫ caramelized | confectioners' sugar |
| ½ cup water ⎭ | 1 oz. each: Kirsch, Curaçao, |
| 3 oz. vinegar | cognac, Triple Sec |
| 1 qt. duck stock (see note) | |

*Note   Prepare as for Chicken Stock,\* using duck bones and trimmings.*

Preheat oven to 425°F. Cut ducks into serving pieces, removing and reserving carcasses. Brown carcasses in oven and reserve. In a skillet, brown duck pieces on all sides in oil. Remove from oil, drain duck segments, and roast 45 minutes in a covered pan. Remove duck from pan and set aside. Discard as much rendered fat as possible and deglaze roasting pan with white wine, scraping to loosen all browned bits. While pan juices reduce, add caramelized sugar to a large pot and, over medium heat, deglaze with vinegar. Then cook over low heat until mixture is reduced by ½. Add reduced pan juices, duck stock, and browned duck carcasses and simmer without boiling for 1 hour. Strain and set aside until all fat rises to surface. Skim off fat, place duck sections in a pan, and pour skimmed sauce over them. Simmer gently, uncovered, for 20 minutes. Meanwhile, sprinkle fruits with confectioners' sugar, glaze under broiler, and arrange on hot serving platter. Skim any remaining fat from duck sauce and remove pieces of duck to serving platter. Stir liqueurs into sauce and pour sauce over duck. Serves 6.


## TARTE AUX POMMES ET À L'ARMAGNAC

*Roger Fessaguet procured this recipe from a colleague in Périgord at the request of a ranking French diplomat and has been using it at La Caravelle ever since.*

1½ lbs. Puff Pastry*
2 Roman Beauty or Eastern
  Delicious apples
4 oz. sugar syrup (see note)

1 oz. Armagnac
1 oz. Cointreau
1 egg yolk beaten with 1½ oz.
  milk

*Note  In a saucepan, bring to boil 1 scant part sugar and 1 part water and continue boiling until syrup barely coats spoon with a light, clear glaze.*

Roll pastry out in 2 thin rounds and trim neatly, using an inverted 12″ pie plate as a template and cutting around it with the point of a small knife. Line a shallow-rimmed 12″ tart pan or pizza pan with 1 circle of the pastry dough and prick the surface in several places to allow steam to escape. Peel, core, and slice apples (very thin slices) and arrange on pastry shell in overlapping circles, leaving a clear border 1″ wide. Blend sugar syrup with Armagnac and Cointreau and brush over apples. Brush pastry border with milk-diluted egg yolk and fit remaining pastry round over tart, pressing around edges to seal. Brush top of tart with milk-diluted egg yolk. Score top of tart by dragging the tines of a fork across it in 2 directions to create a crosshatch pattern (pattern should not extend closer than 1½″ from border). Preheat oven to 375°F. and bake tart 40 minutes, sprinkling surface liberally with granulated sugar after 20 minutes. Serve hot to 6.

*134 East 61st Street*

One of those good things that proverbially come in small packages, Le Lavandou is owned by its chef, Jean-Jacques Rachou, who picked up much of his considerable expertise as *sous-chef* to the incomparable André Soltner (page 74). The setting, with its mirror-sheathed walls, colorful bouquets, and scarlet banquettes, is simple but distinguished, and the cuisine consistently merits superlatives.

## FONDS D'ARTICHAUTS PÉRIGOURDINE

8 medium artichokes
juice of 2 lemons
½ lb. mushrooms, finely diced

2 tbsp. butter
8 slices *pâté de foie gras*
½ cup *Sauce Mornay* (see below)

With a sharp knife, trim tops from artichokes and cook bottoms in boiling water with lemon juice for about 15 minutes, or until tender but firm. Refresh under cold running water. When cooled, remove and discard any remaining "choke" and trim bottoms neatly. Sauté diced mushrooms in butter over low heat, cooking until any water they express has evaporated. Fill artichoke bottoms with mushroom mixture and top each with a slice of *foie gras.* Bake 10 minutes in an oven preheated to 250°F. Top artichoke bottoms with *Sauce Mornay* (recipe below) and brown lightly under broiler. Arrange on small serving dishes and serve with *Sauce Périgourdine* (recipe below).

*Sauce Mornay*
Boil down by ⅓ 1 cup Béchamel Sauce* to which ½ cup heavy cream has been added. Add ¼ cup each grated Gruyère and Parmesan cheese, mix well, and swirl in 3 tbsp. butter.

*Sauce Périgourdine*
Slice 1 or 2 black truffles and sauté in a little butter over very low heat. Season to taste, remove truffles from pan with a slotted spoon, and reserve. Dilute pan juices with 1 cup thickened Brown Sauce.* Simmer briefly, strain, and return reserved truffles to sauce. Add 2 tbsp. Madeira and heat without boiling.

## LA DODINE EN FEUILLETAGE

*Chef Rachou recommends wild rice and a purée of fresh asparagus as accompaniments to this extremely refined dish.*

| | |
|---|---|
| breasts from two 4-lb. chickens | 6 oz. sliced mushrooms |
| ½ cup fine champagne cognac | 1 cup dry white wine |
| 6 oz. dried morels | 6 oz. *pâté de foie gras* |
| 2 whole sweetbreads | 3 egg yolks, beaten |
| 1 large onion, finely chopped | 5–6 green peppercorns |
| 3 oz. butter | Puff Pastry* |

Skin and bone chicken breasts, separate sides, and marinate overnight in cognac. Soak morels in water, white wine, or cognac until soft, drain, and chop fine. Blanch sweetbreads briefly in boiling water and refresh under cold running water. Trim off tissues and dice. Sauté chopped onion in butter until translucent, add mushrooms, morels, and sweetbreads, and cook over low heat until the liquids they express evaporate. Add wine and cognac from the marinade (or, better yet, fresh cognac) and simmer 20 minutes, or until liquids have reduced by about 1½ oz. Add *foie gras* and egg yolks and cook briefly over very low heat, stirring with a wooden spatula. Correct seasonings and add peppercorns. Cook a few moments longer, remove from heat, and allow to cool.

Pound chicken breasts flat and place ¼ of sweetbread mixture on each. Bring up sides of chicken breasts and fold over filling to make a loose envelope. Turn envelopes over, arrange in a baking pan, and leave under broiler or salamander just until flesh is firm and white. Allow to cool, envelop in thinly rolled puff pastry, and seal openings by brushing with a little water-diluted beaten egg and pressing together. Preheat oven to 375°F. Brush tops with same diluted egg mixture and bake 12–15 minutes, until pastry crust is golden. Nap with *Sauce Périgourdine* (preceding recipe) and serve to 4.

## CHOCOLATE CAKE LE LAVANDOU

### *Génoise*

| | |
|---|---|
| 8 oz. flour | 4 egg yolks, beaten |
| 1 cup dry cocoa | 14 oz. sugar |
| 6 eggs, beaten | 8 oz. melted butter |

Preheat oven to 375°F. Sift flour and cocoa together. Using a double boiler, warm eggs, egg yolks, and sugar together over low heat, then beat in a blender until tripled in volume. Add butter and cocoa-flour mixture and blend well. Spread mixture evenly on a baking sheet lined with buttered paper and dusted lightly with flour. Bake 18–20 minutes and allow to cool.

### Buttercream

| | |
|---|---|
| 1 lb. sweet chocolate | 12 oz. sugar |
| 1 pt. heavy cream | 12 oz. softened butter |
| 4 eggs | |

Cut chocolate into small pieces. In a casserole, bring cream to boil, add chocolate, and return to boil. Remove from stove and cool. Meanwhile, beat eggs with sugar, add butter, and cream the mixture until well blended. Add cooled chocolate mixture and blend well.

### Syrup

| | |
|---|---|
| 8 oz. sugar | 3–4 drops vanilla extract |
| 1 pt. water | $\frac{1}{3}$ oz. Grand Marnier |
| 3 slices orange | |

Cook sugar, water, orange slices, and vanilla together for 10 minutes. Strain, add Grand Marnier, and stir well.

### Assembly
Cut cooled *Génoise* into 3 equal rectangles and brush surfaces with syrup. Stack layers of *Génoise,* spreading each with Buttercream, and spread remaining Buttercream over sides of cake. Serves 6.

## La Petite Marmite

*5 Mitchell Place (First Avenue and 49th Street)*

A favorite haunt of United Nations personnel, with a good deal of exotic garb in evidence at lunch, this is one of the most consistently dependable restaurants in the city. Predictable as the menu may be, the old warhorses of *la cuisine française* seem to take on new life as prepared by Gérard Drouet, who owns the restaurant in partnership with Jacky Ruette. The dining room—separated from an inviting bar by a row of graceful arches—is bright, sleek, and comfortable, and the service, all it should be. Ruette, a Norman (as is his partner), is endowed with that ultimate asset of the restaurateur: total recall. Dine here once, and you'll be greeted by name ten years later.

## SAUTÉ DE BOEUF PROVENÇALE

4 lbs. bottom round
$\frac{1}{2}$ cup + 5 tbsp. olive oil
3 tsp. flour
8 garlic cloves, crushed
1 carrot, diced
1 medium onion, diced
1 stalk celery, diced
1 bouquet garni
1 tbsp. tomato paste

1 bottle dry white wine
1 cup water
salt and pepper to taste
$\frac{1}{2}$ lb. mushrooms, diced
30 pearl onions
30 pitted green olives
$\frac{1}{2}$ onion, chopped
5 ripe tomatoes, peeled and
  seeded

Cut meat into $1\frac{1}{2}''$ cubes. Heat $\frac{1}{2}$ cup olive oil in a flameproof casserole, add meat, and sear on all sides. Add flour and crushed garlic, stir well, and cook over low heat 10–15 minutes. Meanwhile, heat 2 tbsp. olive oil in a separate pan, add carrot, the diced medium onion, and celery and sauté until soft. Add vegetables to meat, together with bouquet garni, tomato paste, wine, water, and salt and pepper to taste. Bring to boil while oven preheats to 400°F. When boil is reached, cover casserole and leave in oven 1–1$\frac{1}{2}$ hours, or until meat is tender.

While meat cooks, sauté mushrooms and pearl onions in 1 tbsp. oil over low heat until tender and set aside. Blanch olives briefly in boiling water, drain, and set aside. Sauté remaining onion in remaining oil until wilted, add chopped tomato and salt and pepper to taste, and simmer until liquids are almost completely evaporated.

When meat is done, transfer it with a slotted spoon to a skillet. Add mushrooms, pearl onions, blanched olives, and tomato mixture (which is called *concassé*). Over fairly high heat, reduce sauce that remains in casserole to desired consistency, then strain over meat. Bring to boil briefly and keep hot until ready to serve to 6–8.

# SOUFFLÉ GLACÉ GRAND MARNIER

1 pt. heavy cream
⅓ cup Grand Marnier
3 whole eggs
7 oz. sugar

⅓ cup egg whites
whole strawberries or
  raspberries for garnish

Whip heavy cream with Grand Marnier until peaks form, then chill briefly. In the top of a double boiler, beat whole eggs and ½ the sugar over boiling water until ribbons form. Remove from heat and gradually fold in whipped cream. Refrigerate. Beat egg whites until soft peaks form. In a saucepan heat remaining sugar over very low flame until it melts and coats spoon. Slowly pour resultant syrup into egg whites, stirring, and whip until fairly stiff. Fold into whipped cream mixture, pour into individual soufflé dishes, and chill for 2 hours before serving. Garnish each soufflé with 1 raspberry or strawberry and serve to 6–8.

# Tout Va Bien
*311 West 51st Street*

The original *patronne,* Irès, retired some time back to her native Marseilles, and the restaurant is no longer the gloriously raffish dive described earlier in these pages. The food, however, seems even better now than it did thirty years ago—and hardly more expensive. What you get here is good, straightforward bourgeois fare, served in unpretentious surroundings by matter-of-fact Frenchwomen. Recognizable performers still drop in from time to time on their way to and from the nearby theater district, and the walls are covered with their photographs. The cooking is still meridional for the most part (although Chef Serge Houry hails from Chambord), and the *bouillabaisse* is still one of the city's finest. Nina Migliacco, a Marseillaise, and her Italian-born husband, Carlo, are the present owners and, as the name of the restaurant assures us, all goes very well indeed under their direction.

### COQUILLES MAISON

4 tbsp. butter
3 shallots, minced
1 lb. sea scallops, quartered
¾ cup white wine
¾ cup Chicken Stock* or
Chicken Consommé*
3 tbsp. flour

½ cup half-and-half (milk and
heavy cream)
10 medium mushroom caps,
sliced
2 egg yolks
4 tbsp. grated Parmesan cheese

Heat butter in a pan, add shallots, and sauté over medium heat until lightly colored. Add scallops and cook 3 minutes. Add wine and stock or consommé, stir, and add flour, half-and-half, and mushrooms, mixing ingredients well. (If mixture gets too thick, dilute with additional half-and-half.) Remove from heat and beat in egg yolks and ⅔ of the cheese. Pour mixture into large scallop shells (available at most kitchenware shops and Japanese specialty shops), sprinkle with remaining cheese, and brown lightly under broiler. Serves 4.

### BOUILLABAISSE

*Recipes for this most regal of soups abound, and almost every French restaurant in the city serves what imaginative souls are pleased to call* bouillabaisse, *but a really good one is extremely hard to find. The* bouillabaisse *served at Tout Va Bien, although necessarily a bastardized version of those served in Marseilles and its environs, is the best I've eaten in New York.*

bones, heads, and trimmings of
  at least 2 striped bass and 2
  red snappers
1 whole blackfish
5 tbsp. olive oil
2 stalks celery, chopped
1½ onions, chopped
10 garlic cloves
6–7 ripe tomatoes, roughly
  chopped

1 tbsp. fennel seed, crushed
½ tsp. saffron
peel of ½ orange
water
1 tbsp. tomato paste
salt and freshly ground pepper
  to taste

Place all ingredients in a large pot with water to double level of solids and simmer gently for at least 3 hours. Remove and discard as much skin and bone as possible and work contents of pot through a food mill, grinding as much flesh as possible into the soup to give it body. Return soup to pot and simmer gently while preparing the *Garniture.*

### Garniture

3 live lobsters
1 3-lb. striped bass
1 3-lb. red snapper
30 mussels, in shells

24 small shrimp, unshelled
Pernod to taste
2 tbsp. chopped parsley

Split lobsters and cut fish vertically into inch-thick slices. Scrub and beard mussels. Add lobsters, shrimp, and mussels to soup, cover, and cook 10 minutes. Add fish and cook uncovered 10 minutes longer. Remove fish and shellfish and arrange them on a heated serving platter. Correct soup seasonings and add Pernod to taste just before serving. (There should be a perceptible but not overpowering bouquet.) Place a large round of hard French bread, rubbed with garlic, in each soup plate, pour soup over it, and sprinkle soup portions and seafood with chopped parsley. Serve, with *Rouille* on the side, to 6.

### Rouille

1 garlic clove
1 fresh or dried hot red chili,
  seeded

1 cup mayonnaise

In a mortar, pound garlic and chili together to form a smooth paste, moistening with a few drops of soup, if necessary. Blend thoroughly with mayonnaise and allow guests to spoon *rouille* into soup according to taste.

# LA GRENOUILLE

*3 East 52nd Street*

Gleaming expanses of mirror, red velvet upholstery, pale green walls, and spectacular flower arrangements combine here to blot out three seasons and create *un printemps perpetuel.* This long has been one of the city's gastronomic ornaments; a glittering setting where a chic, moneyed clientele picks daintily at the masterful handiwork of Chef André Joanlanne. The founder, Charles Masson, is, alas, no longer with us, but his gracious widow, Gisele, holds the operation together through a combination of Gallic charm and Gallic acumen.

## CÔTES D'AGNEAU CHAMPVALLON

salt to taste
12 rib lamb chops
2 tbsp. butter
3 onions, thinly sliced
4 potatoes, thinly sliced
bouquet garni including 1 bay
    leaf

1 pinch thyme
2 garlic cloves, crushed
3 cups Beef Consommé*
½ cup dry white wine
chopped parsley for garnish

Salt chops and brown lightly in half the butter. Remove and reserve chops and pan drippings. Add remaining butter to pan and smother with onions, cooking them until translucent over low heat and taking care not to brown them. As onions wilt, mix in potatoes and add salt to taste, bouquet garni, thyme, and garlic. Sauté briefly, remove and discard bouquet garni and garlic, reserving pan drippings.

Combine drippings from both sautés and cook until thickened and light brown. Add consommé and wine, stirring until drippings are dissolved and incorporated, and remove from fire. In a baking dish, arrange a layer of ½ the potato-onion mixture, then a layer of the chops, and, finally, the remaining potato-onion mixture. (If the pan is small and the chops are large, arrange in 2 layers, alternating ingredients in the same sequence.) Add liquids from sauté pan and bring to boil while oven preheats to 375°F. Place in oven and bake uncovered 45 minutes, or until very well done and browned on top, by which time the dish should be moist but not soupy. Garnish with chopped parsley and serve to 4–6, depending on size of chops and appetites.

## OEUFS À LA NEIGE

| | |
|---|---|
| 3 cups milk | 1 cup sugar |
| 6 egg whites | 2 cups *Crème Anglaise** |

Pour milk into a large heavy skillet and bring to simmer. Meanwhile beat egg whites until fluffy. Gradually and gently beat sugar into egg whites and continue beating until mixture is stiffly peaked. With a large spoon, scoop up egg-shaped mounds of the mixture and set carefully into simmering milk. Poach, a few at a time, for 30 seconds, or just until lightly colored. Remove "snow eggs" with a skimmer and drain on napkins until cool. Pour *crème anglaise* into a crystal bowl, mound meringue "eggs" over sauce to form a pyramid, and serve to 4–6.

# The Palace
### 420 East 59th Street

The ultimate in conspicuous consumption, the prix-fixe dinner here—taxes and an obligatory twenty-three percent *pourboire* included—will set you back a hundred smackers a head before you get a look at the wine list. The genius behind the enterprise is Frank Valenza, an actor *manqué* whose only previous experience as a restaurateur had to do with the supervision of a ho-hum establishment called Proof of the Pudding, which he still operates. His premises (if you ignore a collection of decidedly mediocre paintings) are gorgeous, the table appointments are superb, and the service is worthy of royalty. The food—oh yes, the food—is simply exquisite, and well it might be at those prices. Michel Fitoussi is the chef, and only one question remains after inhaling his lush, rarefied handiwork: What can he do with corned beef hash?

*Dinner at The Palace is a leisurely multicoursed affair. The menu that follows is made up of one hot and one cold appetizer, soup, a roast, vegetable accompaniments, and a dessert. Even should a course or two be omitted, it's still quite a meal.*

## PAUPIETTES DE SAUMON FUMÉ À LA CRÈME FRAÎCHE

4 hard-boiled eggs, sieved
1 tsp. minced chives
6 puff paste barquettes, about
  2″ × 4″ (see note)
3 tsp. mayonnaise
½ cup *Crème Fraîche**

6 slices smoked salmon, about
  3″ × 5″, 1 oz. each
4½ oz. caviar
1 tomato, carved in rose shape
12 lemon wedges, seeded

*Note  Puff paste barquettes may be purchased at most French pastry shops.*

Combine sieved eggs and chives. Coat outer edges of each barquette with mayonnaise and roll in chive mixture. Spoon a thin layer of *crème fraîche* into the bottom of each barquette. Coat each slice of salmon with a thin layer of *crème fraîche* and spoon 1 tbsp. caviar onto one end of each salmon slice. Starting at that end, roll up each slice and place in a barquette. Decorate open ends of salmon rolls with piped rosettes of *crème fraîche* and spoon remaining caviar onto salmon rolls. Arrange barquettes on a round silver plate with the carved tomato at its center and with lemon wedges circling its edge. Serves 6.

# BROCHETTES DE ST. JACQUES AUX CÈPES

16 small sea scallops
2 tbsp. olive oil
4 pinches thyme
salt and pepper to taste
3 tbsp. chopped cèpes (see note)
1 tsp. coarsely chopped shallot
¼ tsp. coarsely chopped garlic
1 tsp. coarsely chopped parsley

3 tbsp. sweet butter
1½ cups White Wine Sauce*
3 tbsp. Crayfish Butter*
3 tbsp. heavy cream
4 tbsp. whipped cream
4 very thin Crêpes*
1 tbsp. chopped truffle (optional)

**Note** *Fresh cèpes are, of course, preferable, but hard to find. Tinned cèpes or even domestic mushrooms may be used if necessary.*

Impale 4 scallops on each of 4 small bamboo skewers. Roll skewered scallops in oil, sprinkle with thyme and salt and pepper to taste, and allow to marinate for ½ hour. Lightly sauté cèpes, shallots, garlic, and parsley in 1 tbsp. of the butter and set aside. In a double boiler, bring white wine sauce to boil with crayfish butter, heavy cream, and 2 tbsp. butter. Lower heat, salt and pepper to taste, fold in whipped cream, and keep warm.

In an ungreased cast-iron pan, quickly brown skewered scallops on all sides, allowing no more than 1½ minutes cooking time for the whole process. Lightly butter an ovenproof serving platter and arrange 4 crêpes on it. On the right side of each crêpe, spoon ¼ of the sautéed cèpe mixture, top with a brochette of scallops, and remove skewer. Fold left side of crêpe over right. When all 4 have been filled and folded, pour wine sauce over them, sprinkle with chopped truffle, and run under a hot broiler for a few seconds, until pale golden. For a touch of The Palace's special sort of class, you might garnish the serving dish with lobster legs or crayfish tails and puff pastry crescents. You might also, for that matter, dissolve an orient pearl in each guest's Champagne. In any case, the dish serves 4.

# SOUPE DE MOULES AU SAFRAN

3 lbs. mussels
5 medium shallots, chopped
1 bay leaf
1 pinch thyme
5 twists fresh black pepper
½ cup white wine
½ cup water
2 cups Fish Stock*
6 tbsp. sweet butter

5 tbsp. flour
1 cup heavy cream
2 pinches saffron, boiled in ¼
  cup white wine
¼ lb. bay scallops
2 tbsp. thin julienne strips of
  celery, carrot, and leek,
  blanched in Fish Stock*

Beard and scrub mussels thoroughly and soak them in fresh water 1–2 hours. Drain and place in a large pot with shallots, herbs, pepper, wine, water, and stock. Cover, bring to boil over high heat, and cook just until mussel shells open (about 10 minutes). Reserve mussels for another use and strain cooking broth into an enameled saucepan through a very fine sieve or double thickness of cheesecloth. Over high heat, rapidly boil down broth for about 5 minutes to concentrate its flavor.

In another saucepan, melt 4 tbsp. of the butter and blend with the flour, stirring for 2 minutes over low heat. Remove from heat and slowly add mussel broth, beating with a wire whisk. Return to heat, bring to boil, stirring, lower heat, and simmer gently 15 minutes. (If mixture is too thick, add a little fish stock. If too thin, add a little *beurre manié* made by kneading together equal parts of flour and butter.) When consistency is correct, strain again and return to low heat. Continue stirring and add cream, saffron, scallops, and drained vegetables. Swirl in remaining butter, correct seasoning, and serve immediately to 4–6.

# FILET DE VEAU FLORENTINE

1 6-lb. loin of veal, boned
salt and pepper to taste
5 lbs. spinach, washed and
  trimmed

5 tbsp. butter
1 cup diced Swiss cheese
3 tbsp. vegetable oil
¼ cup chopped onion

| | |
|---|---|
| ¼ cup chopped carrot | 1 cup dry white wine |
| ¼ cup chopped celery | 2 medium tomatoes, chopped |
| ¼ cup chopped parsley | 4–5 cups Veal or Chicken |
| 2 sprigs thyme | Stock* |
| 1 bay leaf, crushed | 1 cup heavy cream |
| 3 garlic cloves, minced | |

Split veal loin lengthwise without separating halves and, with the side of a cleaver, flatten the thickest parts. Sprinkle with salt and pepper. In a large pot, cover spinach with enough water to allow it to swirl freely. Cook 5 minutes until just tender, drain in a colander, and chill under cold running water. Drain spinach well and squeeze a handful at a time until dry. Sauté spinach in 2 tbsp. butter for 2 minutes. Add cheese and blend well. Season with salt and pepper and remove from heat.

Arrange spinach mixture lengthwise down center of the veal. Roll veal tightly and tie at 1″ intervals with butcher's string. Cover ends with aluminum foil and tie securely. Brown veal on all sides in hot vegetable oil and set aside. Over moderate heat, sauté onion, carrot, celery, parsley, thyme, bay leaf, and garlic in 3 tbsp. butter until lightly colored but not brown.

Preheat oven to 350°F. Place veal in a baking pan and add sautéed vegetables, wine, and tomatoes. Pour in stock and bring to simmer over moderate heat. Cover pan and bake in oven for 1½ hours, basting frequently. Transfer veal to a heated dish and keep warm.

Strain pan juices into a saucepan and reduce by half over moderate heat. Stir in cream, correct seasoning, and simmer for a few minutes until sauce thickens slightly. Slice veal in ¾″ thicknesses and arrange on a heated serving platter. Top with sauce and serve immediately to 8–10.

## FAGOTS DE LEGUMES

*Quantities deliberately have been omitted for these engaging vegetable "bundles." Let your needs be your guide.*

carrots

Clarified Butter*

white turnips

salt to taste

trimmed green tops from very
  fresh scallions

Cut carrots lengthwise into ⅛" slices. Cut slices into large "matchsticks," 1" long and ⅛" wide. Briefly blanch in boiling water (they should remain firm and crisp) and refresh under cold running water. Repeat procedure with turnips. Cut scallion greens into strips 10" long and ¼" wide. Blanch in boiling water 5 seconds and immediately plunge into cold water. Across centers of scallion greens, stack carrot sticks two high and three across. Bring ends of scallion greens up over carrot stacks, tie in simple bows, and trim as you would the ribbon on a gift package. Repeat procedure with turnips. Place vegetable bundles in a small pan with clarified butter and salt to taste. Cook, covered, over low heat just until tender, remove carefully from butter, and serve 1 bundle of each vegetable per portion.

## POMMES SOUFFLÉS

Idaho potatoes (1 per serving)        vegetable oil for deep frying

Peel and pare potatoes into cylinders 2" in diameter. Slice cylinders into ⅛" chips and dry chips separately with a clean cloth.

Fill a pot or deep fryer to ⅔ of its capacity with oil and heat to 275°F. Drop potato disks into hot oil a few at a time, swirling oil to prevent potatoes from sticking together but taking care not to let any overflow the pot. After about 5 minutes, potatoes will rise to surface, slightly puffed.

Meanwhile heat a second pot of oil to 475°F. (the oil should be fragrant but should not smoke) and transfer potatoes to second pot where they will puff in seconds. Immediately transfer to a dry cloth to drain, discarding any unpuffed chips.

Just before serving, drop the puffed chips into the hotter of the two oils and remove after a few seconds, or when they have lightly browned. Drain briefly, salt to taste, and serve at once.

# THE PALACE SOUFFLÉ GLACÉ PRALINÉ

*Many and varied are the frozen soufflés served by the city's French restaurants. This is one of the best. Because its preparation is fairly complex, let's take it in easy steps.*

### Step I: Praline Powder

½ cup blanched almonds          1 cup sugar
½ cup shelled filberts          ⅓ cup water

Grease a rimmed cookie sheet just large enough to hold almonds and filberts in a single layer. On a second, ungreased cookie sheet, toast almonds and filberts in a moderate (350°F.) oven until the almonds take color and the filbert skins begin to blister. In a saucepan, dissolve sugar in the water and cook over moderate heat until the mixture takes on a caramel color. Add toasted nuts immediately, pour mixture onto greased cookie sheet, and allow to cool. When cool and set, break the resultant nut brittle into small pieces, pulverize them in a food processor, and reserve.

### Step II: Strawberry Jam

1 dry pt. strawberries, washed          1 cup sugar
  and hulled

In a saucepan, bring berries and sugar to boil, stirring occasionally. Remove from heat and allow to cool.

### Step III: Creamed Italian Meringue

1 cup egg whites          1 lb. sugar
water                     3 cups heavy cream

This requires some tricky timing. Place egg whites in a large Mixmaster bowl and start beating at low speed. Meanwhile, dissolve sugar in a saucepan, using as little water as possible. Bring to boil and cook until soft ball stage is reached (238°F. on a candy thermometer). As sugar cooks, gradually increase mixer speed so as to have egg whites form stiff peaks at the same time that sugar syrup reaches hard ball stage (250–255°F.). As soon as syrup reaches this stage, lower mixer speed to medium and pour syrup into egg whites in a thin continuous stream. Continue to beat mixture until cooled. Whip heavy cream and gently fold in cooled meringue mixture until all is smooth and homogenized.

### Step IV: Assembly

Cut aluminum foil into a 6″ × 24″ strip and wrap around a 2–2½ qt. soufflé dish to form a collar that, when attached, will double the capacity of the dish. Tape collar securely in place. Line bottom of soufflé dish with a thin layer of strawberry jam. Cover jam with ½ the meringue mixture. In succession, cover this with remaining jam and remaining meringue mixture. Freeze for several hours or overnight. When firm, remove foil collar and cover top of the soufflé with reserved praline powder. Serves 8–10.

Le Périgord Park    Le Périgord

*575 Park Avenue*        *405 East 52nd Street*

Willy Krause and Georges Biguet are the owners of these sister-establishments, of which the older is Le Périgord. Both men are descendants, professionally speaking, of the late Henri Soulé (page 36) and the influence of that indomitable perfectionist pervades every facet of both their operations. The glittering, mirror-sheathed, flower-bedecked Périgord is the smaller of the two restaurants, and, if it lacks just a bit of the panache to be found at the more grandly proportioned Périgord-Park (with *its* airy, insouciant decorations by the late Jean Pages), Le Périgord remains a mecca for the city's more exacting gastronomes. The menus, devised by Krause, are virtually interchangeable and the cooking, supervised in both instances by the same Krause, is superb.

## SALADE D'HOMARD

2  3-lb. lobsters, boiled
1  oz. cognac
4  fresh mushrooms, sliced
1  black truffle, sliced
salt and pepper to taste
1  head Boston lettuce

2  cooked artichoke bottoms
1  stalk celery
1  oz. olive oil
1  pinch each: thyme, chopped
   parsley, chopped chervil

Shell lobsters and cube meat. Macerate 4–5 minutes in cognac with sliced mushrooms, truffle, and salt and pepper to taste. (Chef Willy Krause: "Use good cognac and don't macerate the lobster any longer than five minutes, or it will toughen.") Slice lettuce into fine shreds to make a chiffonade. Slice artichoke bottoms and cut celery in julienne strips. Toss chiffonade, artichokes, and celery with olive oil, add to lobster mixture, and sprinkle with herbs. Serve immediately to 6.

## POULET POÊLÉ PÉRIGOURDINE

2  black truffles, sliced
2  3-lb. chickens
salt and pepper to taste
2  slices lard
¼ cup olive oil
¼ cup melted butter
1  onion

1  stalk celery
1  carrot
1  pinch thyme
1  bay leaf
½ cup Madeira
1  cup Brown Sauce*
4  slices *pâté de foie gras,* diced

Insert 4 slices of truffle between skin and breast of each chicken, arranging them 2 to each side and reserving remainder. Salt and pepper birds and place a slice of lard over the breastbone of each. Wrap birds loosely in aluminum foil and refrigerate 3–4 hours so that truffle bouquet may permeate the flesh. In a large casserole, place each chicken on its side, pour mixed oil and butter over them, and cook over low heat (300°F.) 15 minutes, until brown on one side. Turn chickens and repeat, browning second side. Meanwhile chop onion, celery, and carrot into large dice. When chickens are browned on both sides, turn them breasts-up, add diced vegetables, thyme, and bay leaf to casserole, and cook, covered, 15–20 minutes, basting occasionally. When chickens are cooked through and well browned, remove to a serving platter and keep warm. Drain fats from casserole, deglaze with Madeira, and cook until wine evaporates. Meanwhile chop reserved truffle into very fine dice. When wine has evaporated, add brown sauce, bring to boil, and strain. Add diced truffle and *foie gras* to sauce, pour over chickens, and serve very hot to 4.


## POIRE BELLE FRANÇOISE


*Willy Krause created and named this superb dessert for his wife several years ago. It has been a favorite at the restaurants ever since.*

24–30 fresh raspberries
½ cup Armagnac
6 fresh pears
juice of ½ lemon
2 cups sugar

1 vanilla bean, cut in 2–3 pieces
3 cups water
1 tsp. crushed crystallized
   violets


Macerate raspberries in Armagnac 15 minutes, then drain, reserving Armagnac. Peel pears as closely as possible and let stand in cold water to cover, laced with lemon juice, until ready for use. Place sugar, vanilla bean, pears, and 3 cups water in a large saucepan, bring to boil, and simmer 10 minutes, or until pears are tender. Drain, cool, and core pears, discarding poaching ingredients. Insert 4–5 macerated raspberries into hollow core of each pear and set aside while preparing *Barquettes de Nougatine.*

### Barquettes de Nougatine

8 oz. sugar  
juice of 1 lemon

4 oz. blanched almonds, slivered

In a saucepan, cook sugar with lemon juice over low heat until pale brown. Stir in almonds and remove from heat. On an oiled nonabsorbent surface (preferably marble), form mixture into 6 well-spaced patties and roll out in ¼"-thick rounds, using an oiled metal rolling pin or glass bottle. Allow *nougatine* rounds to cool slightly (do not refrigerate), pick them up with an oiled metal spatula, and drape each over a lightly oiled metal *barquette* mold. (Molds should be round and slightly larger in diameter than pears, with fluted sides.) Using a lemon or lime, gently press *nougatine* rounds into molds, effecting a snug fit at all points. Trim off any excess *nougatine* that overhangs mold rims and allow to cool thoroughly without refrigeration. Meanwhile prepare *Mousse à l'Armagnac.*

### Mousse à l'Armagnac

4 egg yolks  
½ cup sugar  
reserved Armagnac from macerate

1 cup heavy cream, whipped

In a blender, beat egg yolks at very low speed. In a saucepan, cook sugar over low heat just until it begins to color. With blender running, pour sugar into egg yolks in a slow thin stream, beating until mixture thickens. When thickened, add Armagnac and leave machine running until mixture thickens again. Turn off blender, pour into bowl, and fold in whipped cream with a wooden spatula, blending gently until all ingredients are thoroughly incorporated.

*Assembly*

Remove *nougatine* cups from molds and place on serving dishes. Stand a pear in each cup and spread *Mousse à l'Armagnac* over pears, using a rubber spatula and coating them lightly and evenly. Decorate pears with crushed crystallized violets and neatly fill *nougatine* cups with remaining *Mousse à l'Armagnac*. Serves 6.

# CAFE ARGENTEUIL

*253 East 52nd Street*

This might be a good country inn outside the asparagus-growing faubourg it was named for. Long a favorite haunt of the publishing crowd, the restaurant may not be quite what it was before the departure of its consummately able chef, Maxim Ribera, for a spin-off establishment in the suburbs. Nonetheless, it is still one of the city's more worthwhile temples of *haute cuisine.* The high-ceilinged dining room is airy, pleasant, and impressively proportioned, with glass dividers, etched in the Art Nouveau style, punctuating the space nicely. Service is formal and expert, and the kitchen rarely can be faulted on its handling of fish and crustaceans.

## GRATIN DE FRUITS DE MER

2 lbs. mussels, scrubbed and bearded
1 cup *Court Bouillon**
1 cup lobster meat
2 tbsp. butter
1 lb. sea scallops

1 cup dry white wine
1 cup heavy cream
2 cups *Sauce Américaine* (recipe below)
4 slices Swiss cheese

In a covered pot, steam mussels in *court bouillon* over medium heat 8–10 minutes, shaking pot occasionally, until shells open. Remove cooled mussels from shells and set aside, discarding any unopened specimens. Sauté lobster gently in butter, just until cooked through, and set aside, reserving pan juices. In a saucepan, gently simmer scallops in white wine and cream for 15 minutes. Remove scallops with a slotted spoon and set aside. Reduce wine-cream mixture by ⅔ over moderate heat, stir in *Sauce Américaine*, and heat thoroughly. Add seafoods to sauce and, as soon as all ingredients are heated through, divide contents of saucepan among four individual serving casseroles or large scallop shells. Top each portion with a slice of cheese and leave under a hot broiler until golden brown. Serve immediately to 4.

*Sauce Américaine*
*Properly, this is an integral part of the dish* Homard à l'Américaine *and is seldom prepared as a sauce per se. This recipe is an adaptation, unauthorized by the restaurant, for home cooks who aren't likely to have quantities of* Homard à l'Américaine *on hand.*

2 medium ripe tomatoes,
  peeled and seeded
pan juices from sautéed lobster
  (above)
1 tbsp. olive oil
2 tbsp. finely chopped onion
2 shallots, finely chopped
⅓ tsp. chopped garlic
½ cup dry white wine

½ cup Fish Stock*
2 tbsp. cognac
⅔ tsp. mixed chopped tarragon
  and parsley
cayenne pepper to taste
lobster coral, intestines, and
  body meat
7 tbsp. butter
1 dash lemon juice

Chop tomatoes coarsely. In the pan previously used to sauté lobster, add olive oil and onion and cook slowly until onion is almost tender, stirring frequently. Add shallots, stir, and hand-squeeze chopped tomatoes into the pan. Add all other ingredients except lobster detritus, butter, and lemon juice, bring to boil, and reduce liquids by ½. Pound lobster innards in a mortar with 1 tbsp. of the butter to produce a fine paste and whisk into sauce over high flame. Remove from flame, still whisking, strain, and swirl in remaining butter, cut into small bits. Correct seasoning and stir in lemon juice.

*Note* Nantua Sauce* *could be substituted in a pinch, although it would change the character of the dish somewhat.*

## PIGEONNEAU BOHÉMIENNE

4 squabs
1 lb. leaf spinach, cleaned
1 lb. mushrooms, sliced
6 oz. butter

½ lb. wild rice
1 cup Madeira
salt and pepper to taste

Remove (or have butcher remove) squab carcasses, leaving birds otherwise intact. Steam spinach just until wilted, drain thoroughly, and set aside. Sauté mushrooms in ½ the butter just until tender and set aside. Simmer wild rice in Madeira until *al dente* (slightly resistant to the bite) and combine in a bowl with spinach and mushrooms. Season to taste and stuff birds with the mixture. Rub birds with salt and, in a skillet, brown on all sides in remaining butter while oven preheats to 375°F. Roast birds 25 minutes, basting frequently with the butter in which they were browned, and serve to 4 with *Sauce Périgourdine* (page 89).

## FRAISES ARGENTEUIL

1½ pts. strawberries
1 oz. Kirsch
1 oz. cognac
2 tbsp. Melba Sauce (recipe
  below)

1 cup confectioners' sugar
1 pt. whipped cream

Wash, hull, and halve strawberries. Blend Kirsch, cognac, Melba Sauce, and confectioners' sugar in a bowl. Add strawberries, mix well, and allow to macerate 15 minutes. Lightly stir in whipped cream and serve to 4.

*Melba Sauce*

¼ cup currant jelly
¼ cup sieved raspberries
½ tsp. cornstarch

¼ cup sugar
1 small pinch salt

In the top of a double boiler, combine jelly and raspberries and bring to boil over direct heat. Mix remaining ingredients, add them to jelly mixture, and cook over hot water until thick and clear. Allow to cool before using.

*Le Madrigal*

*216 East 53rd Street*

Directoire Paris, as interpreted by the muralists Pierre Pages and his late brother Jean, is the setting. The color scheme is mustard yellow and burnt orange, and the rear "garden" (actually a shallow alcove festooned with plastic greenery) looks pretty enough from the dining room proper. If the menu isn't thrillingly original, the cuisine is resolutely *haute* and is prepared with flair under the direction of Chef Gérard Melou.

# POTAGE CRÈME D'AVOCAT

| | |
|---|---|
| 1 onion, chopped | 1 pt. Chicken Stock* |
| whites of 2 leeks, chopped | 1 Idaho potato, diced |
| 2 tbsp. cooking fat (see note) | 1 cup heavy cream |
| 6 ripe avocados | salt and white pepper to taste |

**Note** *If soup is to be served cold, use olive oil; if hot, butter.*

In a skillet, sauté onion and leeks in oil or butter over low heat just until translucent. Remove vegetables from pan with a slotted spoon and set aside. Peel, pit, and dice avocados and sauté over low heat, using the same skillet and taking care not to let them color. Place all sautéed ingredients in a pot, add chicken stock, and bring to boil. Turn heat down low, add diced potato, and cook 15 minutes. Add cream, bring briefly to boil, and remove from stove. Using a blender or processor, purée mixture to a very fine consistency, season to taste, and serve, hot or chilled, to 6.

# DODINE DE CANARD AU POIVRE VERT

| | |
|---|---|
| 2 ducks | 4 pieces caul fat (optional) |
| 1 oz. ground fatback | 1 tbsp. arrowroot |
| 2 oz. + 1 tsp. cognac | 1 tbsp. cooking oil |
| ½ pt. + 1 tbsp. heavy cream | 1 tbsp. Clarified Butter* |
| salt and pepper to taste | 1 tbsp. green peppercorns |

Remove, skin, and separate sides of duck breasts. Remove, skin, and bone duck legs. Brown duck carcasses in oven and make a stock of them (as you would Chicken Stock*). Place breasts (i.e. the ducks') between sheets of waxed paper and flatten them evenly with a mallet or the side of a cleaver. Grind or finely mince boned legs and combine well with fatback, 1 tsp. cognac, 1 tbsp. heavy cream, and salt and pepper to taste. (For a lighter, more flavorful forcemeat, Chef Gérard Melou suggests the addition of a little ground pork and veal.) Divide the mixture into 4 parts, shape them into cylinders, and wrap each in a flattened duck breast. Wrap breasts in optional caul fat, or tie with butcher's string, and refrigerate, covered, until stock is ready.

Preheat oven to 450°F. Dissolve arrowroot in 1 oz. of remaining cognac. Strain off 1 qt. of duck stock, stir in arrowroot mixture and ½ pt. cream, and simmer gently until reduced by half. Arrange filled duck breasts in a roasting pan moistened with oil and clarified butter and bake uncovered 10 minutes, basting frequently. Reduce oven heat to 375°F. and bake 15 minutes longer, basting as before. Meanwhile, add peppercorns to remaining cognac, simmer 2–3 minutes, and flame. Add peppercorn mixture to reduced sauce, mixing well, and pour over duck breasts just before serving. Serve to 4 with wild rice and chestnut purée (page 66).

## TARTE COQUELIN

| | |
|---|---|
| 1 lb. Puff Pastry* | 4 oz. almond paste |
| ½ lb. canned apricots (plus juice) | 3 oz. butter |
| 1 oz. Kirsch | 3 eggs |

Make a thin 10″ tart shell, reserving excess pastry, and refrigerate 1 hour or more. Preheat oven to 350°F. Prick chilled tart shell in several places to allow heated air to escape, bake 10 minutes, and set aside to cool. Gently poach apricots in their juice for 5–6 minutes, drain well, and purée in a blender with Kirsch. When cool, spread apricot mixture over bottom of tart shell. In a blender, cream almond paste and butter together and crack in eggs one by one until thoroughly incorporated. Spread almond cream mixture over apricot mixture and decorate tart with reserved pastry dough cut in lattice strips. Bake 15–20 minutes in a preheated 375°F. oven and serve cold to 6.

## Hermitage

*251 East 53rd Street*

The setting is at once sleekly contemporary and just rustic enough to suggest a fine country inn; the menu combines *haute* and *nouvelle cuisine;* the service is flawless and the clientele, *très chic.* After a leisurely apéritif over a glass-topped trestle table in one of the handsomest—and smallest—of the city's lounges, move on to the half-timbered, mirror-banked dining room and admire the pretty flowers, the pretty women, and such pretty culinary conceits as *barquette de fruits de mer* with two sauces, *terrine de légumes,* and striped bass *au pamplemousse.* Joseph Reyers and Julien Luthi are the *patrons,* and all goes very smoothly under their direction.

## TERRINE DE LÉGUMES

*This very sophisticated recipe will yield far more than you'll require for a small dinner party, but whatever isn't used at once will keep two or three days under refrigeration. And don't overlook its possibilities as cocktail party fare.*

½ lb. string beans, trimmed
6 fresh artichoke bottoms
10–11 baby carrots, scrubbed
11 oz. baby peas
9 oz. lean cooked ham
1 egg white

8 tbsp. vegetable oil
juice of 1 lemon
salt and pepper to taste
4 lemons, peeled and thinly
   sliced

Steam vegetables separately just until cooked through and plunge into cold water (they will be subjected to further cooking later and therefore should be very crisp and bright). Set aside in separate containers. Trim and remove all tendons and connecting tissues from ham. Dice ham and place in a food processor or blender. Add egg white, oil, and lemon juice, season to taste, and blend to a fine purée. Line bottom and sides of a rectangular mold (about 4" × 4" × 14") with lemon slices, fitting them together as snugly as possible. Spread a thin layer of the ham mixture over bottom of mold and successively form layers of the carrots (lengthwise), beans (lengthwise), artichokes, and peas, separating each with a thin layer of the ham mixture. Cover mold with a slightly larger rectangle of wax paper, taping edges tightly under rim of mold. Set mold in a deep pan or poacher and add boiling water to the latter until it reaches to ¾ the height of the mold. Cook 30 minutes over low heat (150°F.). Allow terrine to cool ½ hour at room temperature, then refrigerate until very cold. Unmold and slice with a very sharp knife, allowing 2 ¼" slices per portion. Serve with Cold Tomato Sauce.

*Cold Tomato Sauce*

| | |
|---|---|
| 18 oz. ripe tomatoes | ⅓ tsp. chopped fresh tarragon |
| 1 tsp. tomato paste | ½ tsp. chopped parsley |
| 4 tbsp. wine vinegar | salt and pepper to taste |
| 4 tbsp. olive oil | |

Chop tomatoes into small dice and press through a sieve, discarding watery juice or reserving it for other uses. In a bowl, blend all ingredients well and chill thoroughly before serving.

## TIMBALE DE HOMARD AUX ROGNONS

| | |
|---|---|
| 2 live 2-lb. lobsters | 2 tbsp. butter |
| *Court Bouillon*\* | 2 full clusters of veal kidney, |
| salt and freshly ground pepper | sliced |
| to taste | 1 oz. cognac |
| ½ lb. bay scallops | 1 pt. *Nantua Sauce*\* |
| 2 tbsp. vegetable oil | 1 medium black truffle |

The fell hand of the assassin is required here. Slay the lobsters by plunging the point of a knife into their thoraxes, then poach them 18 minutes in *court bouillon* to cover. Remove shells, cut tail and claw meat into medallions, and toss, seasoning to taste, with raw scallops. Set aside. Heat oil and butter in a skillet and lightly sauté kidneys, keeping them very rare. Remove kidneys from skillet with a slotted spoon and drain. In the same skillet, sauté scallops and lobster medallions for a few moments, just until heated through. Deglaze skillet with cognac and add *Nantua Sauce*. Bring to boil for a few seconds, add kidneys, and boil a few seconds longer. Correct seasoning and transfer contents of skillet to a heated serving dish. Serve, garnished with truffle cut in julienne strips, to 8.

# CLAFOUTI AUX KIWIS

4 eggs
10 oz. *Crème Fraîche**
5¼ oz. powdered sugar

1⅓ oz. plum brandy
10 kiwis
1 unbaked round 9" tart shell

Preheat oven to 375°F. In a bowl, whisk together eggs, *crème fraîche*, sugar, and brandy, blending ingredients thoroughly. Pass mixture through a fine sieve and set aside. Peel kiwis, slice into ¼" thicknesses, and poach in water until tender. Line bottom of tart shell with wax paper, weight with dried beans, and bake 10 minutes. Remove weight and paper and arrange sliced fruit in pastry shell. Turn oven heat up to 400°F., cover fruit with cream mixture, and bake 20 minutes. Remove from oven and dust surface liberally with powdered sugar. Leave under hot broiler until sugar caramelizes. Serve warm to 8.

## PART THREE

# *All'Italiana*

*I*n France, the development of the spit and cauldron—and the cuisine that issued from them—was the natural response to a relatively cold climate and an abundance of fuel. In Italy, where a warmer climate and a paucity of timber (the result of extensive iron smelting by the Greeks and Romans) militated against the use of roaring open fires, a different cuisine evolved. The enclosed charcoal fire was its medium, the sauté pan its basic utensil. It was—and remains—a cuisine in which cereal products such as polenta, rice, and pasta (all unsuitable to both spit and cauldron) loomed large; in which such smaller meat animals as the pig, goat, and calf played a far more important role than beef (for which Italy lacked adequate pasturage); and for which a set of culinary techniques had to be developed that differed radically from those of northern Europe. Supplied with a fine leg of veal, the modern French cook is apt to roast it for hours, whereas the Italian will slice it as thin as possible, pound it even thinner, and sauté it in minutes. Both approaches reflect medieval adaptations to climate and fuel availability.

# IL MONELLO

*1460 Second Avenue*

With few exceptions (notably *osso buco,* which requires a couple of hours of braising), the dishes served in Italian restaurants are cooked to order. As a consequence, the Italian chef can afford the luxury of turning up for work hours later than his French counterpart. At Adi Giovanetti's suggestion, I arrived at Il Monello at ten o'clock on a Wednesday morning. A porter had come in to clean the kitchen four hours earlier, but the chefs were just starting their day.

Giovanetti grew up in Lucca, a Tuscan province renowned throughout Italy for the superiority of its olive oil and—the foregoing generalizations notwithstanding—its spit-roasted meats. (Lucca, according to Waverley Root, "politically an independent state from 1369 to 1847, is gastronomically independent today.") Aristocratic of bearing and impeccably tailored, he is something of a *bon vivant* whose dry wit, smooth urbanity, and analytical turn of mind lend little credence to the notion that his condition might ever have been any humbler than it is today. As it happens, he started his professional career at sixteen, when, just arrived from Italy, he was put to work as the lowliest scullion in the kitchens of Frank Giambelli (page 160).

As was the case with Le Cirque, Il Monello, which Giovanetti opened in the fall of 1974 after working his way up to maître d'hôtel under Giambelli, has been immensely popular from the outset despite an upper East Side location hardly calculated to lure expense-account lunchers from their wonted midtown haunts. Whether it has been as profitable as its capacity dinner crowds might lead one to believe is doubtful. As I was to learn during the course of the day, excellence isn't come by cheaply.

The day's veal arrived shortly after I did. Giovanetti led me to the butcher's table where two double-racks awaited dismemberment. Even had the meat not been stamped "Plume de Veau," its quality would have been obvious. A pale uniform pink, its texture was superb. Giovanetti showed me the purveyor's bill: ninety-six dollars. "We'll get three usable chops from each side," he said. "Twelve chops in all. The three smaller chops on the end can only be used for Valdostana and have to be stuffed." A full veal chop (or, in its flattened form, a *paillard*) sells for eleven dollars at the restaurant—roughly six dollars more than Giovanetti pays his supplier for it. Out of the difference, the eleven highly skilled men who work in his kitchen must be paid every week of the year, vacations and sick leave included, as must the porters, dishwashers, dining-room staff, and bartender. Pension funds, unemployment insurance, and the like also figure into the price of the chop, as do its garniture and sauce. Breakage and spoilage (even the most astute restaurateur can find himself with a lot of very high fish on his hands after a couple of days of unforeseen weather bad enough to reduce significantly the number of dinners he normally would expect to serve) also must be covered, along with linens, uniforms, bread, butter, utilities, rent, flowers, refuse removal, equipment repairs and replacement—the list is almost infinitely extendable and includes everything from the initial investment in heavy equipment down to the last swizzle stick and matchbook. With luck, whatever loss is incurred by service of the chop will be offset by a second round of drinks or a decent bottle of wine.

One of the chefs comes out of a walk-in box bearing a large tray heaped with veal. "For the meat sauce," he says, putting it down on a work counter. What one might have expected to be scraps and trimmings are choice cuts—loins and fillets. To these he adds several large hunks of prosciutto. As nearly as I can judge, the retail price of the combined meats would be somewhere in the neighborhood of fifty dollars. The chef puts them in a large pot to brown, tossing some bay leaves in after them.

Another chef, boning knife in hand, goes to work on a cured ham. Noticing my puzzlement, Giovanetti explains: "In Italy, that prosciutto would be left whole and sliced to order in the dining room. But Americans don't like the parts with the connecting tissue—to me, the parts with the best flavor—so we serve only the center section. The rest is used for meat sauce and soup." The chef has cut away and discarded the leathery skin and thick outer layer of fat. He works the shank bone this way and that, to determine the location of the thigh joint, then quickly cuts it away, and moves his knife up along the femur and around the aitchbone, excising a slab of meat that appears to weigh about four pounds. This, less than a third of what he began with, will be served with melon.

It is not a large kitchen. Like that of Le Cirque, it was inherited from an earlier venture and could do with some reorganization. Five gas ranges occupy the rear of the room, the first three topped with four burners apiece, the fourth with a griddle, and the fifth with a grill. Each is equipped with an oven and all are tented over by an aluminum hood that runs the length of the room. Duckboards cover the floor, at which level it is cold and drafty this early-December morning. The chefs tramp around in heavy work shoes. One of them is butchering a double-rack of veal. He makes an incision along the spine, cuts a sheath of flesh from the ribs on each side, and separates the racks with a cleaver. He then makes a series of long cuts between the ribs, which he pulls slightly apart. Grasping the flesh with a towel, he strips each rib of its thin fleshy covering, as though peeling so many bananas, trims the dangling "peel" from the bone, and separates the chops with a cleaver. They are then butterflied with a lateral flick of the knife and passed to another chef, who will spend much of the morning preparing the day's *scaloppine, costolette,* and *paillards* by rhythmically pounding the meat to the thinness almost of crêpes.

This flattening process is a more demanding art than might be supposed, and watching a master flattener in action (the terminology is my own; if there is an accepted locution for this line of work, I don't know it) is as edifying as witnessing any other virtuoso performance. The chef—in this case, a sinewy, rather phlegmatic young fellow—works with a heavy, long-handled metal disc about the size of a hockey puck, letting it fall more or less of its own weight and imparting an almost imperceptible forward motion to its trajectory in the millisecond before impact. Laying a butterflied chop between sheets of waxed paper, he deals it a series of slightly overlapping blows that eventually triples its area and leaves it looking like an enormously magnified, highly stylized gingko leaf, with the rib bone as its stem. The idea, of course, is to achieve absolutely uniform flatness and a cleanly rounded edge, so that the *costoletta* will cook evenly and quickly. The kid is indeed a master flattener. Mesmerized by his performance, I miss a good deal of the action taking place elsewhere in the kitchen while watching him.

By the time I've come out of my trance, it is 10:40. Chicken stock is simmering on one of the ranges. A béchamel sauce has been started and milk and nutmeg are being added to it. One of the chefs is opening a case (six 108-oz. cans) of Puglisi brand plum tomatoes for the basic tomato sauce. Red wine has been added to the browned meat, onions to the chicken stock. The florist is at work in the dining room, the tomatoes go into the sauce pot. "If I let this burn," the chef says, stirring them, "goodbye, Charlie." *Splat-splat-splat-splat* goes the flattener's mallet, as it will for the rest of the morning.

A forty-three-pound leg of veal is heaved onto the butcher's table at 11:05. Two of them have been delivered this morning, along with a bill for $233. The butcher goes to work on it, attacking the butt end with a boning knife, digging out the end of the spine. "After that's butchered," Giovanetti remarks, "the meat will have to rest for a full day, to drain." The browned meats have been sent downstairs (where the day's pasta is being rolled and cut) to be ground. A chef, working against the grain, cuts leg of veal (butchered yesterday) into pieces for *scaloppine* and passes them along to the flattener. Veal, with its tenacious membranes and slippery immature fat, is a nuisance to work with. Another chef arranges green peppers on a broiler rack. When their skins have blistered sufficiently, they will be slipped off and the peppers will be cut up, to be sautéed with bits of veal. Oil is heating for the meat sauce and into it go the celery, carrots, and onions that were chopped while I watched the flattener. The men—there are six of them in the kitchen now— go about their chores easily, relaxed, saying little but watching one another's moves with respectful, appraising glances, as ballplayers will watch one another at the batting cage or surgeons in an operating theater. One imagines the master carvers at Autun watching Gislebertus in much the same way, as peers appreciative of a colleague's virtuosity. It's an affecting thing to witness.

The kitchen has a good garlicky smell about it. The green peppers have been finished, and now the red—which will be served chilled with anchovies as an hors d'oeuvre—are roasting. Their aroma mingles with that of the garlic and a dozen other substances I have never smelled in this particular combination before to create a bouquet that will haunt me, I suppose, for years to come, and perhaps one day be re-encountered to switch on a Proustian playback of the scene. What an elemental business the preparation of food is! The concern of earth, air, fire, and water, of all five senses.

The morning wears on toward lunch, and the vegetable chef is preparing the zucchini that later will be deep-fried. Only the unpeeled outer portions are usable; the fleshier cores—three-quarters of an inch thick—are discarded. The ground sauce meats have been rebrowned in the oven and returned to the pot, where the sauce begins to thicken. The tomato sauce is thickening too, bubbling sluggishly and taking on color. The veal leg has been reduced to its servable components (about forty percent of the whole), and the butcher begins trimming sliced white bread for *spiedini alla romano.* Sandwiching ham and mozzarella cheese between them, he stacks the trimmed squares high, drives four skewers straight down through each stack, and slices the stacks neatly into quarters. Meanwhile, another chef, working with capers and anchovies, is preparing a sauce for the dish.

By noon, a second double-rack of veal has been passed along to the flattener, the *scaloppine* have been pounded and rolled in wax paper, and a case of zucchini has been sliced into thin wands so uniform that they appear to have been mechanically processed—or would, if any machine were that precise. The flattener's *splat-splat-splat-splat* still echoes monotonously through the room, but now a staccato counterpoint can be heard, as though a beaver had been joined by a woodpecker in an unlikely duet. In a corner of the room, the veal butcher has dumped a mountain of mushrooms—the contents of three seven-pound baskets—onto a small wood-topped counter and, confronted by what looks to me like a full day's work, commences to slice them, his knife going like the very hammers of hell. *Tattattat, tattattat, tattattat*—the sound is almost slurred by its own rapidity. Incredibly, his eyes are everywhere but on his work. It's all done by feel, left hand feeding the right, mushroom slices popping away in hairline uniformity. A waiter comes in with the first lunch order at 12:05.

Lunch turns out to be a desultory affair, with orders coming in at widely spaced intervals. The cooking itself seems almost anticlimactic, incidental to the main business of the day. For the most part, the chefs continue with their preparatory work, occasionally interrupting a chore to turn out an order of *stracciatelle alla romana, salsiccie alla pizzaiola,* or whatever. During dinner the kitchen will look like a Doré illustration for *The Inferno,* with nonstop action at the ranges from six until at least ten o'clock. Now, however, one chef casually puts pasta on to boil and slices something like eight pounds of mushrooms while it cooks (interruptions included, he averages three-quarters of a pound per minute; in thirty-one minutes from start to finish, he will have cooked several dishes and sliced all twenty-one pounds of the fungi). Another dices ham and vegetables for the evening's *pasta e fagioli* between sautés. Several chefs have come up from downstairs, where they have been cutting pasta, stuffing clams, making the filling for *cannelloni,* and the like. There are ten men in the kitchen now, trimming artichokes, cleaning spinach, turning peppers, butchering beef, shucking sauce clams. At one o'clock, a waiter brings in a pot of coffee for all hands. Before pouring himself a cup, the chef in charge of the meat sauce empties his handiwork into a clean pot. He turns to me with an expression of mock relief and says, "Not burned."

In the dining room a few minutes later, Adi Giovanetti suggests *costoletta alla milanese* for my lunch. It's a dish I've never much liked and, with poor grace, I say so. "That," he replies, "is because you've never had it here."

"I've had it at Savini in Milan, and that's about as good as it's supposed to get. It was awful."

"That's because they overheard you speaking English. Once, a waiter there heard me say something in English and served me a meal I had to send back."

His dining room, with its rather florid décor, wrought-iron wine racks, and dreadful closeout-sale pictures, lacks the cool, high-ceilinged cream-and-gold elegance of Savini's. The *costoletta,* as it turns out, is superb.


## CARPACCIO ALL'ITALIANA

*This simple but elegant starter should be prepared at the last moment before serving, so that the meat has no chance to discolor with exposure. Also, the beef should be sliced as thinly as possible, a job you can facilitate by leaving it in the freezer for a couple of hours. The proportions are for a single serving and should be multiplied according to need.*

8 paper-thin slices filet mignon
4 slices white toast, trimmed
   and halved
salt, pepper, and olive oil to
   taste

½ tsp. grated Parmesan cheese
1 pinch finely chopped parsley

Arrange beef slices on toast halves and salt and pepper to taste. Drizzle with a few drops of oil and sprinkle successively with cheese and parsley. *Finito.*


## PAGLIA E FIENO

*It's called Straw and Hay, but you won't find it in many stables.*

½ lb. fresh egg *taglierini*
½ lb. fresh spinach *taglierini*
½ cup heavy cream
whipped butter
½ cup Chicken Broth*

2 slices prosciutto, cut in small
   squares
salt and pepper to taste
2½ tbsp. grated Parmesan cheese

Cook pastas in plenty of boiling salted water for 2–3 minutes (or, if using dried pasta, according to package directions). Drain and place in a serving pan with cream, butter, broth, prosciutto, and salt and pepper to taste. Simmer, tossing, until pasta is well coated with sauce. Add cheese, stir and serve to 4–6.


## VITELLO RIVIERA

1½ tbsp. olive oil
1½ lbs. lean veal, cut in julienne
   strips
flour

3 garlic cloves, chopped
¾ cup dry white wine
¾ cup heavy cream
3 tbsp. *Pesto**

Add oil to a hot skillet and brown veal. Dust lightly with flour, add chopped garlic, and stir well. Add wine, cream, and *pesto,* simmer for a few minutes, and serve at once to 4–6.

*If you prefer chicken to veal, try . . .*

## POLLO MONELLO CAPRICCIOSO

1 small chicken, cut in small
  pieces
flour
4 Italian sweet sausages
2 tbsp. olive oil
1 pinch dried sage
3 shallots, chopped fine
2 tsp. butter

1 cup dry white wine
¾ cup Chicken Broth*
4 ripe tomatoes, peeled and
  chopped
6 pitted green olives
6 pitted black olives
1 tbsp. chopped parsley
salt and pepper to taste

Sprinkle chicken with flour. Slice sausage and sauté in oil with chicken, turning occasionally, until meats are golden brown. Add sage and shallots and sauté 1 minute. Then add remaining ingredients and simmer 10–15 minutes. Serves 4.

# Orsini's

### 41 West 56th Street

The Beautiful People have a way of discovering restaurants, showing up in force for a few weeks or months and then moving on to the next hot property. At Orsini's, they turn up regularly year after year. The restaurant opened, inauspiciously enough, as an overpriced, insufferably snobbish coffeehouse sometime during either the first Eisenhower administration or the papacy of Julius II. Gradually, it was converted to a legitimate, if unabashedly romantic, restaurant and now occupies two floors of a very handsomely appointed town house. Personally, I'm not too fond of the ground-floor dining room, which looks like, and may be, a hideout for adulterous garment tycoons. The upstairs room is an entirely different story, however, with lots of green plants, fine sculpture, internationally known film stars, and some of the planet's most opulent pastries on conspicuous display. The food, surprisingly enough in the circumstances, is excellent.

### SCAMPI ORSINI

4 tbsp. olive oil
4 garlic cloves, halved
12 jumbo shrimp, cut in small
   morsels

4 tbsp. butter
3 tbsp. chopped flat Italian
   parsley

In a skillet heat the oil and garlic. When garlic is light brown, add shrimp and sauté over moderate heat 5 minutes. Discard oil and garlic and add butter. Continue to cook over moderate heat, stirring occasionally, until butter is melted and hot. Serve garnished with a sprinkling of parsley. Serves 4.

# FETTUCCINE ALLA CAPRI

*The sauce for this popular pasta dish can be made in advance and reheated at the table in a chafing dish just before serving.*

2 garlic cloves, halved
4 tbsp. olive oil
4 large red peppers, cut in thin strips
4 anchovies
2 tbsp. capers

1 oz. vinegar
1 lb. fresh fettuccine
2 tbsp. butter
4 tbsp. freshly grated Parmesan cheese
salt and pepper to taste

In a large frying pan, sauté the garlic in oil until it takes on color, then add the peppers. After 5 minutes, add the anchovies and mash them with a fork until they are well blended with the oil. Add the capers and continue to sauté until peppers are tender. Add vinegar, cover pan, and turn heat off. In a large pot, bring plenty of salted water to boil, add fettuccine, and continue to boil about 5 minutes, or until pasta is *al dente*. Drain pasta and discard garlic from sauce. Add sauce, pasta and butter to a chafing dish, tossing ingredients until butter has melted. Add cheese and pepper, toss lightly once more, and serve to 4.

# VITELLO ALLA SORRENTINA

1 large eggplant
salt to taste
1 cup olive oil
8 veal *scaloppine,* pounded very thin
1 cup flour

4 tbsp. butter
8 oz. white wine
2 tbsp. grated Parmesan cheese
8 slices mozzarella cheese, ¼" thick

Peel eggplant and cut into 8 thin slices, reserving remainder for other uses. Salt eggplant slices, place between sheets of paper towel and cover with a flat, weighted pan lid to press out excess water. (This will take an hour or more and can be done a day in advance.) In a large frying pan, brown the drained eggplant in half the oil, then remove and drain on paper towels. Add remaining oil to pan and heat over moderately high flame. Meanwhile dredge veal in flour, shaking off excess. When oil is hot, place veal in pan without allowing pieces to overlap and cook 3–4 minutes. Discard oil, add butter and wine, and let liquid reduce two minutes. Sprinkle Parmesan cheese on each piece of veal, place a slice of eggplant on each and a slice of mozzarella on top of that. Cover pan and cook 3 minutes, or until cheese begins to melt. Serve immediately to 4.

**Nanni** *146 East 46th Street*

**Nanni AL VALLETTO** *133 East 61st Street*

A great many New Yorkers, Luigi Nanni included, will tell you that Luigi Nanni is *numero uno* among the city's Italian chefs. They may be right. Nanni, a transplanted Abruzzese, operates both these restaurants and shuttles between them so artfully that it's almost impossible to dine at either without catching at least a glimpse of his bantam swagger and beetling brows. The 46th Street establishment—the older of the two and a favorite haunt of the publishing world—is physically nondescript and rather cramped, but the food is marvelous. Nowhere in the city will you find better prepared game in season than at the two operations, and nowhere but at Nanni al Valletto will you find more pictures by Mrs. Nanni, an accomplished watercolorist.

## TONNARELLE ALLA PESCARESE

*The difference between* tonnarelle *and such thin, flat egg noodles as* taglierini *and* trenette *is largely one of regional nomenclature. Any of the three will do.*

1 shallot, crushed
2 garlic cloves, crushed
½ cup olive oil
2 tbsp. butter
1 lb. red snapper fillets, diced
2 bay leaves

½ tsp. orégano
6 leaves fresh basil, chopped
8 ripe plum tomatoes
salt and pepper to taste
½ lb. dry (or 1 lb. fresh)
   *tonnarelle*

In a sauté pan, cook shallot and garlic in oil over medium heat until golden. Add butter, snapper, bay leaves, orégano, and basil, cook 10 minutes, and add tomatoes, hand-squeezing them into pan. Add salt and pepper and cook mixture 20 minutes longer. Meanwhile cook noodles in plenty of salted boiling water. (If dried noodles are used, boil about nine minutes, or until *al dente.* Fresh noodles will take about half that time.) Drain pasta when done, toss with most of the sauce, and top with remainder. Serve immediately to 4.

## POLLO ALLA NERONE

*Originated by Chef Nanni, this splendid chicken dish is best accompanied by a good bottle of Pinot-Grigio.*

2 whole 2-lb. chickens
salt and pepper to taste
½ cup olive oil
4 tbsp. butter
2 shallots, sliced
1 sprig rosemary

3 leaves fresh tarragon
2 tsp. Dijon mustard
2 oz. cognac
2 oz. white wine
½ cup Chicken Consommé*

After splitting the spines of both chickens, pry them open, lay them bone side down on a work counter, and flatten them with the side of a heavy cleaver, taking care to leave the skins in place. Salt and pepper chickens. In a large pan (or two if necessary), heat olive oil over high flame until very hot and lower heat. Over a very low flame, add butterflied chickens to pan, cover them with a lid slightly smaller than the pan itself, and weight the lid so that it presses down on the fowl. Cook chickens until golden brown, turn and repeat the process. When chickens are golden on both sides, discard oil and add butter, shallots, rosemary, tarragon, and mustard. Raise heat to medium and, when butter has melted and starts to foam, add cognac and wine. Cook until wine has evaporated, add consommé, and continue cooking for ½ hour, or until chickens are tender. Remove chickens, keep warm, and reduce sauce over medium heat for 7–10 minutes, until thickened. Split chickens in two and serve half a bird, covered with sauce, per person. If my arithmetic is correct, that comes to four servings.

## VEAL CHOPS ALLA CAPRESE

4 1"-thick rib veal chops
flour for dredging
¼ cup vegetable oil
2 tbsp. butter
¼ cup chopped onion
2 whole garlic cloves
1 stalk celery, cut in julienne
strips

1 carrot, chopped
½ cup dry white wine
10 leaves fresh basil
salt and pepper to taste
4 tbsp. Beef Consommé*

Dredge chops in flour, shaking off excess. In a large pan, sauté chops in oil until golden on both sides. Discard oil and add butter. Cook over medium heat until butter just begins to take on color, add onion and garlic, and cook until soft. Add celery and carrot, cook 10 minutes, and add wine, basil, salt, and pepper. Cook until sauce has thickened, add consommé, and cook a few minutes longer. Serve sauce and chops together on warm plates. Serves 4.

## VENISON SALMIS

*This superb game dish requires a wine that will stand up to it. Chef Nanni suggests serving a full-bodied young Barolo.*

| | |
|---|---|
| 1 whole fillet of venison (2–2½ lbs.) | 2 whole cloves |
| 2 lbs. venison bones | 10–15 green peppercorns |
| 2 stalks celery ⎫ | 1 gal. red wine |
| ½ onion ⎬ roughly cut up | ¾ cup vegetable oil |
| 1 carrot ⎭ | flour for dredging |
| 2 shallots, sliced | ½ cup butter |
| 3 whole garlic cloves | 1 cup Beef Consommé* |
| stems from ½ bunch parsley | olive oil for basting |
| 4 bay leaves | pepper to taste |

In a large, deep pan or tray, marinate and refrigerate all ingredients except oil, flour, butter, consommé, and pepper to taste. After 48 hours, remove meat and bones, reserving marinade, and dry them with paper towels. Heat vegetable oil in a casserole, using low flame. Dredge bones in flour, add them to casserole, and cook, turning occasionally, ½ hour, or until they take on color. Discard oil and add butter and vegetables to casserole. When vegetables take on color, add reserved marinade and consommé, bring to low boil, and simmer 1½ hours on low flame. Remove and discard bones. Strain and reserve sauce (if too thick, add a little consommé).

Preheat oven to 350°F. Shape and tie venison with butcher's string and roast in oven 30–45 minutes, to taste. Baste with olive oil, turn meat, and roast 45 minutes longer. Remove meat to a warm platter, wipe dry, and place in casserole. Heat sauce, pour over venison, and let stand 10 minutes. Slice, and pepper to taste (do not salt). Serves 4.

*Note   The chef suggests* papardelle, *a broad ribbon noodle, with the venison. To sauce the pasta, take 3 tbsp. of the salmis sauce per person, reduce it to the desired consistency, and swirl in a little butter.*

## GORGONZOLA WITH PORT

*Simplicity itself, this voluptuous spread ends any meal on a festive note.*

½ lb. good gorgonzola cheese     2 oz. port (or cognac, if preferred)

Mash the cheese with a fork until it is well broken up, add port or cognac, and continue to mash until creamy and free of lumps. Served with toasted Italian bread brushed with Garlic Oil.

*Garlic Oil*
Simply marinate a crushed garlic clove in good imported olive oil for several hours and discard garlic.

# *Patsy's*

### *236 West 56th Street*

Neapolitan food, for generations synonymous with "Italian food" in this country, has been somewhat déclassé since the early '60s, when a lot of gastronomic arrivistes began to acquaint themselves with northern Italian cooking. A pity, for an authentic Neapolitan meal prepared by a sensitive chef still makes for one of life's more edifying experiences. The cuisine at Patsy's is rigorously *alla napoletana,* served *con amore,* and very, very good. (If the thought of it conjures up nothing but visions of thick, overpowering red sauce, try the asparagus *alla parmigiana, insalata di mare,* or seafood or vegetable *fritto misto.*) The restaurant, opened by Pasquale Scognamillo in the '40s, has been luring knowledgeable diners to its present location since 1954. Now operated by the retired founder's sons, Joe and Sal, it has been a haunt for many years of the movers and shakers of American politics, the performing arts (Old Blue Eyes is an habitué), and the media, but first-timers are accorded the same warm welcome presidential aspirants receive.

## LINGUINE WITH WHITE CLAM SAUCE

*Although pasta with white clam sauce appears on most Italian menus in New York, I've seldom found another as good as this— possibly because only tender littleneck clams are used at Patsy's and are shucked and chopped to order. The first time I tried the sauce, I had been invited to lunch with the restaurant's founder, Pasquale Scognamillo, who used to have not* linguine, *but* vermicelli, *with white clam sauce for lunch every day (and, I trust, continues to enjoy it in his well-earned retirement). I still prefer his choice of pasta with the sauce, although the restaurant usually serves linguine.*

2 doz. littleneck clams  
¾ cup olive oil  
6 garlic cloves, chopped fine  
½ cup chopped Italian (flat) parsley  

¼ tsp. dried orégano  
1 lb. linguine or vermicelli  

Open and chop clams just before use, reserving their strained liquor. Heat oil with garlic over low flame in a 4-qt. pot. When garlic begins to color, add clam liquor and an equal amount of water. Add herbs and simmer gently 15 minutes. Start pasta in plenty of boiling salted water. Add clams to sauce and cook over low heat 10 minutes. (Pasta should be *al dente* at about the same time sauce is finished.) Drain pasta and pour sauce over it. Serves 6–8 as a first course or 4 as a main dish.

# BONELESS CHICKEN FRANCESE

2  2½–3 lb. chickens
flour for dredging
2  eggs, beaten
⅓ cup olive oil
1  tsp. chopped parsley
½ cup prosciutto, cut in julienne
   strips

1  cup Chicken Broth*
⅛ lb. (½ stick) butter
juice of 1½ lemons
salt and pepper to taste

Separate legs (with thighs) from chickens, split bodies apart at breastbones, and bone legs and breasts, reserving other parts for other uses (or have butcher do the job for you). Dredge boned sections in flour and dip in beaten egg, coating well. Sauté in hot olive oil, turning once, until brown on both sides. Discard oil, add remaining ingredients, and simmer about 10 minutes, until broth has reduced and thickened. Salt and pepper to taste and serve to 4.

# VEAL SCALOPPINE ALLA MARSALA

*Should you prefer veal to chicken, this is another of those ubiquitous dishes that seems to come off better at Patsy's than at most other restaurants.*

8  veal *scaloppine*, pounded thin
flour for dredging
6  tbsp. olive oil
4  tbsp. butter
4  tbsp. chopped onion

2  tbsp. chopped prosciutto
1  cup sliced mushrooms
⅓ cup Chablis
⅓ cup Marsala
salt and pepper to taste

Dredge veal in flour, shaking off excess. Heat oil in a large sauté pan or skillet (or 2, if necessary, dividing ingredients between them) and sauté veal until lightly browned on both sides. Discard oil, add butter, onion, and prosciutto, and sauté until onion is golden brown. Add mushrooms and both wines, cover pan, and simmer about 12 minutes. Add salt and pepper to taste and serve to 4.

# G·LOMBARDI

*53 Spring Street*

Enrico Caruso ate, Louise Nevelson eats, and Jacqueline Onassis has eaten at Lombardi's, but many a New York restaurant buff is unaware of its existence. So much the worse for them; this is not only one of the oldest, but one of the finest Italian restaurants in the city. Opened by the grandfather of the present *padrone*—both men were named Gennaro for the patron saint of Naples—as a grocery in 1897, it became the nation's first licensed pizzeria in 1905 and has been a full-fledged restaurant since 1928. Recently refurbished in the Art Deco style, with striking collages by Mrs. Nevelson and Robert Indiana (another regular) on permanent view in the second of two dining rooms, the premises somehow retain a turn-of-the-century flavor. Perhaps it's the original marble shop sign mounted on a wall beside the bar. Maybe it's a couple of photographs of the establishment as it looked when immigrant housewives came by for garlic, *stoccafissa,* and, if luck was with them, a glimpse of Caruso. Whatever it is, it works a distinctive spell. The cooking, basically Neapolitan, is distinguished by a refinement and delicacy not always associated with the cuisines of the south.

### FISH SALAD ALLA LOMBARDI

*"Mr. Lombardi," I said, "you left the oil out of this recipe."*

*"There is no oil," Gennaro Lombardi replied. "Some restaurants make their seafood salads ahead of time in big batches and have to add oil to keep them moist. We believe in letting the taste of fresh seafood come through undisguised, but you can add a few drops of oil if you like."*

12 mussels
½ lb. squid, cut in thin rings
½ lb. scungilli (whelk or conch), thinly sliced
1 stalk celery, finely diced
2 lemons, quartered
salt and freshly ground pepper

4–6 leaves Boston lettuce
2 beefsteak tomatoes, quartered
1 red bell pepper, very thinly sliced
8–12 black/green olives, pitted
parsley sprigs for garnish

Clean mussels and remove their beards. Boil seafoods in water 15 minutes, drain well, and cool for 15 minutes. Mix celery and lemon wedges and season to taste. Line a shallow serving dish with lettuce leaves and arrange tomato wedges around edges. Toss seafoods with celery-lemon mixture, add red pepper, and mound in center of dish. Top with olives, garnish with parsley, and serve at room temperature to 4–6.

# ZUPPA PAVESE

| | |
|---|---|
| 1 medium onion, chopped | 4–6 slices buttered white toast |
| 1 tsp. butter | 4–6 eggs |
| 1½ pts. Chicken Consommé* | 1 oz. grated pecorino or |
| 1 pinch salt | Parmesan cheese |

In a saucepan, sauté onion in butter until golden brown. Add consommé and salt and bring to simmer. Pour soup into terracotta bowls and float 1 slice toast atop each bowl. Crack eggs onto toast, centering yolks, sprinkle with cheese, and leave under broiler 5–8 minutes, or until golden. Serves 4–6.

# CONTADINA

*With a few minutes of advance preparation earlier in the day, this toothsome country-style ragout can be readied for an informal dinner party in less than half an hour.*

| | |
|---|---|
| ½ lb. top round beef | ¼ lb. large fresh mushrooms, |
| ½ lb. lean veal | sliced |
| ½ lb. boneless chicken | 4 garlic cloves, peeled |
| 2 sweet red peppers | 2 tsp. butter |
| 2 medium potatoes, peeled | 6 oz. white wine |
| 4 sweet Italian sausages | salt and pepper to taste |
| 2 oz. olive oil | 1 tsp. chopped parsley |

Slice beef thinly, cut slices diagonally, corner to corner, and set aside. Likewise veal. Skin chicken and cut meat into 1″ × 1½″ cubes. Seed peppers and cut into long strips. Cut potatoes in 1″ cubes. In a large skillet sauté chicken, sausage, and potatoes in hot oil 5–6 minutes. Add veal and cook 4 minutes longer. Then set aside meat and potatoes and discard oil. Over moderate heat, sauté mushrooms, sweet peppers, and garlic in ½ the butter for 2–3 minutes. Add ⅔ of the wine, turn heat up high, and boil until wine evaporates. Meanwhile, slice sausages and in a second skillet sauté beef to taste in remaining butter. Add chicken, veal, sausage, and remaining wine to mushroom mixture and cook 10 minutes over low flame. Add beef and turn meats and vegetables out onto a serving dish. Moisten with a soupçon of the pan juices, season to taste, sprinkle with parsley, and serve immediately to 4–6.

*240 Central Park South*

Close by Lincoln Center and done up in ivory and gold, with a graceful arcade affording glimpses of Central Park as one strolls from the bar to the spacious dining room, this is one of the city's more opulent Italian restaurants. Named for Alfredo all'Augusteo, the Roman birthplace of fettucine Alfredo, the establishment is owned by Gianni Minale, a courtly, dapper reformed accountant who hails from Naples but whose menu is made up in large part of such northern specialties as *cima alla genovese, chicche alla Bergonzi, zuppa celestina, tortellini alla panna,* and, of course, fettuccine Alfredo. Galdino LoPezzo presides over the kitchen, and a lighter touch hath no chef.

## TIMBALLO DI ZUCCHINE

1 lb. zucchini
corn oil for frying
1½ tbsp. fine bread crumbs
¼ lb. freshly grated Parmesan
   cheese

½ lb. fresh mozzarella cheese,
   thinly sliced
salt and pepper to taste

Thinly slice zucchini lengthwise and fry in corn oil until soft but not necessarily brown. Butter a baking pan (8″ diameter) and coat bottom with bread crumbs. Cover bottom of pan with a layer of zucchini and successively layer with Parmesan and mozzarella. Repeat process until zucchini is used up. Preheat oven to 350°F. and bake 20 minutes. Serves 4.

## SPAGHETTINI AL CAVIALE

¾ lb. imported spaghettini (see
   note)
1 gal. boiling salted water
4 garlic cloves

5 oz. olive oil
1 sprig parsley, chopped
2 oz. beluga caviar
freshly ground pepper to taste

*Note   One can cast pearls before swine and one can use an inferior domestically manufactured pasta with this regal sauce. My advice would be to forget about the dish altogether if you can't find good imported Italian spaghettini and olive oil. One further injunction: Do not use grated cheese with this dish.*

Add spaghettini to boiling salted water and cook for duration of time specified on package, or until *al dente*, stirring often. While pasta cooks, sauté garlic in oil until browned. Discard garlic and add 2 ladles of boiling pasta water to sauté pan. Add parsley and cook until water evaporates. When spaghettini is ready, drain and turn into a serving obwl. Add parsley sauce and caviar and toss well. Add pepper to taste and serve to 4.

## AGNELLO ALLA TOSCANA

1 small leg of lamb (7 lbs.)
salt and pepper to taste
1½ peeled plum tomatoes
4 garlic cloves

6 oz. olive oil
3–4 sprigs fresh rosemary
2 lbs. fresh peas

Salt and pepper lamb and pass tomatoes through a sieve to remove seeds. Cut garlic in slivers. With the point of a sharp knife, pierce surface of lamb at more or less regular intervals and insert garlic slivers into incisions. Rub outer surfaces of lamb with a little oil, and, in a large pan, brown meat on all sides in remaining oil. Add tomatoes, rosemary, and ¼ cup water to pan, cover and simmer 1½ hours over low heat. A few minutes before lamb is done, cook peas just until tender in salted water. Drain peas and add them to the meat pan. Remove lamb to a serving platter and surround with peas and sauce. Serves 6.

# *Aperitivo*

*29 West 56th Street*

New York has its share and more of fine Italian restaurants, but this—a favorite hangout of performers at the nearby Carnegie Hall—is one of the very best. The atmosphere may not be altogether distinguished, with its plastic flora, adventitious masonry, corny paintings, and prominently displayed exhortations to live it up gastronomically and oeonologically. The food, however, is another story and the simply baked two-

and-a-half-inch-thick veal chop, in particular, is an epic. Paul Magnano, an implausibly bouncy septuagenarian from Liguria, is your host. His partners are Luciano Diminich and Frank Cnapich, both of whom hail from Trieste, and the restaurant's most notable desserts—the twisted crullers called *bougie* and key lime pie (Key lime pie? *That's* Italian?) are the handiwork of his wife, Angiolina.

## MINESTRONE APERITIVO

4 slices lean bacon
2 tbsp. butter
4 tbsp. olive oil
4 qts. water
1 onion, chopped
potatoes
carrots
zucchini ⎱ ¼ lb. each,
string beans ⎰ diced
celery hearts
¼ lb. navy beans (see note)

¼ lb. shelled peas
1 garlic clove, chopped
1 ripe tomato, strained
salt and pepper to taste
1 cup *ditalini* (see note)
½ cup rice
1 tbsp. chopped fresh basil leaves
1 tbsp. chopped parsley
1 cup freshly grated Parmesan cheese

*Note  Navy beans should be precooked according to package instructions until 20 minutes short of doneness. Ditalini is a short macaroni.*

Sauté bacon in butter and oil until brown but not overdone. Wash all vegetables except beans thoroughly and drain. Bring water to boil in a 6-qt. pot and add onion, diced vegetables, beans, peas, garlic, and tomato, and salt and pepper to taste. Allow to boil 8–10 minutes, add macaroni and rice, and boil 12 minutes longer. Remove from heat and stir in basil, parsley, and cheese, adding hot water if needed, although the soup should be quite thick. Let soup stand for a few minutes and serve with additional Parmesan cheese.

## SALSA ALLA BOLOGNESE

*As we shall see on page 185, Italian chefs are notoriously unable to agree on the proper composition of* bolognese *sauce. This is the version used at Aperitivo, and, while you may find many that are different, you'll find few that are better. Use it with any pasta or gnocchi.*

4 tbsp. olive oil
3 tbsp. butter
½ lb. chopped lean beef
3 slices prosciutto, chopped
2 small onions, chopped
1 carrot, chopped
1 stalk celery, chopped
2 pinches chopped parsley

3 bay leaves
1 garlic clove, chopped
1 cup red wine
½ lb. tomato paste (see note)
salt and pepper to taste
3 cups warm Beef Broth*
1 pinch nutmeg

*Note   An equal amount of very ripe fresh tomatoes, peeled, seeded and crushed, would be preferable. If paste is used, dilute in 1 cup warm Beef Broth.**

In a heavy saucepan, heat oil and butter. Add beef and prosciutto and stir with a wooden spoon until beef is well separated. Add chopped vegetables, bay leaves, and garlic and sauté, stirring, until vegetables are golden. Add wine, tomato paste, salt and pepper, and broth. Cover, bring to a slow boil, and cook, stirring occasionally, for 1 hour or more, until sauce reaches desired consistency (if too thick dilute with warm water). Stir in parsley and nutmeg a few minutes before sauce is done.

## PICCATA DI VITELLO

½ cup sifted flour
salt and freshly ground pepper
  to taste
1 lb. lean leg of veal (see note)
½ cup olive oil
⅛ lb. (½ stick) sweet butter

juice of 1 lemon
3 pinches finely chopped
  parsley
½ cup Beef Consommé*
3 oz. dry white wine

*Note   Paul Magnano recommends Provini brand veal. If this isn't available, choose the palest, tenderest veal your butcher can provide and have him slice it thinly, with the grain, and pound it to form paper-thin scaloppine.*

Blend flour, salt, and pepper and sprinkle lightly on both sides of *scaloppine*. Heat oil in a hot skillet, add veal, and sauté, turning frequently, until golden on both sides. Remove meat, set aside, and clean pan. Heat butter and return meat to pan. Sauté briefly on both sides, add remaining ingredients, and allow to simmer for a minute or two. Remove veal and keep warm. Quickly reduce liquids over high heat, pour over meat, and serve to 4.

## ANGIOLINA'S KEY LIME PIE

1  can condensed milk          1  tsp. grated lime rind
2  egg yolks, beaten           1  prebaked 6″ pie shell
juice of 2 fresh limes         whipped cream

Pour condensed milk into 2 qt. bowl, add egg yolks, and stir for a few minutes. Add lime juice and grated rind. Stir 1 minute longer and refrigerate mixture overnight. Transfer lime mixture into prebaked pie crust, spread with a rubber spatula to level, and top with as much fresh whipped cream as your conscience will allow. Serves 4.

# Il Menestrello

*14 East 52nd Street*

It's an ill wind indeed that blows nobody good. When Le Mistral, a once-vaunted French restaurant named for the gale that howls down the Rhône valley and across the Midi, blew itself out of existence in mid-1977, it was replaced by the roughly homonymous Il Menestrello (The Minstrel). The premises—complete with inherited mural views of Provence—were left as they were, and, as a consequence, one is served not *bouillabaisse* but *zuppa di pesce* beside the Old Port at Marseilles; not Châteauneuf-du-Pape but Corvo di Casteldiccia in the shadow of Avignon's Palace of the Popes. The split-level setting remains that of a fine old southern-French inn, with dark wooden beams, roughly plastered walls, and gleaming copper utensils much in evidence. The food, however, is resolutely Italian—and spectacularly good. There is no more sumptuous a pasta dish in the city, if not the world, than Chef Luigi Strazulli's *linguine al frutti di mare,* or a better veal choice than . . . but why go on? Just about everything on the menu, from the paper-thin beef *bresaola* to the high-Baroque pastries, merits superlatives.

## VONGOLE PARTENEOPEA

*This succulent clam dish makes a marvelously fragrant prelude to a meal distinguished by its contrasting aromas. The ideal conclusion would be fresh fruit and a bit of good Italian cheese.*

| | |
|---|---|
| 2 tsp. finely chopped shallots | ½ cup dry white wine |
| 2 tsp. finely chopped garlic | 2 cups peeled plum tomatoes |
| 8 tsp. olive oil | 2 cups Chicken Broth* |
| 24 littleneck or small cherrystone clams | salt and pepper to taste |

Lightly brown shallots and garlic in oil. Scrub clams and add to pan. Add wine, turn heat up fairly high, and cook until wine has reduced considerably. Squeeze tomatoes by hand, adding them to the pan. Add broth, salt, and pepper; cook, covered, over medium heat until clams open. Serve clams in their shells with pan sauce. Serves 4.

## TRENETTE AL PESTO

| | |
|---|---|
| 1 lb. trenette (thin noodles) | 2 cups Chicken Broth* |
| 2 tsp. finely chopped garlic | 8 oz. butter |
| 8 tsp. olive oil | salt and pepper to taste |
| 8 tbsp. *Pesto** | grated Parmesan cheese to taste |

Precook noodles until *al dente* (fresh pasta is preferable), drain and keep warm. In a saucepan, lightly brown garlic in oil and then add *pesto*, broth, butter, salt, and pepper. Allow the mixture to boil 3–4 minutes. Toss noodles with sauce (preferably at the table, using a chafing dish), correct seasoning, and sprinkle with cheese. Serves 4.

## COSTOLETTE DI VITELLO AL CARTOCCIO

*A real showpiece of a dish that emits a cloud of fragrance when served.*

| | |
|---|---|
| 4 thick rib veal chops, trimmed of fat | 1 cup Marsala |
| 8 tsp. olive oil | 12 mushroom caps, sliced thin |
| 2 tsp. finely chopped shallots | 8 tsp. Brown Sauce* |
| 1 clove garlic, minced | salt and pepper to taste |
| 4 oz. butter | 4 No. 10 brown paper bags, oiled |

Sauté chops in oil almost to desired degree of doneness. Lightly brown shallots and garlic in butter, add Marsala, mushrooms, brown sauce, and seasonings, and cook over high heat 3–4 minutes, or until liquids thicken. Coat chops with thickened liquid, top each with one-quarter of the mushrooms, and carefully place them in individual paper bags. Roll and crimp bag openings to seal tightly and bake in a very hot oven 5–8 minutes, or until bags inflate. Slit bags open at tableside, carefully remove chops, and serve to 4.

## *Giambelli* 50th
### *46 East 50th Street*

Frank Giambelli is affectionately known as "The Godfather" to a number of younger men around town who, after perfecting their skills in his employ, went on to open fine restaurants of their own. They couldn't have had a better mentor. Giambelli accumulated his own expertise in the course of an exhaustive professional odyssey that took him from his native Milan to the better hotels and restaurants of France, Switzerland, Czechoslovakia, Germany, and ultimately New York, where he opened Giambelli 50th in 1960. His town house establishment, divided into several attractive public and private dining rooms, is one of the city's most popular, and deservedly so. The softly lighted premises are inviting, the service is impeccable, and the food is remarkably good. Outstanding dishes here include *zuppa di pesce Capri, vitello Principe Filippo* (created expressly for the Duke of Edinburgh, who failed to show up for a scheduled dinner, thereby depriving himself of one of life's more gratifying experiences), and *trenette al pesto,* which is sauced with basil grown on the roof, picked at the peak of perfection, and rushed downstairs to the chef. The wine cellar, by the way, is one of the finest in town.

## SCAMPI GIAMBELLI

| | |
|---|---|
| ½ cup olive oil | juice of 1 lemon |
| 16 imported Italian *scampi* (see note) | salt and pepper to taste |
| flour for dredging | 8 very thin slices prosciutto, halved |
| ¼ lb. butter | 16 thin slices mozzarella cheese |
| ½ cup white wine | ½ cup grated Parmesan cheese |

*Note  Various shrimp from American waters often are served as* "scampi" *in this country. They are not, never have been, and never will be* scampi, *which are indigenous to the Old World. For this dish, Frank Giambelli insists, frozen* scampi *are preferable to any fresh crustacean masquerading as the genuine article.*

In a sauté pan, heat but don't burn the oil. Dredge *scampi* separately in flour and sauté until golden brown. Drain off oil, add butter to pan, and cook over low heat until melted. Add wine, lemon juice, salt, and pepper and sauté 2 minutes, stirring continuously. Turn off heat, remove *scampi* from pan, and roll each in a half-slice of prosciutto. In a baking dish, align *scampi* closely in 2 rows and cover them with their cooking sauce. Blanket *scampi* with mozzarella slices; evenly sprinkle mozzarella covering with Parmesan cheese. Bake in a preheated oven at 425°F. until cheese is golden brown. Serve to 4 with Sauce Giambelli.

### Sauce Giambelli

| | |
|---|---|
| 1 shallot | 1 tbsp. chopped parsley |
| 1 garlic clove, chopped | ½ cup white wine |
| 2 tbsp. butter | 1 dash lemon juice |
| 2 anchovies, finely chopped | ½ cup Brown Sauce* |
| 5 capers | salt and pepper to taste |

Sauté shallot and garlic in butter until golden brown. Add anchovies, capers, and parsley and cook 5 minutes over moderate heat. Add wine and lemon juice, mix well, and stir in brown sauce. Season to taste.

## CAPELLI D'ANGELO GRANZEOLA

| | |
|---|---|
| 2 tbsp. olive oil | salt and pepper to taste |
| 2 tsp. chopped shallots | 2 tsp. chopped parsley |
| ½ tsp. chopped garlic | 1 lb. imported angel's hair pasta |
| 1 lb. lump crab meat | ¼ lb. whipped sweet butter |
| 8 oz. peeled plum tomatoes, coarsely chopped | |

Heat oil in a large skillet over low flame. Add shallots and garlic and sauté until garlic is golden. Discard garlic. Add crab meat and mix thoroughly, taking care not to break up chunks. Add tomatoes, mix gently, and continue to sauté 5 minutes. Add salt and pepper to taste and, finally, parsley.

Place pasta in 5 qts. boiling salted water and stir at once to prevent sticking. Boil 1–2 minutes, or until *al dente,* and drain immediately. In a large warmed pan or serving bowl, toss pasta with butter and half the crab meat sauce. Serve and top each portion with remaining sauce. Serves 6 before entrée or 4 as a main course.

# PANETTONE

*Just why this veal and eggplant dish bears the same name as the traditional Italian Christmas cake it in no way resembles is debatable. Its merits, however, are unarguable.*

| | |
|---|---|
| 8 veal *scaloppine* (uniform size) | 1 cup white wine |
| salt and pepper to taste | 1 small eggplant, peeled |
| flour for dredging | 8 oz. tomato sauce |
| 2 eggs, beaten | 8 very thin slices prosciutto |
| 4 tbsp. olive oil | 6 oz. mozzarella cheese |
| 2 oz. butter | grated Parmesan cheese |

Have butcher pound *scaloppine* very thin. Dredge *scaloppine* in seasoned flour and dip in beaten egg, coating thoroughly. Sauté in half the oil until golden brown on both sides. Drain oil from pan, add butter and wine, and cook 2 minutes over low heat. Remove from heat and set aside. Slice eggplant $\frac{3}{16}''$ thick (the area of each slice should match that of each *scaloppine*), dredge successively in flour and beaten egg, and sauté in remaining oil until tender and golden, adding more oil if needed. Drain eggplant on paper towels.

Arrange *scaloppine* in a large casserole and evenly distribute tomato sauce over meat. Place a slice of eggplant atop each *scaloppine* and a slice of prosciutto over each slice of eggplant. Add a final layer of thinly sliced mozzarella, sprinkle with grated Parmesan cheese, and place under broiler until cheese turns golden brown. Serve at once to 4.

# ZABAGLIONE CAMIA

*At the restaurant, this dessert, which is named for Giambelli's very capable maître d'hôtel, is served semifreddo, or half-cold. I prefer it that way, and, although it takes a bit more elbow grease, the restaurant's version can be duplicated by removing the dish from the heat early, placing it over a bowl of crushed ice, and then whisking the bejabbers out of it.*

| | |
|---|---|
| 5 egg yolks | 4 oz. Marsala |
| 5 tsp. sugar | |

Fill bottom half of a 2-qt. double boiler with water and bring to boil. Place all ingredients in top half and beat well with a wire whisk until the mixture thickens to the consistency of soft custard. Pour into champagne glasses and serve to 4.

# GIAN MARINO
## 221 East 58th Street

One of the best. The menu, an anthology of regional classics with a few of the eponymous *padrone's* inventions thrown in for good measure, is comprehensive and consistently interesting. Service, under the direction of the very able Giovanni diSaverio, is friendly and expert. The premises are pleasant enough, if somewhat trite, and usually packed—for good reason. Vegetables are particularly well handled here, with stuffed artichoke, sautéed escarole, and an absolutely sensational *linguine* with broccoli and zucchini among the standouts. Filet mignon Caruso, *mezzani al siciliana,* and *soglio fiorentina* also are memorable.

## RIGATONI ALLA RICCI

| | |
|---|---|
| 3 oz. ground ham fat | salt and pepper to taste |
| 1 onion, chopped | ½ cup red wine |
| 2 oz. prosciutto, shredded | 1½ lbs. medium *rigatoni* |
| 3 oz. sliced mushrooms | 2 tbsp. chopped fresh basil |
| 3 oz. whole chicken livers | 3 oz. butter |
| 1 lb. tomatoes, crushed | 4 oz. grated Parmesan cheese |

In a pot, heat ham fat, add onion, and sauté until onion is soft but not browned. Add prosciutto, sauté 2–3 minutes, and successively add mushrooms, chicken livers, and tomatoes. Salt and pepper to taste and cook over moderate heat 15 minutes, occasionally turning off flame for a few moments. In another pot, reduce wine by ¼ and add it to the sauce. Meanwhile cook *rigatoni* in lightly salted boiling water until *al dente*. Drain *rigatoni* and transfer to a large warmed serving dish. Sprinkle pasta with chopped basil, dot with butter, and cover with sauce. Top with Parmesan cheese and serve to 4–6.

# SOLE WITH CHIANTI

5 oz. butter
2 lbs. fillet of sole
4 cups Chianti

salt and pepper to taste
½ oz. flour
juice of ½ lemon

Melt 2 oz. of the butter in a sauté pan, add sole fillets outer sides down, and cover with wine. Dot with 2 oz. of the butter, salt and pepper to taste, and bring quickly to boil. Remove pan from heat, cover with wax paper, and leave in a moderate oven 15–18 minutes. Transfer fillets with a slotted spatula to a hot plate and reserve wine. Knead remaining ½ oz. butter with the flour and, in the meantime, boil wine mixture down until reduced by ½. Add butter-flour mixture, boil a few seconds longer, and remove from heat. Stir remaining butter and lemon juice into sauce, season to taste, and pour over fish. Serves 4.

# FILET MIGNON ALL'ITALIANA

4 thick slices filet mignon
4 slices mozzarella cheese
4 slices prosciutto
4 thick slices white truffle (see note)

5 tbsp. melted butter
bread crumbs for dredging
salt and pepper to taste
½ cup Marsala

*Note   The white truffle, which may be the most sublime edible substance known to man or dog, is harvested in the Piedmont district of Italy from late October to early January and can be found in the better American specialty shops during those months. According to Giovanni diSaverio of Gian Marino, it can be frozen for a month or two with no ill effects. If you don't freeze your truffles, store them in short-grain Italian rice for a few days. This not only keeps the truffles in good shape but makes ambrosia of the rice.*

With a sharp knife, make an incision in a side of each filet to form a pocket. Insert a slice each of mozzarella, prosciutto, and truffle in each pocket. Dip steaks in ½ the melted butter, coating them thoroughly, then dredge in bread crumbs. In a sauté pan, cook steaks in remaining butter over a fairly high flame (they should remain rosy inside). Remove to a hot plate and salt and pepper to taste. Add Marsala to pan juices and reduce liquids by ⅓ over high heat. Cover steaks with sauce and serve to 4.

# MONSIGNORE II
## *61 East 55th Street*

Jimmy Aufiero, a gentleman of the old school, sat down and reconsidered his orientation after a 1975 fire inflicted serious damage on the establishment he had operated for twenty years. When he reopened the place a few months later, one of the city's dowager restaurants had undergone an astonishing face-lift. Several acres of chokingly stuffy red plush had been replaced by an airy, autumnal color scheme; an equally dated torch singer and her fiddler-consorts were no longer in evidence; a cliché-ridden "Continental" menu had been jettisoned. Its prolonged identity crisis over and done with, Monsignore today is one of the city's sprightliest Italian restaurants. In the dining room, man's journey through life, sardonically depicted on a series of metal panels by Franco Gracco, appears to be a Cook's tour of the planet's more decadent wateringholes. In the kitchen, Chef Vincenzo Mariani conducts a cook's tour of his own, turning out various regional dishes—and a few of Aufiero's own devising—with unerring intelligence and flair.

### FETTUCCINE JESSICA

*This excellent pasta dish was named for Jimmy Aufiero's small daughter when she was too young to partake of it. Growing older has its rewards.*

| | |
|---|---|
| 1 lb. egg fettuccine | ¼ cup heavy cream |
| ½ onion, sliced | salt and pepper to taste |
| ½ cup sliced mushrooms | ¼ cup bread crumbs |
| ½ cup minced prosciutto | 1 cup freshly grated Parmesan |
| 8 tbsp. sweet butter | cheese |

Use fresh fettuccine if possible. While pasta cooks in lots of rapidly boiling salted water until *al dente,* sauté onion, mushrooms, and prosciutto in butter until mushrooms are tender. In an ovenproof pan, toss drained pasta, contents of sauté pan, cream, and salt and pepper until cream is absorbed. Sprinkle successively with bread crumbs and cheese and brown until golden under a hot broiler. Serves 4–6 as a first course.

### PETTO DI POLLO MARIANI

| | |
|---|---|
| 4 large chicken breasts, skinned and boned | flour for dredging |
| salt and pepper to taste | 2 tbsp. finely chopped shallots |
| 4 slices Fontina cheese | 6 slices cooked tongue, cut in julienne strips |
| 4 slices prosciutto | 1 cup dry white wine |
| 6½ tbsp. sweet butter | 2 cups Brown Sauce* |
| 1 beaten egg | |

With a smooth-surfaced mallet, beat chicken breasts between sheets of wax paper until they have spread out in very thin *paillards*. Lightly pepper centers of breasts, lay a slice of cheese on each and then a slice of prosciutto, and dot with ½ tbsp. butter. Roll up the breasts, coat them with beaten egg, and dredge in flour. Melt 2 tbsp. butter in a saucepan and sauté chicken breasts over medium heat for 3 minutes, rolling them to cook evenly. Remove from heat and keep warm. In a separate saucepan, cook shallots in 2 tbsp. butter until golden brown. Add tongue and wine and cook until liquids reduce by half. Add brown sauce and remaining butter, correct seasoning, and pour sauce over chicken breasts. Sauté for 1 minute and serve immediately. Serves 4.

## Parioli
## Romanissimo
### 1466 *First Avenue*

Rubrio Rossi, a reformed architect, is the prime mover here, and his restaurant was accurately described several years before its opening by John Milton, who wrote, "Oh how comely it is and how reviving/ To the spirits of just men long opprest!" The cuisine is northern Italian and very stylish, the premises are romantic as all get-out (with love seats, no less, at shadowed rear tables), and the service, rendered by what looks like the cream of Renaissance aristocracy, is impeccable. The tariffs, it might be added, are pretty steep, but it would be hard to find better food at any price.

## FUNGHI FARCITI

| | |
|---|---|
| 1 lb. large, very fresh mushrooms | salt and pepper to taste |
| 2 cups tinned Spanish pimientos | 2 garlic cloves, finely chopped |
| 1½ cups pitted black olives | 2 tbsp. olive oil |
| 8 anchovy fillets | 2 cups chopped ripe tomatoes |
| ¼ cup grated Parmesan cheese | chopped parsley to taste |
| | 2 tbsp. butter |

Remove stems from mushrooms. Chop stems with pimientos, olives, and anchovies. Blend chopped ingredients with cheese, season to taste, and reserve. Sauté garlic in olive oil just until it starts to color, remove from heat, and reserve. In a saucepan, simmer tomatoes and parsley about 10 minutes. Add reserved garlic and oil, season to taste, and simmer 10 minutes longer. Fill mushroom caps with reserved pimiento-olive mixture and place in a shallow baking dish. Pour tomato sauce over mushrooms and dot with butter. Bake 15 minutes in a preheated oven at 400°F. Sprinkle with parsley and serve very hot to 6.

## RACK OF VEAL WITH ROSEMARY

| | |
|---|---|
| 1 rack of veal | salt and pepper to taste |
| 6 slices bacon | 3 cups white wine |
| ½ cup olive oil | 1 cup Chicken Broth* |
| 1 tbsp. dried rosemary | 2 tsp. butter |

Preheat oven to 450°F. Cover meaty side of rack with bacon slices, tie them in place with butcher's cord, and place veal, bone side down, in a roasting pan. Drizzle entire surface with oil, sprinkle with rosemary, and season to taste. Roast about ½ hour, or until golden brown, basting frequently. Turn meat over, reduce heat to 350°F., and roast 15 minutes longer, basting as before. Add wine and chicken broth and roast another 15 minutes. Remove from oven and transfer pan liquids to saucepan. Add butter to sauce and reduce to desired consistency over high heat. Pour sauce over roast and serve to 6–8.

## PATATE AL DIAVOLICCHIO

*This zingy potato dish would make a fine accompaniment to the foregoing rack of veal.*

| | |
|---|---|
| 1 tsp. chopped garlic | 2 *pepperoncino* (see note) |
| ½ cup olive oil | 1 tsp. dried rosemary |
| 2 tbsp. butter | |
| 6 medium Idaho potatoes, thinly sliced | |

*Note  A small, hot pickled pepper available at all Italian groceries and many supermarkets.*

Sauté garlic in the oil and butter until soft. Add all other ingredients, cover pan, and cook over medium heat until browned. Serves 6.

**Ponte's**

*37 Desbrosses Street*

The most improbably located restaurant I've ever encountered stood in a small, sudden jungle clearing in Assam, in the northeastern corner of what was then British India. There, in a neighborhood populated by Naga headhunters, slouched a mud-walled shambles, its disintegrating thatched roof lurching this way and that. A grinning, apron-clad Chinese stood in the doorway, a few scrawny chickens scratched disconsolately beneath a banana tree in the front yard, and the menu in its entirety consisted of fried chicken and banana fritters. The name of the establishment, conferred on it by a crumbling sign salvaged from an abandoned outpost of empire, was Water Closet.

Offhand, I'd say the *second* most improbably located restaurant I've run into is Ponte's. Without the restaurant, Desbrosses Street, which few New Yorkers have heard of and nobody knows how to find or pronounce, would be about as heavily trafficked as the dark side of the moon. With it, this narrow, grimy waterfront thoroughfare is chockablock with chauffeured. limousines at peak dining hours.

Don't look for subtlety here. The downstairs reception area wouldn't be out of place in a Barbary Coast whorehouse, and the sprawling second-floor dining rooms, ayawp with the keening of a strolling minstrel, beggar description. For the most part, the cuisine, perhaps best described as steakhouse Italian, is simple and straightforward. The lobsters are enormous and the sirloins gross; the pastas, copious and robustly sauced. Delve more deeply into the menu, however, and it turns out that Chef Sabatino Sammerone, a native of Abruzzi, is capable of considerable delicacy. His striped bass *mare chiare* is a marvel of understatement, his potato *gnocchi* are ethereally light, and his stuffed breast of veal (which can be leaden if mishandled) practically levitates off the plate. A favorite hangout of the sporting set.

## ZUPPA DI POLLO

*Despite the proprietary claims of Jewish mothers, every ethnic group except perhaps the Eskimos has its own ways of preparing chicken soup. This is the simple but satisfying version served at Ponte's.*

| | |
|---|---|
| 1 3-lb. chicken, quartered | 2 medium onions, chopped |
| 2 medium carrots, halved | salt to taste |
| 1 small celery knob, halved | 2 ripe tomatoes, diced |

Place all ingredients except tomatoes in a large pot with 1½ gals. water. Bring to boil and add tomatoes. Lower flame and simmer

1 hour. Remove chicken and carrots and strain contents of pot through a fine sieve or cheesecloth. Dice carrots, pick meat off chicken in small pieces, and return both to strained broth. Bring to boil and serve piping hot.

*Note  This recipe will yield more than you're likely to need for a single meal, but the soup keeps well under refrigeration.*

## COMBINATION PONTE

4  4-oz. slices filet mignon
4  full capon breasts, boned and
    halved
5  oz. olive oil
6  tbsp. butter
4  oz. sliced mushrooms
4  tbsp. proscuitto, cut in
    julienne strips
2  tbsp. flour

4  tsp. finely chopped onion
⅔  cup white wine
4  cooked artichoke bottoms,
    sliced
⅔  cup Chicken Stock*
2  tbsp. chopped Italian parsley
6  pitted black olives, sliced
salt and pepper to taste

Over fairly high heat, sauté steaks and capon breasts in oil until browned on both sides. Discard oil, add butter, mushrooms, and prosciutto, and sprinkle with flour. Stir thoroughly, add all other ingredients, and cook over low flame 2–4 minutes, stirring constantly. Serves 4.

# *Romeo Salta*

### 30 West 56th Street

For some time, the cry around midtown Manhattan was "Oh Romeo, Romeo, wherefore art thou Romeo?" Romeo, it turned out, had embarked on a belated wanderjahr and, in his absence, the establishment that bears his name had gone pretty much to pot. To the relief of an army of temporarily malnourished admirers, the boss is back minding the store now, and all's well with the world. This is one of the priciest Italian restaurants in town and has been since 1953, when Salta, who had operated a very successful West Coast venture, came east to pamper a clientele that had been wooed thither from Hollywood by the New York-based television industry. It is also one of the most colorful restaurants of any genre, with a gaggle of celebrities in more-or-less permanent residence, a highly visible glass-sheathed kitchen, and a pair of outsized aquariums, one for lobsters and one for trout, out of which latter disoriented specimens have been known to flip onto the tables of astonished diners. The cuisine is northern Italian, the menu is imaginative, the cooking is extremely stylish, and the veal, in particular (which Salta raises on his New Jersey farm), is flawless.


## BLACK AND WHITE CROSTINI

12 round slices French bread, ½″ thick
2 boiled chicken breasts, sliced in 12 pieces

salt and pepper to taste
12 slices black truffle

Preheat oven to 350°F. In a shallow buttered baking dish, arrange bread rounds as closely as possible. Cover each with a slice of chicken breast, salt and pepper to taste, and top with truffle slice. Bake in oven 15–20 minutes, taking care not to burn undersides of bread. Serve immediately to 4–6.


## TAGLIERINI CON SALMONE

1 lb. egg *taglierini* (preferably fresh)
4 tbsp. olive oil
2 shallots, minced
4 oz. smoked salmon, cut in julienne strips

7 oz. plum tomatoes (see note)
4 oz. heavy cream
1 pinch nutmeg
salt to taste

*Note* *Tomatoes should be peeled, seeded, and hand-squeezed.*

While *taglierini* cooks in boiling salted water, warm oil in a 4-qt. saucepan on a slow fire. Add shallots, sauté until translucent, and add all other ingredients. When pasta is cooked *al dente,* drain thoroughly, and add to saucepan. Toss well with sauce and simmer gently 2–3 minutes. Serves 4.

## VEAL PAILLARDS GIACOMO

| | |
|---|---|
| 2 large shallots, chopped | salt and pepper to taste |
| ½ tsp. dried thyme | 4 veal *paillards* (see note) |
| 1 tbsp. red-wine vinegar | 12 button mushrooms |
| 1 tbsp. Chicken Broth* | 2 tbsp. butter |

*Note* A paillard *is a rib veal chop pounded flat, as described in the article on Il Monello (page 129). Ideally, the trimmed rib bone should remain attached.*

In a bowl, mix all ingredients except mushrooms, butter, and meat. Add *paillards* and allow to marinate 1 hour, turning occasionally. In an iron skillet, sauté mushrooms in butter until tender, remove them from butter, and set aside. Remove *paillards* from marinade, pat dry, and sauté 10 minutes on each side in the same skillet. Pour marinade over meat and cook, covered, over low heat for 20 minutes. To serve, place 3 mushrooms on each *paillard* and add pan sauce to taste. Serve immediately to 4.

## FRESH LIME DESSERT

*Ideal for spur-of-the-moment get-togethers, this refresher can be made in advance in batches and kept frozen until needed.*

| | |
|---|---|
| 4 large green limes | 4 oz. Galliano or triple sec |
| 4 tbsp. grated almonds | 4 tbsp. lemon sherbet |

Cut off lime tops at a depth of one inch and reserve. Remove pulp from limes with a small spoon without breaking rinds. Break up lime pulp slightly in a bowl and add almonds, liqueur, and sherbet. Mix quickly with a spoon and fill each lime shell with the mixture. Replace lime caps and store in freezer for 24 hours before use. Remove from freezer 15 minutes before serving to 4.

# FORLINI'S

*93 Baxter Street*

Although obscurely located at the juncture of Chinatown and Little Italy, this traditional haunt of New York pols is worth seeking out. To my chagrin, a recent refurbishing has made a model of prefabricated banality of what used to be magnificently scruffy premises where you sat cheek-by-jowl with friendly strangers. The food, however, is every bit as good as it was when an earlier generation of Forlinis came here from Piacenza to introduce spaghetti-jaded New Yorkers to the delights of risotto and polenta. If there's a better grilled trout to be had in the city than the one served here, I've never found it. Nor have I found other versions quite as good as the restaurant's *anolini in brodo, baccalà* with polenta (try it with sautéed *broccoli di rapa* on the side) or its tadpole-shaped *tortellini con la cua.*

## GNOCCHI ALLA BOLOGNESE

| | |
|---|---|
| 1 lb. Idaho potatoes | 1 small egg yolk |
| ⅔ lb. flour | 1 pinch salt |

Place potatoes, unpeeled, in a pot fitted with a steamer. Add water enough to steam potatoes without immersing their behinds and cover pot successively with cloth toweling and lid. Steam potatoes until tender but still firm, peel, and put through ricer or mash with flour, egg yolk, and salt, blending ingredients well. Roll dough into long cylinders about the diameter of a cigar and cut into ¾″ lengths. Corrugate each piece by rolling it outward on the tines of an ordinary table fork and, just as each piece leaves the end of the fork, indent it slightly with the thumb, forming a shallow well to hold sauce. (If dough is too moist, add a little potato flour.) Poach *gnocchi* in plenty of boiling water, remove to serving dish as they rise to the surface, and serve with *Bolognese Sauce.* Serves 6 as a first course, 4 as a main dish.

### Bolognese Sauce
*As has been noted elsewhere in these pages, nobody agrees on the proper composition of this sauce. This, more or less, is the way it's made at Forlini's. The quantities represent educated guesses, since no one at the restaurant thinks in terms limited enough to apply here. The results I've obtained have been excellent.*

¾ lb. ground beef
¼ lb. ground pork
3 tbsp. olive oil
2 tbsp. butter
½ cup finely chopped onion
¼ cup grated carrot
¼ cup finely chopped celery
5–6 dried imported
   mushrooms, broken up

½ tsp. chopped parsley
3 cups Burgundy wine
6 plum tomatoes, hand
   squeezed
1 tbsp. chopped fresh basil
½ tsp. minced garlic
salt and pepper to taste

In a large heavy-bottomed saucepan, brown meats in oil and butter, breaking them up with the edge of a large spoon. Add onion, carrot, and celery and sauté for a few minutes, stirring. Then add mushrooms and parsley and mix well. Add wine and then tomatoes and simmer gently 2 hours, adding basil, garlic, and salt and pepper to taste a few minutes before sauce is done.

**Note** *Do not oversauce gnocchi.*

## FAGOTTO DI VITELLO

4 large veal cutlets (from leg)
salt and pepper to taste
eight 4" × 4" slices prosciutto
four 4" × 4" slices Swiss cheese
flour for dredging
2 eggs, beaten

4 tbsp. olive oil
2 tbsp. butter
¼ lb. fresh button mushrooms
¼ cup Chicken Stock*
¼ cup white wine
1 tsp. chopped parsley

Pound (or have butcher pound) veal into 8"-square *scaloppine.* Sprinkle meat lightly with salt and pepper. Successively layer each of the *scaloppine* with squares of prosciutto, cheese, and prosciutto, centering each square on the veal. Fold edges of veal over ham-cheese stacks to form envelopes, pressing edges to make them adhere. Dredge each envelope in flour and dip in beaten egg, coating thoroughly. Drain off excess egg while oil heats in a skillet. When oil is hot, sauté veal envelopes 3 minutes on each side, remove to serving dishes, and keep hot. Drain oil from skillet, add butter, and sauté mushrooms until tender. Add chicken stock and wine and simmer 5–6 minutes. Add parsley and reduce sauce to desired consistency. Pour sauce over veal and serve immediately to 4.

## MACEDONIA

*No quantity specifications are necessary here. The thing to remember is that the three liqueurs should be equal in quantity and in a sufficient amount to leave whatever quantity of fruit is used wallowing in at least half its depth. The sugar should be used very sparingly and the lemon juice just in sufficient quantity to make its presence felt.*

Stock brand mandarino liqueur     sugar
Stock brand blackberry julep     lemon juice
Stock brand maraschino liqueur
Fresh strawberries, oranges,
    peaches, pineapple, etc., diced

In a serving bowl, pour liqueurs over fruits, sprinkle with sugar and lemon juice, and refrigerate for half an hour or so, turning once or twice. Don't overchill.

## PART FOUR

# *In the Chinese Manner*

*T*o the gastronomic enrichment of her citizenry, France developed a truly national cuisine. The process was assimilative and to all intents and purposes began in relatively recent times—in 1533, to be precise, with the arrival on French soil of Catherine de Médicis and her retinue of Italian chefs. Later, the country's regional (and a good many foreign) dishes and techniques gradually were absorbed into the national repertory. While easily recognizable regional styles persisted, as they do to this day, it was something like a point of honor for the French to know and love the entire spectrum of their cookery and to incorporate its disparate elements into a systematized corpus that all the world now acknowledges to be distinctively French.

Such was not the case in Italy, where foreign influences were absorbed much earlier, where regional idiosyncrasies remained largely regional, and where nobody bothers to codify anything. (As one observer quoted by Waverley Root put it, "Order Béarnaise sauce in 200 different French restaurants and you will get exactly the same sauce 200 times. Ask for Bolognese sauce in 200 different Italian restaurants and you will get 200 different versions of ragú.") Nor, certainly, was such the case in China, where almost no outside influence was felt by the populace at large and where little regional exchange took place outside Peking. What both the Italians and Chinese developed was not a cuisine but a multiplicity of cuisines, and to generalize about either is (as we've seen in the case of Luccan spit-roasting) to tread on very slippery ground.

Still, it safely can be said that the arts of cooking and eating in Italy and China share some striking similarities. Both diets, for example, are far more farinaceous than that of the French (if, as some observers believe, future contention for world political supremacy finds the meat eaters aligned against the grain eaters, it isn't inconceivable that the Italians might find themselves in the latter camp); in both countries noodles were independently discovered (notions of Marco Polo's having brought them home from China notwithstanding) and are much used; pork plays a larger role in both Italy and China than in France, as does rice, while the confected dessert plays a much smaller one, at least as the conclusion to a meal. Beef, the most popular meat in France by far, is little used in Italy and hardly at all in China, whereas the smaller marine crustaceans, regarded as mere hors d'oeuvres and garnishes in France, are the chief components of any number of major dishes in both other countries.

The most pronounced similarity of all, though, has to do with an underlying culinary philosophy born of a shared exigency. In Italy, a paucity of fuel led to the development of the sauté pan as the fundamental cooking utensil. In China, the wok was the logical response to a fuel shortage perennially so acute that more often than not it necessitated the cooking of an entire meal over a momentary flare-up of tinder. Both implements depend for their effectiveness on elaborate advance preparation of raw ingredients; preparation that to somewhat varying degrees exposes far more surface area than bulk to heat. And if Italian cooking can be described as a logical alternative to the spit- and cauldron-derived fare of France, Chinese cooking, broadly defined, is the diametrical opposite of the French.

The wok, in essence a footless metal bowl, is probably the

most efficient and versatile cooking utensil ever devised. It heats uniformly and quickly, cleans easily, and lends itself to at least five basic culinary techniques: stir-frying, deep-frying, braising, sautéing, and (augmented by a bamboo basket) steaming. As used in a professional kitchen, it is also a sink and laundry basin, and to watch a really accomplished chef work with it is as breathtaking an experience as witnessing a Stan Kenton working with the tools of *his* trade, or a Muhammad Ali, when he had it all together, with his.

# SHUN LEE PALACE

*155 East 55th Street*

China's nearest equivalent to a national cuisine is Mandarin cooking, a co-optive style that evolved in Peking, largely as a means of alleviating the homesickness of provincial officials posted to the Imperial City. It is China's *haute cuisine* and its foremost exponent in this country may well be Tsung Ting Wang, who, in a nomenclatural inversion, is known to New Yorkers as T. T. Wang. Trained in Peking, Chef Wang also has been one of the prime movers in a gastronomic upheaval that during the past decade has toppled Cantonese cooking from its traditional position of preeminence and won thousands of New York China hands over to the fiery cooking of Hunan and Szechwan provinces. He is part-owner of three of the city's most highly regarded restaurants and has been described by Craig Claiborne, the resident *bec fin* of *The New York Times,* as "conceivably the most successful Chinese chef in the United States." At his mealtime work station in the crowded kitchen of Shun Lee Palace—a station roughly analogous to that of a football running back—he appears to the casual visitor to be neither more nor less successful than the three other stir-fry chefs with whom he lines up to produce the vast majority of the restaurant's cooked-to-order dishes. A laconic, rather dour-looking man of middle height and indeterminate age who speaks no English, he is flanked by a wizened veteran on his right and on his left by a tall young fellow with the carved face of a T'ang dynasty Buddha. At the fourth set of woks, a burly, gray-haired, potbellied chef of about fifty-five, the last of the morning's arrivals, takes up his position at 11:55. Centered between this lineup and a bewildering array of minced, chopped, shredded, diced, and sliced raw ingredients, all laid out in trays in a line of their own, is a fifth chef who seems a younger, smaller copy of Wang and to whom I would assign the title Quarterback the moment he went into action.

I had turned up at eleven o'clock at the invitation of an old friend, Michael Tong, the restaurant's manager and maître d'hôtel. By that time, the bulk of the morning's preparatory chores—some forty man-hours of precision cleaver-work included—had been finished and various employes—waiters, captains, chefs, cooks, and dishwashers—were drifting toward a large pot at the center of the kitchen floor. *"Congee,"* Tong explained. "Water-rice. We all have some before it gets busy." He filled a small bowl for himself, garnished it with a few sprigs of watercress, and picked at it with chopsticks as he wandered out for a final check of the dining rooms.

Physically, the restaurant is one of the larger, more tastefully decorated of the city's Chinese establishments, a meandering split-level layout with glittering crystal chandeliers set off against a shimmer of silver-and-gold wallpaper. Economically, it may not be quite as robust as its unusually heavy dinner trade would seem to suggest it is. "Costs are skyrocketing," Tong remarked, "and that hurts us far more than it does the French and Italian restaurants." The problem is rooted in part in ethnic custom. The city's Chinese restaurants depend heavily on a Jewish clientele made up of big eaters and light drinkers. In the past, cheap unorganized labor kept operating costs down, but today's soaring food prices have pretty much offset that edge. "It isn't liquor that's the problem," Tong continued in response to a question. "These days, everyone has a cocktail before the meal and we probably sell as much liquor as anyone else. The difference is that the French and Italian places make their money on wines. But who drinks wine with a Chinese meal?"

The first of the lunch patrons were arriving and Tong rose. "Our profit margin is extremely thin," he added as he prepared to greet them. "If we ever had to unionize, it would be the end of every Chinese restaurant in the city. Chinese restaurant workers are against unionization, though, because every last one of them hopes to open a place of his own some day."

By the time I returned to the kitchen the stir-fry chefs were at work on the day's first orders. The decibel count had risen considerably with the sizzle of the deep fryers, the snarl of boiling oil in the woks, the explosive hiss of water on hot metal, the clatter of steel against steel. I took up as unobtrusive a position as I could find, directly behind the potbellied chef at the end of the line. He sang as he worked, but the tune was inaudible in the general din.

Although a substantial portion of the American public has familiarized itself with the use of the wok during the past few years, the difference between its employment in the average home kitchen and a major restaurant is roughly that between a nine-year-old's kazoo rendition of "Happy Birthday" and a performance of Beethoven's *Ninth* by the New York Philharmonic. The elapsed time between reception of a waiter's order to his pickup of the finished dish rarely exceeds two minutes and can be as little as forty seconds flat. In such periods of time literally hundreds of bits of food must be manipulated as though each were being cooked separately and to a precisely calibrated degree. A really expert stir-fry chef combines the talents of a juggler and magician, disposing his various ingredients in relatively hot and cool, wet and dry sectors of the wok—even keeping some of them airborne—while everything remains in constant motion that from moment to moment changes from centrifugal to centripetal, from tumbling to an abrupt sort of rug-pulled-out-from-under-itself reversal that neatly somersaults the whole business. At Shun Lee Palace, the woks—a couple of feet in diameter—are set in fire holes on the sheet-steel range top. Behind them a gutter and backboard run the length of the range. A tall steel oil pot stands beside each pair of woks, surmounted by a shallow colander.

A waiter comes in and slides a written order across a steel shelf. The Quarterback reads it and goes into action, taking a serving dish from the shelf with his left hand and plucking with his right at the required dry ingredients as he moves from tray to tray, fingers bunching beaklike at each stop. Pluck, pluck, pluck—chicken, celery, scallions; pluck, pluck, pluck—garlic, ginger, water chestnuts, each item arranged so that it can be flicked from dish to wok in a sequence predetermined by its required cooking time. He executes a half-turn and hands the dish off to Chef Wang, who ladles the required amount of oil into his wok and goes to work. His tools, a long-handled spatula and shallow ladle, seem prehensile extensions of his arms. He attacks the wok like an assassin, elbows high, forearms working in pistonlike jabs as the oil sloshes alarmingly close to the rim of the wok, rears in the air like a golden version of Hokusai's "Great Wave," and crashes back down over the food.

The Quarterback hands off another dish to the chef nearest my vantage point. I move in for a closer look as the latter transfers a gummy wad of raw shrimp from dish to wok with a short backhanded flip of the spatula, and catch the end of his song: ". . . please don't take my sunshine away." His movements seem more casual, less incisive than Wang's, and full of unnecessary flourishes. In five seconds the shrimp have taken on definition and color. They are scooped up with the ladle and spatula and dumped onto the colander to drain. The Music Man clacks ladle and spatula together, flips vegetables from dish to wok, ladles a bit of tomato sauce over them, and launches into his next number. "I'm a Yankee Doodle Da-a-andy," he sings. "A Yankee Doodle-do or di-e-ie." Meanwhile, Buddha-face, stationed between Wang and the Music Man, has gone to work on a noodle dish and turns out to be the real hot dog of the group—a bravura stylist who chivies his materials all over the wok in a coruscating whirl that quickly accelerates into a multicolored blur. Although I can't get a clear view of him, the old-timer at the far end of the line also seems to have a distinctive working style. His movements are languid, almost somnambulistic, his gaze is averted from his wok and, for all I can tell, fixed on some point deep in mainland China in the days of Chiang Kai-shek. Nonetheless, his dishes remain in the wok no longer than anyone else's.

Some ninety seconds after receiving its raw components, Chef Wang, ladle and spatula cupped together like the hands of a small boy holding a large toad, is finishing his chicken dish. This operation, too, follows a predetermined sequence designed to distribute the ingredients (and, consequently, colors, textures, and flavors) evenly in the serving dish, with a few choice morsels reserved for a last decorative fillip. A sudden geyser of steam *whooshes* up from his wok; turning to pass the dish to the pickup shelf, he has flicked a swiveling water faucet into position, automatically turning it on. He scrubs out the wok with a couple of flat circular passes of a cloth, sloshes the water against the backboard, returns the faucet to the "off" position, and is handed another dish by the Quarterback.

Another *whoosh* as the Music Man—now singing "Clementine"—finishes his dish, followed almost simultaneously by two more as Buddha-face and the old-timer finish theirs. It is 12:40 now, and the waiters are blitzing the Quarterback in twos and . threes. The stir-fry chefs are working two dishes at a time, and a young, bushy-headed backup quarterback has materialized at the preparation counter. His responses, too, seem almost instinctive. Pluck, pluck, pluck—shrimp, broccoli, *bok choy;* pluck, pluck, pluck—black beans, chili peppers, bean sprouts. There is never a moment's hesitation or indecision on anyone's part. The action is furious now, the din terrific, with boiling oil sloshing, swirling, pinwheeling, leaping free of the woks, and crashing back down into them. The Music Man, sweating copiously and singing "When Johnny Comes Marching Home," is stirring one wok with his left hand while sliding batter-coated shrimp into another with his right. The right-hand dish, shrimp puffs, is particularly tricky, since each of the adhesive globs must be kept separated from the others until a crust begins to form. Once it does, he stirs them furiously with a counter-clockwise motion while his left hand, working more slowly, moves the contents of the other wok in a clockwise direction. Astonishingly, the chefs are getting ahead of the waiters, with finished orders piling up on the pickup shelf.

By this time, the hors d'oeuvre chefs have finished with lunch and are starting the preparatory work for dinner. What I'd guess to be about a hundred chickens have been dumped onto a high work counter at one side of the kitchen, and a couple of men who previously had occupied themselves with the cold, deep-fried, and steamed appetizers are now skinning the birds. Gradually, the pace at the woks slackens and, one by one, the stir-fry chefs abandon the range to help with the chickens. The Music Man ambles over, cleaver in hand, and, as the bushy-headed kid passes trimmed chicken breasts to him, he slices them with surgical precision, singing, "It's a long way to Tippera-a-a-a-r-ry, it's a long way-y-y to go-o. . . ."

It's a long way to dinner, too, but there will be barely enough time to get everything ready for the busiest hours of the working day.

*Chinese meals do not conform to Western notions of progression, with courses served in a fixed order. Also, it is difficult to determine the number of servings a given recipe will yield, because diners are expected to take as much or as little of each dish as they want. Thus it should be borne in mind that it is hardly necessary to serve the dishes that follow in the order given, and that the number of servings indicated for all dishes is approximate, at best.*

## HOT AND SOUR SOUP

2 large dried black mushrooms
6 tree ear mushrooms
4 dried tiger lily stems
1 tbsp. peanut oil
$\frac{1}{4}$ cup finely shredded pork
$\frac{1}{2}$ cup finely shredded bamboo
  shoots
5 cups rich Chicken Broth*
1 cake fresh white bean curd,
  shredded

3 tbsp. dark soy sauce
3 tbsp. vinegar
1 tsp. white pepper
$\frac{2}{3}$ tsp. salt
1 tbsp. sesame oil
2 eggs, lightly beaten
2 tbsp. cornstarch mixed with 3
  tbsp. water
2 tbsp. chopped scallions
1 tsp. minced fresh coriander

Place mushrooms, tree ears, and lily stems in a mixing bowl, pour in boiling water to cover, and let stand at least 15 minutes before draining. Cut off and discard black mushroom stems and thinly slice mushroom caps and tree ears. To a hot wok or skillet add peanut oil and pork, stirring just until strands of pork separate. Add mushrooms, tree ears, lily stems, and bamboo shoots, stir quickly, and successively add chicken broth and bean curd. Bring to boil, add soy sauce, vinegar, pepper, and salt. After 10 seconds add sesame oil and turn off heat. Add eggs gradually in a thin stream while stirring soup with a circular motion. Stir in diluted corn starch. Garnish with scallions and coriander and serve piping hot to 4–6.

## CHICKEN SOONG

| | |
|---|---|
| 1 head iceberg lettuce | 2 tsp. chopped garlic |
| 1 boned chicken breast (about 1 lb.) | 3 tbsp. finely chopped scallions |
| | 2 tbsp. dry cooking Sherry |
| ½ tsp. salt | ½ tbsp. soy sauce (see note) |
| 1 egg white, beaten | 1 tsp. hot chili paste (optional) |
| 2 tbsp. cornstarch | 1 tsp. sugar |
| 10 water chestnuts | 1 tsp. MSG (optional: see note) |
| ½ cup finely diced celery | 2 cups peanut oil |
| 3 tbsp. diced carrot | ½ tsp. sesame oil |
| 1 tsp. peeled and chopped fresh gingerroot | |

*Note   MSG (monosodium glutamate) is always optional as far as the recipes in this book are concerned. As far as I'm concerned, this supererogatory flavor enhancer should be rigorously eschewed. It is not only suspected as a possible carcinogen in some quarters (as what isn't?), but can induce a vague malaise known variously as the Chinese Restaurant Syndrome and Chinese Temples.*

*Unless otherwise specified, light soy sauce should be used in all recipes.*

Core lettuce, separate leaves, arrange on a serving platter, and set aside. Using a sharp knife or Chinese cleaver, divide chicken breast laterally into thin slices. Stack slices and cut lengthwise into shreds, then cut crosswise into tiny cubes (there should be about 2 cups). Using the fingers, thoroughly blend diced chicken, salt, egg white, and 1 tbsp. of the cornstarch. Cut water chestnuts into tiny cubes, as you did the chicken. In a bowl combine water chestnuts, celery, carrot, and gingerroot and set aside. In another bowl combine garlic and scallions and set aside. In a small, deep dish combine Sherry, soy sauce, optional chili paste, sugar, and optional MSG and set aside. In a similar dish mix remaining cornstarch with 1½ tbsp. water.

In a wok or skillet, heat peanut oil over high flame. When oil is hot, add chicken and cook, stirring constantly, 1½ minutes. Immediately drain contents of wok through a colander mounted on a receptacle to catch the oil. Return 2 tbsp. oil to wok and add water chestnut mixture. Cook, stirring, 30 seconds and add scallions and garlic. Cook, stirring, 10 seconds longer and return chicken to wok. Continue to stir-fry 30 seconds and add Sherry mixture and sesame oil. Quickly stir cornstarch mixture until smooth, add it to wok, and stir rapidly for 30 seconds. Transfer mixture to a hot platter. Serve immediately with lettuce on the side.

At this juncture the guests take matters into their own hands, each placing a spoonful or so of the chicken mixture onto a lettuce leaf, folding the leaf around the chicken and eating the resultant package with the fingers. Serves 4 as a first course, 8–10 as an accompaniment to cocktails.

## HEAVENLY FISH FILLETS

| | |
|---|---|
| 1 sea bass, about 2 lbs. | ¼ tsp. sesame oil |
| 1 egg white, beaten | 3 cups peanut oil |
| 1 tbsp. cornstarch | 1 garlic clove, coarsely chopped |
| 10 snow peas | 1 heaping tbsp. minced fresh |
| 10 water chestnuts | gingerroot |
| ¼ cup dry cooking Sherry | 2 chopped scallions, green tops |
| 2 tbsp. sugar | included |
| ½ tsp. salt | ½ tbsp. cornstarch mixed with 1 |
| 1 tsp. MSG (optional) | tbsp. water |

Have fishmonger cut sea bass into fillets about 3″ long and 1¼″ thick. In a bowl toss fillets in a mixture of the egg white and

1 tbsp. cornstarch, coating them thoroughly, and set aside. Combine snow peas and water chestnuts in a dish and set aside. In a shallow bowl, mix Sherry, sugar, salt, optional MSG, and sesame oil and set aside. Heat peanut oil in a wok or skillet and, when quite hot, add fish fillets one by one, taking care not to let them overlap. When all fillets are in wok, turn off heat, and stir them gently for 1 minute. Turn on heat as high as possible, add snow peas and water chestnuts, and cook 20 seconds. Drain through a colander set on a receptacle to catch oil, leaving about 1 tsp. of oil in the wok. Add garlic, gingerroot, and scallions to wok, stir-fry 20 seconds, and return fish fillets, snow peas, and water chestnuts to wok. Add remaining ingredients and cook, stirring, for 30 seconds longer. Serves 2–8, depending on the size of the entire meal.

 **DAVID K's**

# CHUNG KUO YUAN
*1115 Third Avenue*

The indefatigable David Keh, who has known both the thrill of victory and the agony of defeat, has never settled for halfway measures. With Chung Kuo Yuan (page 39) he has gone for broke in the confident expectation that his clientele would do likewise. Dinner here can produce a tab that approaches the national debt, but you won't find a more stunning setting or more civilized service in any other Chinese restaurant in the known universe.

*The meal that follows can be prepared in advance and cooked in a trice. With fresh fruit for dessert, it would make an ideal tête-à-tête supper after an evening at the theater.*

### IMPERIAL NOODLES

½ lb. egg noodles
1 tsp. sugar
2 tbsp. soy sauce
1½ tbsp. wine vinegar
1 tbsp. sesame oil
1 tsp. chili oil
1½ tbsp. creamy
   peanut butter  } blended
2 tbsp. water

1 pinch minced scallion
1 pinch peeled and minced
   fresh gingerroot
1 pinch minced garlic

While noodles cook in plenty of boiling salted water, blend all other ingredients thoroughly. Bear in mind that Chinese noodles are usually cooked to a slightly softer stage than they would be for Italian pasta dishes, and add a minute or two to the cooking time specified on the package. When noodles are done, rinse and drain twice, using cold water, and serve, topped with sauce, to 2.

## BEEF WITH BROCCOLI

½ lb. boneless sirloin, sliced thin
1 lb. broccoli, minus thick stems

1 pt. peanut oil
2 large black Chinese mushrooms, soaked and drained

*Chef Chou's Beef Sauce*

1 tbsp. Sherry
3 tbsp. soy sauce
1 tsp. sugar
1 pinch peeled and minced fresh gingerroot

1 pinch minced scallion
1 tbsp. cornstarch, diluted with a little water
2 tbsp. Chicken Broth*

First, prepare sauce by blending all its ingredients thoroughly. Slice beef ⅛" thick. Separate broccoli into flowerets. In a wok or skillet, heat oil slowly until simmering (do not boil). Add beef to wok and stir-fry 30 seconds. Add broccoli and stir-fry 15 seconds longer. Pour contents of wok into a colander mounted on a receptacle to catch oil. When well drained, return beef and broccoli to wok, add mushrooms, and stir 5 seconds. Add sauce and stir briskly 10 seconds longer. Remove at once and serve with steamed rice to 2.

# HOUSE of CHAN

*Seventh Avenue at 52nd Street*

After feeding chow mein and chop suey to the senior prom crowd and newly bar mitzvahed since around the time of Marco Polo, the House of Chan revamped its menu a few years ago and now serves some of the most interesting and best-prepared Chinese food in the city. The party responsible is Stanley Chan, the late founder's son, who combined a computer-sharp intellect and a reverence for tradition to produce a bill of fare based on recipes that, in some cases, go back as far as the Han dynasty. His restaurant sprawls all over the street floor and basement of a sizable building not far from the theater district and comprises a number of handsome rooms, of which the largest is quite stately, with its fine wood paneling, lofty ceiling, and dignified gray napery. Others, with their murky lighting, filigreed screens and more intimate proportions, afford the sort of protective coloration favored by middle-aged businessmen given to romancing their secretaries, but the lower-level refectory is all up-front hustle and bustle.

## GRANDMA NG'S BANQUET

*Many of the dishes served at the House of Chan are the products of Chan family recipes, most of them handed down to Stanley Chan by his grandmother. As Chan describes the meal that follows, it was traditionally prepared for such occasions as "New Year's, graduation, son's job promotion, baptism, confirmation, son/daughter bringing home a fiancé(e), anniversary." Individual dishes, Chan adds, "were not served in courses per se [but] when they were ready. The entire meal is designed to feed eight people to near discomfort."*

### WINTER MELON SOUP

| | |
|---|---|
| 1  4-lb. section Chinese winter melon | 4 oz. (or 1½ doz.) whole dried oysters |
| 4 oz. preserved dried fish air bladder | ¾ oz. dried tangerine peel |
| | 1½ gal. Chicken Stock* |

Remove seed mesh and cut melon into 2" cubes. Cut rind from melon or not, according to taste (Stanley Chan: "I was taught there was nourishment in leaving the skin on"). Bring all ingredients to boil, reduce to simmer, and cook until stock is reduced by ⅓. Do not stir after boil has been reached.

# CRISPY SKIN DUCK

2 tbsp. crushed rock sugar or
corn syrup
2 tbsp. *ng ka py* (or gin)
2 tbsp. white vinegar
6 tbsp. hot water

1 4½–5½-lb. fresh duck
2 tsp. five-spice powder
3 tbsp. salt
3 qts. cooking oil
2 lemons, cut in wedges

In a saucepan, combine sugar (or syrup), *ng ka py* (or gin), vinegar, and hot water and cook over very low heat until blended. While the mixture is still hot, pour it over the duck, working it into the skin until the bird is well coated. In a dry pan over low heat, stir-fry five-spice powder and salt about 1 minute, or until mixture turns brown. Rub inside of duck with spice-salt mixture and refrigerate uncovered duck overnight.

Select a heavy pot large enough to accommodate duck and oil within half the pot's depth and heat oil to 350–375°F. When oil is sufficiently hot, deep-fry duck for about 20 minutes, turning when necessary to crisp skin on all sides but taking care not to puncture the skin. During the last 2–3 minutes of frying process, turn heat up as high as possible for maximum crisping effect. Remove duck from oil (which can be reserved for other uses) and allow to drain for a minute or two. Carve duck into convenient serving pieces, arrange on a platter, and garnish with lemon wedges.

# BRAISED HAM KNUCKLE

1½ oz. medium dried oysters
1 3½–4½-lb. fresh ham knuckle
(skin intact)
3 tbsp. dark soy sauce
2 cups cooking oil
2 oz. dried black mushrooms
1 oz. dried hair seaweed

4 sprigs coriander
1 qt. (or more) Chicken or
Beef Stock*
½ teaspoon salt
2 tbsp. crushed rock sugar or
corn syrup

Soak oysters overnight in cold water to cover. Rinse knuckle and pat dry. Rub knuckle thoroughly with dark soy sauce. Over a moderate flame, heat the oil in a large skillet. Add knuckle, brown it on all sides until golden, and set it aside to drain. Soak mushrooms and seaweed ½ hour in separate bowls of water to cover. Snip off and discard mushroom stems. When seaweed is soft and loose, add 2 tsp. cooking oil to water, let stand 10 minutes, and rinse seaweed in a fine sieve under cold running water. Wash coriander and break into 1" pieces. To a Dutch oven, add stock and salt and bring to boil. Carefully add knuckle, taking care not to pierce skin, and if necessary add enough stock to cover. Bring stock to boil and reduce to slow simmer. Add all other ingredients except coriander and simmer, covered, for 1½ hours, or until liquid has been reduced by two-thirds. (If liquid is not sufficiently reduced, continue to simmer until it is. Stanley Chan: "My grandmother cooked the knuckle just until its skin was on the point of breaking.") Transfer knuckle to a large soup tureen and cover with broth. Sprinkle with coriander and serve.

## CHICKEN WITH SOY SAUCE

| | |
|---|---|
| 2 pieces star anise | 1 tbsp. peeled and mashed |
| 4–5 tbsp. crushed rock or cane | fresh gingerroot |
| sugar | ⅔ tbsp. *ng ka py* (or gin) |
| 1 pt. light soy sauce | 1 4½-lb. fresh-killed chicken |
| 3 pts. dark soy sauce | 4 scallion heads (white part |
| 1 pt. water | only) |
| preserved peel of ¼ tangerine | scallion greens, cut in slivers |

In a large pot, combine all ingredients except chicken and scallions and cover. Bring to boil, reduce heat, and allow to simmer 15–20 minutes. Place chicken in the pot (which should be of a size to allow liquids to cover the fowl) and continue to simmer gently so that chicken skin doesn't break for 50–60 minutes. Remove chicken carefully and allow to cool for 10–15 minutes. With a sharp knife, slit the scallion heads from tops downward to form brushes. Chop chicken into serving pieces, garnish with scallion brushes and slivers, and serve.

*Note   Cooking liquid may be reserved, refrigerated, for future use.*

# DOUBLE BOILER STEAMED MUSHROOMS

3 doz. medium dried black
mushrooms, the thicker the
better
½ cup rendered chicken fat
¼ tsp. salt
1 pt. Chicken Stock*

1 tsp. corn syrup
1 tsp. minced Virginia ham (see
note)
2–3 sprigs fresh coriander,
chopped

*Note* A one-inch cube of ham should be cut in quarters and parboiled
with 1 tsp. sugar in 1 cup water for 30 minutes, then dried and minced.

Place mushrooms in a bowl with water to cover. Soak for about
½ hour, drain the mushrooms, and squeeze out as much water
as possible without breaking them. In a covered double boiler,
simmer all ingredients except ham and coriander for 2 hours,
stirring occasionally, or until mushrooms have absorbed all
liquids. Serve mushrooms sprinkled successively with ham and
coriander.

# POACHED SEA BASS

*For this dish, the fish must be irreproachably fresh, with clear eyes
and odorless gills.*

1 2–2½-lb. whole sea bass,
scaled, definned, and gutted
salt to taste
3 tbsp. cooking oil
2 tbsp. peeled and shredded
fresh gingerroot

2½ oz. canned sweet cucumber,
preserved in syrup
2 whole scallions cut in 3″
slivers
3 tbsp. soy sauce

Place fish in a poacher or Dutch oven large enough to hold it
comfortably and add salted water to cover by ¼″. Remove fish,
bring water to boil, and reduce to a slow simmer. Lower fish
into water, simmer for about 10 minutes, and transfer to platter.
(Chan: "My grandmother taught me to watch the eye of the
fish to determine when it was done. When the eye began to
bulge and turn white, that was the time to remove the fish to
a platter.") In a saucepan, heat the oil until it begins to smoke

and add the gingerroot. Cook until it begins to turn brown and remove from heat. Drain all accumulated liquids from the fish platter, pour hot ginger-oil mixture over the fish, and sprinkle fish with salt. Cut drained cucumbers into 1½″ julienne strips and sprinkle them and scallions over fish. Finally, sprinkle fish with soy sauce and serve.

## FLOWER-CUT CHICKEN GIZZARDS

gizzards from 4–5 chickens,
  cleaned and peeled of gristle
1 tbsp. cooking oil
½ garlic clove, minced
salt to taste
¼ cup Chicken Stock*
¼ cup finely diced carrots

¼ cup fresh green peas
¼ cup roasted unsalted cashew
  nuts
1 tsp. each cornstarch and
  water, blended
1 tbsp. finely diced scallions
1 tsp. oyster sauce

Quarter each gizzard and, with a sharp knife or cleaver, cut each piece in a deep crosshatch pattern, taking care to leave it intact. Parboil gizzards in water for about a minute, or until they assume a set, flowerlike shape. Rinse under cold running water for 5 minutes and drain. Set aside. In enough hot oil to thinly cover the bottom of an 8–10″ skillet, add the garlic and salt. Stir-fry garlic briefly until aromatic, add gizzards, and continue to stir-fry vigorously for a few seconds. Add stock and carrots and cover until stock boils. Add peas and cashews, stirring briefly, and fold in cornstarch mixture, stirring continually, until all ingredients are thinly coated with sauce. As soon as sauce has thickened sufficiently, add scallions and oyster sauce, stir briefly, and serve at once.

## SAUSAGE FRIED RICE

3 cups long-grain rice
6 links Chinese pork sausage
3 tbsp. cooking oil
pinch of salt
½ medium onion, finely chopped
¼ lb. fresh bean sprouts, drained

2 eggs, firmly scrambled
¼ cup finely chopped scallion
  tops
½ cup finely chopped lettuce
1 tbsp. soy sauce

In a heavy deep-sided saucepan, wash the rice in cold running water until water in pan clears. Add enough water to cover rice by "the depth of a thumbnail [the measure is Stanley Chan's; I assume that he means an average thumbnail, and not the outrageously attenuated affairs once cultivated by Chinese aristocrats] as it gently lies on the surface of the rice." Cover the pan and bring to a boil "until steam, escaping from the edge of the lid, slows to a gentle wisp." (Chan, who can wax practical as well as poetical, adds, "If you want to cheat a bit, as my grandmother did at times, quickly peek into the pot and see if there are holes in the risen rice. If there are, reduce heat to lowest setting and let cook for an additional 15–20 minutes.") When the rice is done, allow it to cool slightly and run a fork through it until the kernels are loosened.

Parboil the sausage in water for 10 minutes and remove. Allow to cool and cut in $\frac{3}{8}''$ slices. In a large skillet or wok, add oil and salt and stir-fry all ingredients except scallions, soy sauce, and lettuce until onions just begin to wilt. Add scallions, stirring, then lettuce, still stirring, and, finally, soy sauce. Stir the whole business quickly and thoroughly and serve in a large bowl.


## TANGELO PEEL STEAMED SPARERIBS

2  1½-lb. sheets of spareribs,          4–6 oz. canned preserved
    trimmed of fat and gristle              tangelo peel in syrup

Separate ribs with a heavy cleaver. Chop into $1\frac{1}{2}''$ lengths. Parboil the ribs in water for 3 minutes to remove excess fat and drain. Place ribs in a large mixing bowl, add tangelo peel and syrup, and knead ribs until well permeated with syrup. Arrange in one layer (or, if necessary, two) on an ovenproof serving platter or roasting pan and place the receptacle in an aluminum roasting pan large enough to accommodate it easily. Add water to larger pan until halfway to the top of the smaller pan, cover larger pan, and place over high heat until it begins to steam. Steam, covered, for 10–15 minutes, or until meat slides easily from bone. When done, place platter on a trivet and fall to.

# DRY STIR-FRIED SHRIMP

1 tsp. mashed cooked black
   beans
cooking oil
2 doz. "16–20" white headless
   shrimp, unshelled (see note)
1 small garlic clove, mashed
2 tbsp. peeled fresh gingerroot,
   slivered

1 tsp. soy sauce
1 tbsp. dry Sherry
2 tbsp. Chicken Stock*
1 doz. scallion heads (white part
   only)

*Note* "16–20" *refers to number of shrimp per pound.*

Make a smooth paste of mashed beans and ½ tsp. oil. With sharp scissors, slit backs of shrimp shells and devein shrimp. Coat bottom and sides of a large skillet or wok with oil and put pan over high heat until oil begins to smoke. Add shrimp and turn rapidly and continually until shells begin to singe. Quickly add bean paste, garlic, and gingerroot, stirring to distribute the mixture evenly over the bottom of the pan. Before bean mixture burns, add soy sauce, Sherry, stock, and scallions and cover immediately. Vigorously slide pan back and forth over fire, so that shrimp "scrub" its bottom for about 30 seconds. Lower heat as far as possible and continue cooking, covered, for 3–5 minutes. Serve immediately.

# Mandarin Inn
眞北京

*14 Mott Street*

# Mandarin Inn Pell
眞
北
京

*23 Pell Street*

The atmosphere at both these walk-up establishments in the heart of Chinatown is cheerfully scruffy, but the food is first-rate, as a great many New Yorkers make abundantly evident by their massed presence most nights. Peter Wong, the most visible of the owners and a master of sleight of hand, drifts from table to table (possibly at both restaurants at once), dazzling customers with his card tricks and incomprehensibly proliferative sponge-rubber balls. Brass gongs herald the arrival of particularly elaborate dishes, and a good time is had by all, particularly when the minimal check is presented.

## SPICY PICKLED SALAD

*This Szechwan hors d'oeuvre, a specialty of the Mandarin Inn restaurants, can be prepared days—or even as long as two weeks—ahead of time and kept refrigerated in a covered jar until needed. The number of servings is indeterminate, but whatever is left over can be returned to the marinade for future use.*

1  small head cabbage
2  green peppers
2  carrots
1  cup white rice vinegar
1  cup sugar
2  2″ cubes peeled fresh
   gingerroot, crushed

8  garlic cloves, crushed
8  dried red chili peppers,
   halved and seeded
1  qt. water

Cut cabbage and green peppers into 1″ squares and carrots into ½″ diagonal slices. Place vegetables in a 4-qt. mixing bowl. Combine all other ingredients and pour over vegetables. Select a plate or lid that will fit closely inside mixing bowl, place it over the salad, and press down hard. Refrigerate 3 days, turning salad occasionally. Remove chilis, garlic, and ginger before serving.

## CORN SOUP

*This velvety preparation is a specialty of Shantung province.*

4  cups Chicken Broth*
1  tsp. salt
8  oz. canned creamed corn
1½ tbsp. cornstarch dissolved in
   3 tbsp. water

1  tbsp. dry Sherry
2  egg whites, beaten until fluffy
1  whole scallion, thinly sliced

Bring broth to boil and add salt and creamed corn, stirring constantly until mixture returns to boil. Stir dissolved cornstarch and add to soup. Stir until thickened, about 1 minute. Add Sherry, stirring. Remove from heat and add egg whites, stirring gently. Garnish with scallion and serve immediately in individual bowls to 4–6.

## TEA EGGS

| | |
|---|---|
| 8 eggs | 1 tbsp. salt |
| ¼ cup black tea | 1 tsp. star anise |
| 3 tbsp. soy sauce | |

In a saucepan, cover eggs with cold water, bring to boil, and simmer 30 minutes. Drain and rinse in cold water. Press eggs against kitchen counter-top, rolling, to crack shells all over, taking care not to let any pieces of shell break off. Place eggs in a saucepan, cover with cold water, and add remaining ingredients. Bring to boil, cover, and simmer 1½ hours. (The eggs will take on a marbled appearance.) Allow eggs to cool at room temperature and refrigerate. When ready to serve, peel eggs and quarter them. Serves 6–8.

## SHANGHAI DUCK

*You won't find this dish on the menu, but it will be prepared if ordered a few days in advance.*

| | |
|---|---|
| 1 4–5-lb. duckling | 2 tsp. star anise |
| vegetable oil | ¼ cup dry Sherry |
| 4 rounds fresh gingerroot, ⅛″ thick | 4 tbsp. soy sauce |
| 2 scallions, cut in 2″ lengths | 2 tsp. sugar |
| | 1 cup water |

Place duck breast-down in an oil-rubbed casserole. Place gingerroot and half the scallions in duck cavity and strew remainder over duck along with star anise. Combine Sherry, soy sauce, sugar, and water and pour over duck. Turn heat to high and bring to boil. Cover, turn heat to low, and simmer 1½ hours, turning duck onto its back after 30 minutes. Remove from heat and let stand 30 minutes. Remove duck from liquid and refrigerate, uncovered, overnight. Refrigerate cooking liquid separately.

Carve the duck and the skin in thin slices and arrange on a serving platter. Serve with Steamed Bread and Shanghai Sauce, allowing guests to make sandwiches of duck and bread, spooning a little sauce over top. Serves 6.

### Shanghai Sauce

Remove jellied cooking liquid from refrigerator and discard layer of fat from its surface. Bring jelly to boil and cook vigorously until reduced to ½ cup. Strain and serve warm in a small bowl.

### Steamed Bread

| | |
|---|---|
| 1 or 2 pkgs. refrigerated biscuits | sesame oil |

Shape each biscuit into 4" rectangle, slightly narrowed at the center, and brush surfaces with sesame oil. Fold biscuits in half, bring a cup or so of water to boil in a steamer, and place each folded biscuit on a 3" × 3" square of wax paper, leaving space between biscuits for expansion. Steam 10 minutes.

# Uncle Tai's
# HUNAN YUAN
### *1059 Third Avenue*

One of the most durable—and perhaps the best—of the several restaurants opened around town at one time or another by the redoubtable David Keh, Uncle Tai's is named for its chef, whose personal culinary odyssey began in his native Hunan province in his ninth year and subsequently took him to Peking, Shanghai, Taipei, Japan, and the Philippines before he finally settled in the Big Apple. The large dining room, although comfortable enough, is less than distinguished, but the same charge can't be leveled against either the service or food. In China, "Uncle" is an honorific conferred only on veterans of universally acknowledged ability. Uncle Tai's vegetable pie, corn-and-crab soup, cold peppered rabbit, paper-fried squab, Lake Tung Ting shrimp, and frogs' legs with lichee nuts amply confirm the legitimacy of his claim, but so, for that matter, does just about every dish on the restaurant's extensive menu.

## LAKE TUNG TING SHRIMP

*Lake Tung Ting is situated in northeastern Hunan, expands to cover an area of some 4,000 square miles at high water in summer, and shrivels almost to nothingness in winter, when rice is grown in its bed.*

$\frac{1}{2}$ lb. "21–25" shrimp (see note)
1 tbsp. salt
Marinade (recipe below)
$\frac{1}{2}$ head broccoli
4 water chestnuts (optional)
2 ōz. cooked ham, preferably Smithfield
2 scallions
5 large egg whites

2 tbsp. cornstarch
1 tbsp. water
Sauce (recipe below)
3 cups vegetable oil
1 cup warm Chicken Stock*
1 tsp. peeled fresh gingerroot, cut in paper-thin $\frac{1}{4}''$ squares
$\frac{1}{2}$ tsp. sesame oil

*Note   Figures refer to approximate number of shrimp per pound.*

Shell shrimp, halve them lengthwise, and devein. Place shrimp in a colander, mix thoroughly with salt, and rinse under cold running water until free of salt. Drain, pat dry, and place in a mixing bowl. Prepare Marinade.

*Marinade*

$\frac{1}{2}$ egg white
1 tbsp. dry Sherry or Shao-Hsing wine

$\frac{1}{4}$ tsp. salt.
1 tbsp. cornstarch
white pepper to taste

In a small bowl, beat ½ egg white with Sherry and salt until frothy. Mix with reserved shrimp. Add cornstarch and pepper to taste and stir vigorously with the hand until starch is completely dissolved. Allow to marinate at least 20 minutes. (If preparing long in advance, refrigerate marinating shrimp and warm to room temperature before cooking.)

Cut off top inch or two of broccoli and separate into flowerets. Rinse and drain, reserving remaining broccoli for other uses. Peel and wash optional water chestnuts, slice in ⅛″ rounds, and cover with cold water until ready to use. Slice ham in ⅛″-thick julienne strips. Cut scallions into ½″ bits. Beat 5 egg whites until just broken up and barely foaming. Dissolve 2 tbsp. cornstarch in 1 tbsp. water, gently but thoroughly beat mixture into egg whites, and set aside. Prepare Sauce.

### Sauce

| | |
|---|---|
| 2 tsp. cornstarch | 4 tbsp. Chicken Stock* |
| 4 tbsp. dry Sherry or Shao-Hsing wine | ¼ tsp. salt |
| | ¼ tsp. MSG (optional) |

In a small bowl, dissolve cornstarch in 1 tbsp. of the wine. Stir in remaining wine, stock, salt, and optional MSG.

In a wok or skillet, heat vegetable oil to 280°F. Turn heat down a bit and pour in reserved egg-white mixture, using a circular motion. Stir gently from bottom up and when egg whites are just set (5–10 seconds) pour contents of wok into a strainer set over a receptacle to catch oil. Shake strainer gently to drain off as much oil as possible. Return oil to wok, heat to 280°F., and add shrimp, stirring constantly to separate. As they begin to take on color, add drained water chestnuts, broccoli, and ham and stir gently 20–30 seconds, or until broccoli is bright green and shrimp are just firm. Drain off oil as before.

Rinse egg whites in strainer with warm stock, washing off as much oil as possible. Return 1 tbsp. oil to wok, turn heat up high, and add scallions and ginger. Sizzle for a moment and return shrimp, ham, and broccoli to wok. Quickly stir sauce to redistribute starch and add to wok. Stir constantly 15–20 seconds. Add set egg white and toss 15–20 seconds, until everything is piping hot. Turn off heat, gently mix in sesame oil, and serve to 2.

## SLICED LAMB HUNAN STYLE

| | |
|---|---|
| 1 lb. boneless lamb (leg or sirloin) | 1 bunch watercress |
| Marinade (recipe below) | Sauce (recipe below) |
| 1 tsp. minced garlic | 3 cups + 2 tbsp. vegetable oil |
| 2 scallions cut in $\frac{1}{3}''$ lengths | 12 small dried hot chili peppers |
| $\frac{1}{2}$ tsp. peeled fresh gingerroot, cut in paper-thin $\frac{1}{4}''$ squares | 1 tsp. vinegar |
| | 1 tsp. sesame oil |
| | salt to taste |

Trim lamb well of fat and membranes. Freeze to facilitate cutting. Remove lamb from freezer 20 minutes before cutting and, when just thawed enough to slice, cut against grain in slices $2'' \times 1'' \times \frac{1}{8}''$. Place slices in mixing bowl, allow to thaw completely, and drain off any liquid that accumulates in bowl. Prepare Marinade.

*Marinade*

| | |
|---|---|
| 1 egg white | $1\frac{1}{2}$ tbsp. dry Sherry |
| $\frac{1}{4}$ tsp. salt | $1\frac{1}{2}$ tbsp. cornstarch |

Beat first 3 ingredients until lightly foaming and mix with meat. Add starch, stirring vigorously with the hand until completely dissolved. Cover and refrigerate at least 20 minutes, or up to 24 hours. (The texture will improve noticeably the longer the mixture is marinated.)

Ready garlic, scallions, and gingerroot. Pick over watercress, trim and discard 1" from stems, and reserve remainder. Prepare Sauce.

## Sauce

| | |
|---|---|
| 1½ tsp. cornstarch | 1 tsp. vinegar |
| 3 tbsp. soy sauce | 1 tsp. sugar |
| 1½ tbsp. dry Sherry | |

Dissolve starch in 1 tbsp. of the soy sauce, then stir in remaining ingredients.

In a wok or skillet, heat 3 cups of the vegetable oil to 280°F. Turn heat up to maximum and quickly add marinated lamb, stirring constantly to separate slices. Stir for 30 seconds after lamb changes color, then drain in a colander set on a receptacle to catch oil. Return 1½ tbsp. oil to wok and add dried chilies, stirring over high heat until they turn a deep mahogany-brown. Quickly add garlic, ginger, and scallions and sizzle for a moment. Add lamb and stirred sauce and cook, stirring constantly, until sauce has thickened and food has heated through. Stir in vinegar, then sesame oil, transfer mixture to a serving platter, and keep it warm. Wash wok and place over high heat. When quite hot, add remaining 2 tbsp. vegetable oil, swirling around edges of wok. Add cress and salt to taste and stir-fry until just wilted and deep, bright green. Drain and garnish one end of serving platter with greens. Serve immediately to 4–6.

# SHUN LEE DYNASTY

*900 Second Avenue*

T. T. Wang (page 188) is the principal owner of this gathering place for U.N. personnel, which is endorsement enough for any restaurant. The décor, by Russel Wright, is colorful and animated, with hanging ornaments activated by any stray breeze that happens to tickle them and with bold silhouettes of edible fauna—updated versions of the traditional Chinese art of paper-cutting—ranged over translucent wall panels. An eclectic menu is made up chiefly of Mandarin, Pekingese, Szechwan, and Hunanese specialties, with a hot appetizer assortment, sizzling rice soup, fiery sea bass with shrimp roe, and sea scallops "Wang style" eminently worthy of investigation.

## FRIED DUMPLINGS

*Served as an accompaniment to cocktails, this recipe's yield should take care of at least ten guests. As a first course, four dumplings per person are adequate, and proportions should be modified accordingly.*

3 cups flour
¾ cup warm boiled water
¾ tsp. minced fresh gingerroot
5 oz. tender scallion heads
6 oz. ground pork
2 tsp. MSG (optional)

1 tsp. salt
1 tbsp. soy sauce
1 tbsp. sesame oil
½ garlic clove, chopped
⅓ cup plus 3 tbsp. peanut oil
⅔ cup cold water

In a mixing bowl blend flour and boiled water thoroughly, knead for 5 minutes, and allow to stand, covered with a cloth, for 30 minutes. Fine-chop gingerroot and scallion and mix with ground pork, 3 tbsp. water, optional MSG, salt, soy sauce, sesame oil, and garlic. Set aside. Roll out dough in a long rectangular sheet and cut into 40–50 pieces. Flatten each piece with the heel of the hand and roll it out, forming a very thin round pancake. Spoon a bit of the meat mixture, slightly off-center, onto each pancake, fold over half the dough to make a semicircle and pinch edges to seal. Heat a large frying pan (not a wok), add 3 tbsp. of the peanut oil, and swirl to cover bottom of the pan thoroughly. Arrange dumplings to cover bottom of pan without overlapping and sauté over medium heat until undersides are golden. Lower heat, add ⅔ cup of water, and cook 5–10 minutes until water has evaporated. Add ⅓ cup peanut oil to pan, fry until dumpling bottoms are brown and crisp, and drain off oil. Serve immediately.

# CELLOPHANE NOODLE AND MEATBALL SOUP

½ cup ground pork
1 tbsp. soy sauce
1 tbsp. dry Sherry
1 oz. dried cellophane noodles

3½ cups Chicken Broth*
1 tsp. salt
¼ tsp. MSG (optional)
1 whole scallion, chopped

Mix pork with soy sauce and Sherry and form into 8 meatballs. Soak noodles in warm water to cover for 20 minutes. In a large pot, heat chicken broth with salt and optional MSG. Bring to boil, add meatballs, and cook 5 minutes. Add noodles, cook a few moments longer, until noodles are tender, and serve, garnished with chopped scallion, to 8.

# CHICKEN WITH PEANUTS

*Sauce*

1 lb. boned chicken breast
1 egg white, beaten
1 tbsp. cornstarch
5 cups peanut oil
6 dried red chili peppers
½ cup skinless peanuts
½ tsp. peeled and chopped fresh gingerroot
½ tsp. chopped garlic
1 tbsp. diced scallion greens

2½ tbsp. dark soy sauce
1 tbsp. Sherry
½ tbsp. vinegar
1 tbsp. sugar
1 tbsp. cornstarch
½ tsp. sesame oil
½ tbsp. hot chili paste

} blended

Cut chicken into ¾" cubes, combine with egg white and 1 tbsp. cornstarch, coating chicken thoroughly, and refrigerate 30 minutes. In a wok or large skillet, heat peanut oil to 450°F. for about 4 minutes. Add chicken cubes and stir-fry for 30 seconds, until chicken takes on color. Using a colander mounted on a receptacle to catch oil, drain wok. Return 2 tbsp. oil to wok and fry peppers, stirring, until they darken almost to black. Add peanuts and continue to stir-fry 15 seconds. Add ginger, garlic, and scallions, followed immediately by chicken. Stir quickly, add sauce, and cook 10 seconds longer, stirring to coat chicken thoroughly with sauce. Serve immediately to 4–6.

# HUNAM

*845 Second Avenue*

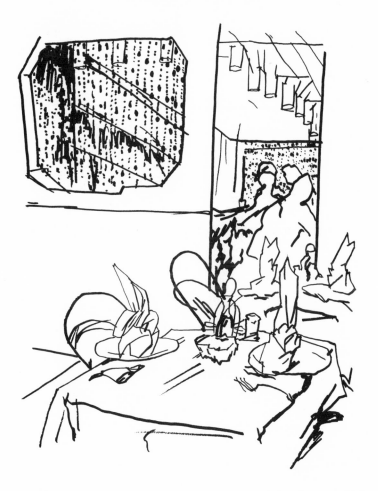

Neither the plastic-crowned façade nor the rather lugubrious gilded interior is very inviting, but the food—which can be blisteringly spicy—more than makes up for the indifferent ambiance. Hunanese cooking (which is essentially a countrified version of Szechwan cooking) has enjoyed quite a vogue these past few years, largely thanks to this restaurant's proselytism of the genre.

# HACKED CHICKEN

*Immoderate indulgence in this excellent cold appetizer has been known to blister the lips and bring tears to the eyes.* Caveat gustator.

1 lb. young chicken breast
½ tsp. pulverized brown
   Szechwan peppercorns

½ tbsp. peeled and chopped
   fresh gingerroot
½ tbsp. chopped garlic

### Sauce

2 tbsp. sesame paste
3 tbsp. soy sauce
1 tbsp. vinegar
1 tbsp. sesame oil

1 tbsp. red pepper oil
2 tsp. sugar
½ tsp. MSG (optional)

In a large pot of boiling water, cook the chicken breast for 15 minutes, drain, and allow to cool. Hack the chicken into pieces 1½″ long and ⅜″ thick and sprinkle with peppercorn powder, gingerroot, and garlic. Mix sauce ingredients thoroughly, pour over chicken, coating it well, and serve to 4–6.

# HUNAM BEEF

¾ lb. trimmed flank steak
1 tbsp. cornstarch ⎱ blended
1 beaten egg white ⎰
1 tbsp. dark soy sauce
½ tsp. sugar
⅛ tsp. sesame oil
1 tbsp. Szechwan paste (see
   note)

¼ tsp. chopped garlic
½ tbsp. cornstarch ⎱ blended
½ tbsp. water ⎰
½ tsp. MSG (optional)
3 cups peanut oil
½ cup torn watercress
⅛ tsp. salt
2 tbsp. dry Sherry

*Note Szechwan paste, available at Chinese specialty shops, is an incendiary blend of chili paste and garlic.*

Place the steak on a flat work surface and using a sharp knife slice it thinly across the grain. Place the meat in a mixing bowl and add 1 tbsp. cornstarch and 1 egg white, blended together. Mix well and set aside. In another bowl blend soy sauce, sugar, sesame oil, Szechwan paste, garlic, starch blended with water, and optional MSG and set aside. In a wok or skillet, heat peanut oil at 400°F. for 4 minutes, then add beef, and stir-fry about 30 seconds. Drain thoroughly in a colander mounted on a receptacle to catch oil. Return beef to wok, turn up heat as far as it will go, and add soy sauce mixture. Cook, stirring vigorously, 15 seconds. Drain wok as before and put beef on the left side of a serving dish. Clean wok and return 2 tsp. peanut oil. Over high heat, add watercress, salt, and Sherry and stir-fry 20 seconds. Arrange watercress on right side of serving dish and serve to 4.

# PEKING PARK

*100 Park Avenue*

Parts of this sprawling complex might easily be mistaken for Stanley Kubrick's vision of the next century, and you may prefer to be seated where you won't be distracted by the slide-show travelogue flashed onto a centrally located screen. The peculiar ambiance notwithstanding, this is one of the very best Chinese establishments north of Canal Street, and its manager, Alexander Chang, is one of the city's most gracious hosts.

# SPICY CUCUMBER

*Cool as the proverbial cucumber and then some, this will get the meal off to a very refreshing start*

4 medium cucumbers
2 tsp. salt
4 tsp. sugar
½ red bell pepper
1 tbsp. sesame oil
4 small dried chili peppers

3 oz. peeled fresh gingerroot, shredded
½ tsp. brown Szechwan peppercorns
2½ tbsp. rice vinegar
½ tbsp. soy sauce

Trim ends from washed cucumbers and cut in half lengthwise. Remove and discard seed cores, cut cucumbers in wands about ½" thick, and place in a large bowl. Add salt and 1 tsp. of the sugar. Mix, rubbing salt and sugar into cucumbers with the fingers for about 5 minutes, and set aside for 20 minutes. Wash cucumbers again in cold water, then drain. Cut red bell pepper into very fine julienne strips and reserve. In a wok or skillet, heat sesame oil to 375°F., add chili peppers, and stir-fry until slightly scorched. Add chilies, red bell pepper, and gingerroot to cucumbers, then add remaining sugar, peppercorns, vinegar, and soy sauce. Toss well and marinate in refrigerator 8 hours. Serve cold to 4–6.

# WINE-SOUSED CHICKEN

1 broiler (2½–3 lbs.)
2 tbsp. salt

2½ cups dry Sherry or Shao-Hsing wine

Thoroughly wash and rinse chicken under cold running water and pat dry with kitchen towels. Rub chicken evenly, inside and out, with salt and let stand 2 hours in a cool place. Put chicken in a deep heatproof bowl, set bowl in a covered steamer, and steam with 1 cup water over high heat for 30 minutes, replenishing water as needed. Remove chicken from steamer, allow it to cool, and cut into 6–8 pieces. Place chicken parts in a deep bowl, pour wine over them, and add stock from steamer.

(If necessary, add Chicken Stock* to cover meat.) Cover and refrigerate at least 24 hours. Before serving, cut chicken into smaller pieces. Serve cold to 4–8, depending on number of courses in meal.

## MINCED SQUAB PACKETS

1  2-lb. fresh-killed squab
1  egg white, lightly beaten
1  tbsp. cornstarch
1  tbsp. dry Sherry
$\frac{1}{4}$ tsp. salt
8  unblemished lettuce leaves
2  cups peanut or vegetable oil
2  oz. cellophane noodles
$\frac{1}{4}$ cup heart of celery ⎫
$\frac{1}{4}$ cup bamboo shoots ⎪
$\frac{1}{4}$ cup Chinese mushrooms (see note) ⎬ chopped fine
$\frac{1}{4}$ cup water chestnuts ⎭

1  tbsp. soy sauce
1  tsp. sugar
$\frac{1}{4}$ tsp. black pepper
$\frac{1}{4}$ tsp. MSG (optional)
1  tsp. sesame oil

*Note* Soak whole dried Chinese mushrooms in warm water 10 minutes to soften, then squeeze out water before chopping.

Rinse squab inside and out in lukewarm water and pat dry. Using a sharp knife, skin and bone squab, discarding tendons and any loose fat. With a very sharp cleaver or kitchen knife, mince meat very fine (don't use a machine for this job, tedious as it may be). In a mixing bowl, thoroughly blend minced squab, egg white, cornstarch, Sherry, and salt and refrigerate 30 minutes or more. Wash lettuce, leaf by leaf, under cold running water and pat dry. Arrange leaves around edge of platter, leaving center of platter clear, and keep cool.

In a wok or skillet, heat peanut or vegetable oil to 375°F. Drop noodles into oil, stirring briefly to separate, and lift out with a slotted spoon as soon as they puff. Drain well on paper towels and transfer to center of platter. Pour off and reserve for other uses all but 2 tbsp. of the oil. Heat remaining oil until it starts to smoke and add chopped vegetables. Stir constantly 30 seconds, add refrigerated squab mixture, soy sauce, sugar, pepper, and optional MSG, and stir-fry, separating squab mixture, 2 minutes. Finally, add sesame oil, stir-fry a few seconds longer, and heap contents of wok over noodles. Serve immediately, allowing each guest to spoon 2–3 tbsp. of squab-noodle mixture onto center of a lettuce leaf, which then should be rolled into a loose cylinder and eaten with the fingers. Serves 4–8, depending on the size of the entire meal.

# 彭園
# Peng's
*219 East 44th Street*

The décor, with its red and black lacquer reliefs and calligraphic hanging scrolls, is nothing to get wildly excited about, but the service at this large establishment is punctilious and the cooking is superb. Chang-Kwei Peng, a venerable but youthful-looking Hunanese who speaks no English, is the owner and executive chef and was so respected in his homeland that he was appointed personal chef to Chiang Kai-shek when he and the generalissimo decamped for Taiwan in 1949. His minced squab soup, served in a bamboo cup and much imitated around town by erstwhile disciples who arrived in this country before Peng did, shouldn't be missed, and the cuisine in general is as rigorously authentic as it is delicious.

*For some reason or other, the Chinese have named a great many chicken dishes for their military heroes. On second thought, perhaps they weren't heroes at all and the dishes merely echo the taunts of the troops. Here, in any event, is*

## GENERAL TSO'S CHICKEN

| | |
|---|---|
| 4 chicken legs | 4 tsp. soy sauce |
| 1 tsp. cornstarch | 4 tbsp. white vinegar |
| 1 egg, beaten | 4 tbsp. water |
| 1 garlic clove, chopped | ¾ cup corn oil |
| 1 tsp. peeled and chopped fresh gingerroot | 4 dried hot chili peppers |

Skin and bone chicken legs and cut each into 6 pieces. In a bowl mix cornstarch and egg to a smooth consistency, add chicken, and stir to coat thoroughly. Mix garlic, ginger, soy sauce, vinegar, and water. Pour oil into a wok or skillet, heat over high flame until very hot, and add chicken. Stir-fry chicken until crisp, remove, and drain in colander. Pour off all but 1 tsp. oil (reserving discard for future use). Return wok to fire, add chili peppers, garlic mixture, and chicken and stir-fry 2 minutes. That's it. Serves 2–4, depending on the number of dishes included in the meal.

## PENG'S SHRIMP WITH GINGER SAUCE

| | |
|---|---|
| 1 lb. jumbo shrimp | ¾ tsp. peeled and finely chopped fresh gingerroot |
| 1 tbsp. catsup | |
| ½ tsp. sugar | 1 cup corn oil |
| 1 tsp. hot red pepper oil | 1 scallion, chopped |

Shell and devein shrimp. Mix sauce, using all ingredients except shrimp, corn oil, and scallion. Heat corn oil in a wok or skillet over medium flame; before oil gets very hot, add shrimp, and stir rapidly for 1 minute. Drain contents of wok into a colander mounted on a receptacle to catch oil. Return wok to fire, add shrimp, sauce, and scallion, and sauté 5 minutes, stirring constantly. Serves 2 as a main dish.

## PART FIVE

# *The World Is Your Oyster*

*W*hat follows is a conscientious sampling of those New York restaurants that lie outside the realms of the three major cuisines. In some cases, the menus are eclectic. In others, they represent a distinctly ethnic orientation. Still others—products of the melting pot—are adherents of an emergent style best described as American. Finally, a few are simply Major Institutions whose presence in the city transcends any gastronomic considerations. A few indubitable institutions, it should be added, have been omitted, either because any recipes they might have contributed would have been too trite (which isn't necessarily a reflection on their quality) or because their attractions, such as they may be, are lost on me.

**THE FOUR SEASONS**

*99 East 52nd Street*

Under the inspired direction of Tom Margittai and Paul Kovi, this remains what it was when Joe Baum dreamed it up (page 41): *sui generis,* the stateliest of all pleasure domes, the best of all possible worlds. Seppi Renggli is the resident alchemist and his every dish is a wondrous transmutation. A marvelously innovative menu, magnificent setting, superb cellar, and crack service corps—in short, the Compleat Restaurant.

# AVOCADO SOUP WITH AVOCADO SHERBET

*Chef Renggli's antidote to anyone's dog day afternoon is simple, original, and aristocratic.*

2 ripe avocados
¼ cup sour cream
¼ cup *Crème Fraîche*\*
1/16 tsp. ground thyme
6 drops Tabasco sauce
1 pinch coriander

1 tsp. salt
juice of ½ lemon
1 cup heavy cream
2 cups Chicken Consommé\*
1¼ cups avocado sherbet

Peel and pit avocados and purée pulp with a food mill, blender, or processor. In a bowl beat sour cream, *crème fraîche,* seasonings, and lemon juice into avocado purée. Beating constantly with an electric mixer or by hand, add heavy cream. Still beating, add consommé in a slow stream. Strain and chill. Serve in small bowls garnished with a scoop of Avocado Sherbet. Serves 8.

*Avocado Sherbet*

1 ripe avocado
¼ cup sugar

1¼ cups cold water
juice of ½ lemon

Peel and pit avocado and purée pulp with a food mill or blender. Whisk sugar in water until dissolved, then beat in avocado purée and lemon juice. Freeze in an ice cube tray, beating several times as mixture sets, to break up ice crystals.

# CHICKEN AND OYSTERS WITH NANTUA SAUCE

12 chicken fillets (see note)
12 chicken oysters (see note)
8 oz. crayfish tails (see note)
2 shallots, minced
4 tbsp. Lobster Butter\*
4 tbsp. cognac

½ cup white wine
salt and pepper to taste
12 oysters with their liquor
⅔ cup cèpes, sliced (see note)
1 cup Nantua Sauce\*

*Note* Chicken fillets are the small, easily detachable flaps of meat found on the undersides of boned halved chicken breasts (suprêmes). Chicken oysters are the tender nuggets of dark meat found on either side of the backbone, just above the thighs. Fresh raw crayfish are preferable. Fresh cèpes ditto.

Sauté chicken fillets, chicken oysters, crayfish tails (if fresh), and shallots in lobster butter for 1 minute. (If using frozen crayfish tails, add them after 1 minute and cook just long enough to heat them through.) Turn out onto a hot serving dish and set aside. Add cognac to sauté pan and flame. When flame has subsided, add wine, salt, and pepper and reduce over high heat for about 1 minute. Add oysters with their liquor and cèpes and simmer 30 seconds longer. Then add Nantua sauce and simmer for another minute. Spoon reserved ingredients back into pan, toss thoroughly, and serve immediately to 4.

## CREAM CHEESE AND RIESLING SOUFFLÉ

4½ tbsp. sweet butter
4½ tbsp. flour
1½ cups boiling milk
6 eggs, separated, plus 2 egg
   whites

4 oz. cream cheese
2 tbsp. Riesling wine
½ cup sugar

Preheat oven to 375°F. In a double boiler, melt butter and blend in flour to a smooth consistency. Add milk and cook, stirring constantly, until mixture thickens. Add egg yolks and beat well. Allow mixture to cook slightly and remove from heat. Beat cream cheese with a wire whisk until it is creamy and beat wine into cheese a little at a time. Combine cheese and soufflé mixture and stir well. Beat egg whites until they hold soft peaks, then gradually add sugar, and continue beating until peaks are stiff. Fold into soufflé mixture. Dust a lightly buttered 9-cup soufflé dish with sugar. Pour in soufflé mixture and bake in preheated oven 35 minutes, or until puffed and lightly browned. Dust top with powdered sugar and serve immediately with a sauce of softened vanilla ice cream thickened with whipped cream. Serves 6.

## Sea·Fare
### of the Aegean

*25 West 56th Street*

The population of Volos, a fishing port in eastern Thessaly, would be 41,707, instead of 41,706, had Christos Bastis not emigrated to this country in the 1930s. If the statistical differential seems trifling, look at it this way: Had Bastis stayed home, the number of first-rate New York seafood restaurants would be significantly smaller than it is today. Bastis opened Sea Fare of the Aegean in 1963 and, in a city where great fish houses are scarce as clams' teeth, we can all be thankful he did. A theatrically designed, monumentally proportioned place that might be the setting for a Cecil B. De Mille costume epic, the restaurant serves as a showcase for both Bastis's superb art collection and for some of the freshest fish to be found above sea level. Gus Hallas, a native of the Cycladic island of Andros and a colleague of Bastis' for more than three decades, is the chef, and, while the cuisine is Greek-accented, such Yankee standbys as New England clam chowder and broiled shad roe are prepared as skillfully as are *avgolemono* and shrimp Santorini.

## TARAMA SALAD

2 slices white bread, crusts removed
4 oz. Russian type tarama (carp roe)
½ cup olive oil ⎫
¾ cup vegetable oil ⎬ mixed

1 oz. fresh lemon juice
2 oz. cold water
1 tbsp. finely chopped onion

Soak bread in a small bowl of cold water, then squeeze as dry as possible. In a blender or processor, mix bread and tarama, gradually adding in succession half the mixed oils, the lemon juice, half the remaining oil, 2 oz. cold water, and remaining oil. Finally, add onion and blend a few seconds longer. Chill and serve on Melba toast or sea toast. Serves 6 or more.

## STRIPED BASS SYROS

1 small onion, sliced
1 cup stewed tomatoes
juice of ½ lemon
2 oz. Sherry
1 bay leaf
¼ tsp. chopped garlic
2 oz. olive oil

1 tsp. chopped dill and parsley (combined)
4 small potatoes
salt and pepper to taste
2 qts. Fish Stock*
4 12-oz. fillets striped bass

Spread onion over bottom of a deep skillet, add all ingredients except bass, and cook over medium heat for 20 minutes. Place one fish fillet and ¼ of cooked ingredients in each of four serving casseroles and cook over medium heat for another 20 minutes. Serve immediately to 4.

## FLOGERA

3 eggs, separated
1 pt. milk
¼ cup flour
¼ cup cornstarch
1 tsp. vanilla extract

½ cup sugar
1 pinch salt
rind of ½ lemon, grated
1 cup butter, melted
18 sheets *phyllo* (see note)

*Note*  Phyllo *(sometimes spelled "filo") is sold in most Greek and Middle Eastern bakeries and food shops. Commercially prepared leaf strudel, which is virtually identical, can be used instead. The dough should be kept covered until used.*

In a mixing bowl, combine egg yolks and ½ the milk and beat with a whisk for a few seconds. Add flour, cornstarch, and vanilla and beat until smooth. In another bowl, beat egg whites until frothy, then fold into egg yolk mixture, and set aside. In a deep pot combine the remaining milk, sugar, salt, lemon rind, and 1 tsp. of the butter and bring to boil, stirring constantly. Lower heat and gradually add egg mixture, stirring vigorously until very smooth. Remove from heat, cover successively with a paper towel and lid, and set aside to cool.

When the filling has cooled, brush butter over surfaces of 1 full sheet and 1 half-sheet of 8″ × 12″ *phyllo.* Cover half the larger sheet with smaller sheet and spread 3 tbsp. of the custard filling over the smaller sheet, leaving edges uncovered. Fold unfilled half of large sheet over filled half-sheet, fold over edges, and press together to seal. Repeat until phyllo—and, if all goes well, filling—is used up. Brush with butter, arrange in a shallow baking pan, and bake at 350°F. just until golden brown. Serve warm, covered with Syrup (recipe below) to 12.

### Syrup

¾ cup sugar
½ cup water
1 tsp. lemon juice

1 oz. brandy
3 cloves (optional)

In a small saucepan, combine sugar, water, and lemon juice. Bring to boil over high heat, stirring until sugar dissolves. Cook briskly for 15 minutes, add brandy and optional cloves, and remove at once from heat. Serve warm.

## *Tres Carabelas*
### *314 East 39th Street*

The three ships in question are the *Nina, Pinta,* and *Santa
Maria,* and the establishment named for them, though somewhat
off the beaten track, is well worth a voyage of exploration. This
is in every way the most authentic of the city's Spanish restaurants, which is hardly surprising, for it was conceived as a
gathering place for Spanish expatriates and is partially subsidized
by the Spanish government. Housed in the strikingly handsome
complex that comprises the Casa y Circulo Cultural de España
and managed by the very gracious Ramón San Martin, the
restaurant is strongly reminiscent of the government-operated
*paradores* to be found throughout Spain and, indeed, turns out
to have been designed by the architect in charge of those
excellent caravansaries. Don't look here for the kitsch with
which most Spanish restaurateurs in New York festoon their
premises. The dining room is distinguished by simplicity,
sobriety, and dignity. A few still lifes painted in the dark tones
of Zurbarán and Ribera are disposed on cream-white walls,
heavy antique chandeliers hang from dark beams, and everything
about the place will remind you of your favorite restaurant in
Barcelona or Madrid (or will if you've avoided the tourist traps).
The service is gravely formal and the food blessedly inexpensive,
with *callos a la madrileña, pollo al chillindrón, fabada,* and
*villagodio a las brasas con tuéteno* among the outstanding dishes.

### COCIDO MADRILEÑO

*The Spanish equivalent of the French* pot au feu *or Italian*
bollito misto, *this dish (actually a two-dish meal from a single pot)
is rarely found in restaurants, even in Spain.*

| | |
|---|---|
| 2 cups dried chick-peas | 1 *morcilla* (blood sausage) |
| ½ chicken | ½ lb. pork belly, sliced ¼″ thick |
| 2 *chorizos* (Spanish sausages) | ½ lb. beef shin |

### Bola

| | |
|---|---|
| ½ lb. ground veal | 2 whole eggs |
| 1 garlic clove, minced | salt and pepper to taste |
| 2 tbsp. parsley, minced | flour for dredging |
| 1 tsp. dried orégano | 1 egg, lightly beaten |
| 1 cup fresh bread crumbs | 2 oz. olive oil |

### Soup and meat garnish

| | |
|---|---|
| 1 head cabbage | 1 hard-boiled egg, chopped fine |
| 8 small potatoes, peeled | 1 cup tomato sauce (optional) |
| 2 large carrots, peeled | chopped parsley |
| 1 cup vermicelli | |

Soak chick-peas 12 hours with 3 tbsp. salt in lukewarm water to cover. Wash chick-peas in lukewarm water to remove salt, then place in a 6–8-qt. soup pot. Add 2½ qts. lukewarm water and place over medium heat. Just before water comes to boil, add chicken, sausages, pork, and beef shin. Bring to a very light simmer, reduce heat, and cover. Cook 2 hours, adding lukewarm water as needed to cover ingredients and skimming fat as it rises to surface.

As the meats cook, prepare the *bola,* a large caseless sausage or meatball. Combine veal, garlic, parsley, orégano, bread crumbs, whole eggs, and seasoning, working ingredients together and shaping them into a large oval sausage approximately 5″ × 3″. Dredge the *bola* in flour, roll it in the beaten egg, and sauté in olive oil until browned on all sides (about 4–5 minutes). Add *bola* to soup pot 45 minutes before other meats are done. Cook cabbage, potatoes, and carrots separately in boiling salted water until tender. Drain broth into saucepan from soup pot and check seasoning. Add vermicelli to broth and simmer until noodles are tender.

Serve broth with noodles as a first course, garnished with chopped hard-boiled egg and chopped parsley. Divide meats and vegetables into equal serving portions and serve with olive oil to taste or tomato sauce. Serves 4 generously.

# CREMA CATALANA

3 cups milk
1 stick cinnamon
zest of ½ lemon (see note)
strip of orange zest
3 egg yolks

2 tbsp. cornstarch
2 tbsp. sugar
1 tbsp. anisette
5 drops vanilla extract

*Note*  *The yellow outer portion of the rind, all white removed.*

In a small saucepan, bring milk to boil with cinnamon and citrus zests and simmer gently 10 minutes. In another pan, beat remaining ingredients together until smooth. Strain milk into egg yolk mixture, stirring constantly. Bring just to boil over medium heat, stirring constantly, and remove from heat at once. Chill and strain custard. Divide mixture among 4 shirred-egg dishes, sprinkle with a little sugar, and run under a hot broiler to glaze tops. Chill well before serving. Serves 4.

*Box Tree Restaurant*
**242 East 50th Street**

"In small proportions," Ben Jonson wrote, "we just beauties see/ And in short measures life may perfect be." He might have been describing an evening of wine and roses at this flawless gem of a restaurant, which, despite its minuscule dimensions and location in a tenement, is exquisitely appointed and terribly chic. Amenities within this forest-green snuggery include tea roses at each place setting (the settings themselves are easily the most distinguished in town), fine antique furniture, luxurious fabrics, first-rate art, impeccable service, a superb cellar, and an exceptionally refined cuisine. Calla lilies and candlelight, Stilton cheese and Port—what more could anyone ask? Well, a bit more elbow room, perhaps, but you can't have everything.

## TERRINE OF DUCK LIVER

| | |
|---|---|
| 1 large onion, sliced | 1 oz. brandy |
| ¼ lb. butter | ¼ lb. softened butter |
| 1 garlic clove, sliced | 4 oz. heavy cream |
| 1 lb. duck livers | truffle slices for garnish |
| salt and pepper to taste | Port Aspic* |

Over low heat, sauté onion slowly in ¼ lb. butter, add garlic, and cook until transparent. Turn up heat, add livers, and sear on all sides. Reduce heat and sauté livers until cooked on the outside but reddish-pink within. Place contents of pan in a blender and purée. Strain purée, season with salt and pepper, and add brandy. Add softened butter and heavy cream and stir until butter melts. Pour into a serving terrine (or individual terrines) and chill until set. Garnish with truffle slices, glaze with a ⅛″ film of semiliquid aspic, and allow aspic to set before serving. Do not unmold. Serves 10–12.

## ORANGE AND TOMATO SOUP

| | |
|---|---|
| 2 qts. very ripe tomatoes | 1 pt. heavy cream |
| 2 oranges (pulp and rind) | salt and pepper to taste |
| 1 large onion, sliced | ½ pt. heavy cream, whipped |
| ½ lb. butter | julienne strips of orange peel |
| 3 oz. flour | for garnish |

Peel and seed tomatoes. Seed oranges and, in a blender or processor, purée orange pulp and rinds. Sauté onion in the butter until transparent. Add flour and cook over low heat 4–5 minutes, stirring. Add tomatoes and orange purée, bring to boil, and simmer 10 minutes. Transfer cooked mixture to blender and purée. Strain purée, season, and finish with 1 pt. heavy cream. Serve hot or cold (if cold, dilute to desired consistency with Chicken Stock\*) to 6, garnished with whipped cream and orange peel.

## POACHED SALMON WITH SAUCE MOUSSELINE

| | |
|---|---|
| ¼ lb. butter | 1 small pinch cayenne pepper |
| 3 egg yolks, whipped until thick | juice of one garlic clove |
| juice of ½ lemon | ½ cup whipped cream |
| salt and pepper to taste | 4–6 ¼"-thick salmon steaks |

Boil butter briefly and add drop by drop to whipped egg yolks. Add lemon juice drop by drop. Season with salt, pepper, and cayenne and add garlic juice. Beat in whipped cream.

Cover salmon steaks with water and bring to boil. Reduce heat and simmer 4–6 minutes, until bone loosens from meat. Drain salmon, remove and discard skin and bones, and reassemble steaks. Pour sauce over fish and serve one salmon steak per portion.

## COCOTTE DE FRAMBOISES

| | |
|---|---|
| 1¼ pts. fresh raspberries | 4 oz. old Port |
| raspberry juice (see note) | ¾ cup crème chantilly (see note) |
| 3 tbsp. sugar | 4 oz. brown sugar |

*Note  For raspberry juice, mash ¼ pt. of the raspberries, add sugar and Port, and allow to steep 2 hours. Crème chantilly is heavy cream whipped just until it holds its shape. Ideally, the cream should be allowed to thicken for a day or so in an uncovered refrigerated container before it is whipped.*

Fill four 5½-oz. ramekins to ⅓ their depth with raspberries and juice. Cover berries with *crème chantilly*, smoothing surfaces with a rubber spatula. Sprinkle brown sugar over *crème chantilly* in an even layer about ⅓" deep. Burn the sugar by lightly pressing a very hot salamander iron onto the surface. Serves 4.

*308 East 86th Street*

If your idea of Greek food is overcooked lamb and limp gray vegetables, you're in for a pleasant surprise here. Stravros Tsillas spent sixteen years as personal chef to the late Aristotle Onassis, who, Lord knows, could afford the best. Now, the rest of us can, too; prices at the restaurant are negligible. The setting, with its rough whitewashed walls, stone floors, and colorful hangings, is that of a typical *taverna*. And the cooking is absolutely first-rate. Tiny deep-fried Brazilian smelts, when available, shouldn't be missed, but the same might be said for dozens of dishes, among which *levraki plaki, kalamarakia rafinas, synagrida,* and rack of lamb are particularly memorable.


## SKORDALIA

*This makes a fine prelude to dinner. Whether it's an acceptable prelude to anything of a more intimate nature is debatable; three crushed garlic cloves aren't precisely the equivalent of a dab of Chanel No. 5.*

½ loaf stale Italian bread, at least 3 days old
3 garlic cloves, peeled and crushed
⅓ cup blanched almonds
1 tsp. salt
juice of 1 lemon

⅓ cup white vinegar
3 tbsp. mayonnaise
⅔ cup olive oil
6 small zucchini, sliced either in rounds or sticks
flour for dredging
corn oil for deep frying

Soak bread in cold water until soft and squeeze out as much water as possible. Put all ingredients except oils, zucchini, and flour into a food processor, start machine, and pour in olive oil in a slow, steady stream, until a creamy consistency is reached. Dredge zucchini slices in flour, deep-fry in hot corn oil, and drain on paper towels. Serve piping hot with sauce on side. Serves 6.


## SPETSIOTA

1 8-lb. striped bass, scaled, cleaned, and cut into 6 steaks
6 slices feta cheese (see note)
6 ripe tomatoes, sliced
1 garlic clove, crushed

salt and pepper to taste
2 tbsp. finely chopped parsley
6 oz. white wine
⅔ cup olive oil

*Note  Feta, a white cheese used extensively throughout Greece and much of the Levant, is sold in most specialty food shops.*

Arrange fish in an oiled baking dish and top each piece with a slice of cheese. Cover with an even layer of tomato slices. Spread with crushed garlic, sprinkle with salt, pepper, and parsley, and add wine and oil. Bake 30 minutes in a preheated 350°F. oven. Serve immediately to 6.

## YOUVETSI

3 lbs. lean leg of lamb, cut in 1½″ cubes and washed in cold water
6 ripe tomatoes, peeled and diced

1 tbsp. tomato paste
salt and pepper to taste
1½ lbs. *orzo* (see note)

*Note* Orzo *is a ricelike Greek pasta available at most Middle Eastern specialty shops. Use Fantis brand if you can find it.*

In a covered pot or Dutch oven, bake all ingredients except *orzo* for 1 hour in a preheated 350°F. oven. After 55 minutes, put *orzo* into a large pot of boiling salted water and cook 5 minutes. Drain and add *orzo* to lamb mixture, distributing it evenly. Cover and continue to bake ½ hour longer. Serve immediately to 6.

## BOUGATSA

⅔ cup farina
5 eggs
1 qt. milk

¾ lb. *phyllo* (see note)
25 oz. sweet butter, very soft
sugar or honey to taste

*Note* A very thin leaf pastry available unbaked in Greek and Middle Eastern food shops. Use 12″ × 12″ leaves.

Place farina and eggs in a bowl while milk warms in a saucepan. Gradually pour warmed milk into the bowl, beating constantly until all milk has been added and mixture is well blended.

Butter a 6″ × 10″ baking pan and lay a single leaf of *phyllo* on its bottom, allowing excess pastry to overhang sides of pan. Brush surface of *phyllo* thoroughly with butter and repeat process until 6 layers of buttered *phyllo* have been built up in pan. Spread farina mixture evenly over top layer, using all of it, and place 4 more layers of *phyllo* over this, buttering each as before. Fold overhanging *phyllo* back into pan, brush surfaces with butter, and bake 1 hour, or until brown, in a preheated 350°F. oven. Dust pastry with sugar to taste or pour honey to taste over it. Cut into rectangles and serve to 6.

# EL PARADOR

### 325 East 34th Street

Its popularity among Americans notwithstanding, Mexican food isn't much understood in this country, where a cuisine of great variety and considerable subtlety has been reduced to a relative handful of tasty but mostly inconsequential dishes. If El Parador isn't precisely a center of higher learning, it's still a standout among the city's Mexican restaurants. Packed each night with an attractive, mostly youngish crowd of aficionados, the establishment occupies two floors and the cellar of a colorfully appointed town house and has been operated since its opening two decades ago by Carlos Jacott, a ruggedly handsome Mexican-born ex-actor whose gallantries have a way of mildly unhinging even the most self-possessed women. What little flattery Jacott himself doesn't dispense is provided by the soft glow of pierced-tin hanging lamps. If these latter tend to throw more shadow than light, thereby making one's *mole poblano* somewhat elusive, their effect on milady is salutary. The effect on *anyone* of the restaurant's excellent Margaritas shouldn't be discounted either.

## GUACAMOLE

*Although the classic avocado dip is simple, some care should be taken in choosing and ripening the avocados. On that subject, Carlos Jacott has this to say: "Some do not lend themselves to the dip and have a soupy consistency. The 'Calavos' from the West Coast are truly the best. They are small, like an orange, and dark greenish in appearance. Avocados must be soft. They give to gentle pressure when ripe, like a pear. Buy them hard and allow four to five days for softening at room temperature."*

| | |
|---|---|
| 1 garlic clove, mashed | 2–3 dashes Louisiana chili sauce |
| 1 pinch salt | 1 ripe avocado |
| ½ tsp. vegetable oil | 2 tbsp. chopped onion |

Mash garlic and salt together in oil and add chili sauce to mixture. Mash peeled and pitted avocado well with a fork or potato masher (do *not* use a machine), add garlic mixture and onion, and mix thoroughly. Serve with fried tortilla chips to 4–6.

## POLLO PARADOR

8 garlic cloves
1 tsp. olive oil
2 small frying chickens, quartered
2 tbsp. paprika
2 tbsp. orégano
2 tbsp. crushed bay leaves

2 tbsp. salt
1 cup wine vinegar
2 $\frac{1}{2}''$ slices Bermuda onion
flour for dredging
oil for frying
cooked peas for garnish

Mash garlic in olive oil to produce a smooth paste. Rinse chickens inside and out in cold water and pat dry. Using a brush (or, "better yet," according to Carlos Jacott, "with the fingers") paint outer surfaces of chicken with garlic paste, reserving any not used and making more, if necessary. Arrange chicken in a large pot and add blended remaining ingredients (except frying oil, peas, and flour) a little at a time, shaking the pot vigorously to flip chicken parts over several times, coating them thoroughly with the mixture. Cover and refrigerate overnight.

Remove chicken parts from pot with a slotted spoon, reserving marinade. Pat semidry and shake with flour (preferably buckwheat) in a large paper bag, coating them evenly. Pour $\frac{1}{2}''$ frying oil into a large skillet (or two, if necessary), add chicken, and sauté over fairly high heat 5 minutes, or until golden brown. Repaint chicken with garlic paste and return to skillet. Add sliced onion from marinade and bring heat down very low. Cover and cook 20–25 minutes, or until nearly done. Add 3–4 tablespoons of the reserved marinade. Replace cover, turn heat up high, and fry briskly 4–5 minutes. Remove from heat and transfer chicken to hot serving plates with a slotted spoon. Top portions with separated onion rings, garnish with cooked peas, and serve to 4–6.

# NATILLA (SPANISH CREAM)

| | |
|---|---|
| 1 cup sugar | 3 eggs, well beaten |
| 3 tbsp. cornstarch | 2 tbsp. butter |
| ¼ tsp. salt | 1 tsp. vanilla extract |
| 1 qt. milk | powdered cinnamon |

In a bowl combine sugar, cornstarch, and salt. Stir in ¼ cup of the milk to make a smooth paste. Add beaten eggs and stir until smooth. Scald remaining milk in the top of a double boiler, slowly add egg mixture, and cook over boiling water, stirring constantly with a wooden spoon until mixture thickens just enough to coat spoon. Stir in butter and vanilla, pour mixture into individual serving cups, and chill. Sprinkle tops with cinnamon just before serving to 6–8.

# CAFÉ MENDOZA

*An after-dinner libation that goes down with more ease than some of its enthusiasts get up.*

Pour 1 shot of tequila and ½ shot of Kahlúa into a whisky sour glass. Fill with hot espresso coffee and top with fresh whipped cream. *Salud!*

*1 World Trade Center*

Joe Baum's improbable spaceship (page 43) hovers 1,350 feet and 107 stories above mean sea level, lighting up the skies over lower Manhattan, affording patrons lucky or influential enough to come by reservations with a view that stretches from here to the general vicinity of Salt Lake City, and feeding three hundred in the main dining room with no discernible sweat. From this height, the Statue of Liberty looks like a toy soldier, the Verazzano Narrows Bridge like a necklace in Tiffany's window, and all of Manhattan like an amoeba seen through a microscope. In short, the Ultimate High. Inside, the atmosphere is that of a high-budget 1930s musical with a vaguely nautical motif. The food, considering the volume of traffic, is much finer than might be expected and the wines are outstanding.

## TOMATO CONSOMMÉ WITH WILD THYME

*Try serving this soup for all seasons hot, with a Freemark Abbey Chardonnay, or refrigerate it and serve it à la madrilène with a chilled Beaujolais.*

1 qt. strong Beef Stock*
¾ lb ground beef
6 large ripe tomatoes, chopped
½ onion, sliced
6 whole peppercorns
½ leek, sliced (white part only)
1 stalk celery

2 egg whites, beaten
1 small garlic clove, crushed
2 tsp. salt
1 cup tomato juice
2 tbsp. fresh (or 1 tsp. dried) thyme

Mix all ingredients well and place in a heavy pot. Bring to simmer and cook 35 minutes. Strain through a cheesecloth, chill, and remove film of fat from top. Serve hot or well chilled with a sprinkling of thyme. Serves 6.

## PÂTÉ DE CANARD À L'ORANGE

*Onion dip has its virtues, but panache may not be one of them. Try this on your party guests instead. It's worth the effort.*

2  4½-lb. ducks
3  oz. rum
5  shallots, peeled and minced
1  tbsp. chopped parsley
2  tbsp. salt
8  twists fresh pepper
½  lb. duck livers plus livers from
   the 2 ducks
1  cup milk
2  lbs. pork shoulder
10  oz. fatback
½  bunch parsley, finely chopped
1  medium onion, finely
   chopped

1  tbsp. butter
2  pinches powdered rosemary
1  pinch each ground { coriander / thyme / marjoram / cardamon / clove }
2  garlic cloves, crushed
4  oz. white wine
5  small juice oranges
8  oz. fatback sliced as thinly as
   possible
4  ¼" strips fatback

*Two days before party*

Skin and bone ducks, leaving skins whole. Slice one of the four breast pieces into ½" strips and place in a marinade of 2 oz. rum, shallots, 1 tbsp. chopped parsley, a pinch of salt, and 1 twist of black pepper. Refrigerate. Wrap remaining duck meat tightly in foil and refrigerate. Combine livers with milk and refrigerate. Wrap and refrigerate duck skins.

*One day before party*

Drain livers, wash in cold water, and pat dry. Cut off string membranes and soak livers in 1 oz. rum. Remove and reserve as much fat as possible from inside of duck skin, taking care not to pierce skin. With the skin, line a 3-qt. loaf pan, 11¾" × 5⅝" × 3¼", arranging outside of skin against pan and using as little skin as possible but allowing an inch of skin to overhang pan edges. Cut rectangular piece of skin just large enough to barely cover top of pan and reserve it. Cut any remaining skin into 1" squares, put them in a heavy pot with reserved fat, and cook over very low heat until fat is rendered.

*The farce, or stuffing*

Cut remaining duck meat, pork shoulder, and 10 oz. fatback into ½" cubes. Using finest disk of a meat grinder, feed meats through it one at a time, then repeat process. (If using a processor, grind $\frac{1}{3}$ of the mixture until puréed and chop remaining $\frac{2}{3}$ to consistency of fine hamburger.) Place meats in a bowl and add remaining parsley. Sauté onion in butter until golden and add to meats. In a stoppered bottle, combine herbs and spices, garlic, and white wine and shake vigorously. Add mixture to meats, then add salt, pepper, and 3 tbsp. rendered duck fat, mixing all ingredients thoroughly.

Cut livers in half laterally, trim evenly, and add trimmings to mixed meats. Peel oranges and remove all white membrane. Cut tops and bottoms off oranges, stand them on end, and trim with a sharp knife to form cylinders that, when laid end-to-end, form a smooth column. On a large square of wax paper, overlap the thin slices of fatback to form a sheet that is 9″ wide and long enough to accommodate the oranges when they are laid end-to-end. Cover the fatback with a $\frac{1}{8}$″ layer of the farce and place oranges end-to-end in the center of the farce. Gently lift the wax paper at a side parallel to the row of oranges and roll fatback and farce tightly around the oranges, detaching the paper as you go. Refrigerate the resultant roll. Spread a $\frac{1}{4}$″ layer of farce on bottom and sides of skin-lined pan and arrange a layer of duck liver slices down its center. Cover this with a thin layer of farce, pressing it down lightly. Remove fatback-and-orange roll from refrigerator, center it in the pan, and coat lightly with additional farce. On either side of the roll, build up layers of marinated duck breast, $\frac{1}{4}$″ strips of fatback, and farce until a final layer of farce is level with the top of the roll. Make a layer of remaining liver slices and cover with farce to fill pan. Place reserved rectangle of duck skin, fat side down, over pâté and fold edges of skin lining the pan over it.

*Cooking the pâté*
Bring a pot of water to boil while preheating oven to 325°F. Set pâté mold in a large baking pan and place in oven. Carefully pour boiling water into baking pan until it reaches a level 1″ from top of pâté mold. Bake 95 minutes. Remove from oven, place a weighted board, marble slab, weighted loaf pan, or the like over the pâté, and allow to cool. Refrigerate, with weight in place, overnight.

*The day of the party*

Dip pâté mold briefly into hot water. Invert platter over pâté mold and flip platter and mold over, allowing pâté to fall onto platter. With a sharp knife, remove solidified fat from around pâté. Refrigerate pâté until ready to serve, then slice with a very sharp knife and garnish to taste. Serves 10–30, depending on host's generosity and guests' restraint or lack thereof.

## SALMON IN RED WINE

*Served with a full Bordeaux or light Burgundy—the restaurant recommends an American wine, Heitz Cabernet Sauvignon—this is a dish for the gods.*

| | |
|---|---|
| 1 7-lb. salmon | 2 tbsp. butter ⎱ kneaded |
| 13½ cups *Court Bouillon** | 2 tbsp. flour ⎰ together |
| 16 mushroom caps | 1½ tbsp. butter, cut in small bits |
| 1⅓ cups Red Wine Sauce* | |

Measure fish lengthwise at its thickest point. Place on rack in fish poacher and add *court bouillon.* Cover poacher and bring to boil. Reduce heat to simmer and continue to cook, allowing 10 minutes per measured inch of fish, fractions included. While fish is poaching, put mushroom caps in a small pan with a few tbsp. *court bouillon* and simmer briefly until tender. Using poacher rack, remove fish to a serving platter. Decorate fish with mushroom caps. Heat wine sauce and stir in butter-flour mixture. Swirl in remaining butter until melted. Pour a few tbsp. of wine sauce over fish, and serve remainder in a sauceboat. Serves 6–8.

## FRIED ZUCCHINI

*A fine accompaniment to the fish.*

| | |
|---|---|
| 2½ lbs. small zucchini | 12 oz. bread crumbs |
| 5 oz. flour | peanut oil sufficient to nearly fill |
| 6 eggs, beaten and seasoned | deep fryer |
| with salt and pepper to taste | salt |

Wash and dry zucchini and trim off ends. Cut them lengthwise into $\frac{3}{8}''$ strips. Dredge zucchini strips in flour, a handful at a time, coating them evenly and shaking off excess. Dip floured strips successively in egg batter and bread crumbs, coating them evenly and then patting them with paper towels so that bread crumbs adhere. Lay on paper towels until ready for fryer. Heat fat to 325°F. Fry zucchini in batches small enough to allow them to rise to top of oil in one layer. Remove finished zucchini with a skimmer, drain on paper towels, and keep warm while frying remaining batches. Place in a serving dish lined with a cloth napkin, sprinkle with salt, and serve immediately. Serves 8 generously.

## GOLDEN LEMON TART

2½ tbsp. cornstarch
1½ cups water
⅔ cup fresh lemon juice
⅓ cup sugar
7 egg yolks
1½ tbsp. butter
1–1¼ cups heavy cream, whipped

6 macaroons, coarsely crushed
1 9″ prebaked pie or quiche crust
3 lemons, seeded and sliced very thin
1 cup apricot glaze (see note)

*Note   A simple glaze can be made by warming 1 cup apricot jam with 1 tbsp. lemon juice and passing the mixture through a sieve.*

Dilute cornstarch in 2 oz. water. In a pan, bring lemon juice, sugar, and remaining water to boil, cooking until sugar is thoroughly dissolved. Gradually stir in diluted cornstarch, mixing well, and in a bowl add resultant syrup to egg yolks little by little, beating constantly. Pour egg mixture into top of double boiler and cook, stirring constantly, until bubbles appear. Remove from heat, stir in butter, and cool rapidly over a bowl of ice, stirring occasionally. When mixture has cooled, fold in whipped cream and crushed macaroons and carefully fill pie crust. Dip lemon slices in apricot glaze and arrange them in a single layer on top of tart filling. Chill well and allow to return to room temperature before serving to 8.

# the brazilian pavilion

*141 East 52nd Street*

A sleekly designed cellar done up in the national colors of the Estados Unidos do Brasil, this is where the girls from Ipanema—and displaced Cariocans in general—drink their *batidas* and dispel their homesickness over *bacalhao, churrasco gaucho, farofa,* and *feijoada.* Joaquin Gonzales, an expatriated Galician who grew up in Brazil and later operated the first of Gotham's Brazilian restaurants, opened this one in 1973 and has been playing to packed houses ever since. Little wonder; the food and service are first-rate and the tariffs are minimal.

## CALDEIRADA DE PEIXE

½ lb. *bacalhao* (salt cod)
10 clams
½ lb. striped bass
1 lb. whiting or fresh cod
½ lb. medium shrimp
1 lb. cleaned squid
1 onion, diced
2 tomatoes, diced
2 green peppers, diced

½ cup vegetable oil
1 cup tomato sauce
¼ cup white wine
3 bay leaves
salt and pepper to taste
2 lbs. potatoes, diced
2 tomatoes, sliced
½ onion, sliced
1 green pepper, sliced

Soak salt cod in cold water 48 hours, then rinse. Steam clams open and remove from shells. Cut all fish but salt cod into large chunks, shell and devein shrimp, and cut squid into 1″ lengths. In a pot, sauté diced onion, diced tomato, and diced pepper in the oil until onions are golden. Add shrimp, clams, squid, and water to cover. Cover pot and simmer 15 minutes. Add bass, whiting, ¾ cup tomato sauce, wine, and bay leaves. Season to taste and simmer 8–10 minutes longer. Remove bay leaves.

Meanwhile, in a separate pot, arrange potatoes, sliced tomatoes, sliced onion, sliced pepper, and salt cod. Add ¼ cup tomato sauce and enough water to bring liquids to ¾ the depth of the solids. Cover and simmer 20 minutes, or until potatoes are tender. Remove salt cod and discard or reserve for other uses. Add contents of second pot to first, mix gently but well, and simmer another 5 minutes. Serves 4–5.

## COCADA

8 oz. Baker's "southern style" coconut
3 cups boiling water
7–8 tbsp. sugar

½ cup water
3 egg yolks, beaten
6 slices fresh mild white cheese

Add coconut to boiling water and simmer, uncovered, 45–60 minutes, until coconut is soft and moist and most of water has evaporated. Heat sugar and ½ cup water over high flame until mixture is light brown (about 10 minutes). Add resultant syrup to coconut, blend well, and allow to cool. Add egg yolks to coconut mixture, stir well, and refrigerate. Serve with sliced cheese to 6.

### Mr.&Mrs. Foster's Place

*242 East 81st Street*

Should you wish you were in the land of Dixie, this is the place—the Old South behind an upper East Side storefront. Pearl Byrd Foster is the heroine of a thousand romantic potboilers: the embattled widow somehow holding the plantation together against all odds, the Old Dominion aristocrat forced by cruel circumstances to take in paying guests. She also happens to be one of the most astute and innovative cooks on the scene today, with a sure grasp of underlying culinary principles that enables her triumphantly to combine ingredients that in less skilled hands might make an utter shambles of a meal. Architecturally, the restaurant isn't exactly Jeffersonian—motel moderne would be more like it—but the service has an antebellum graciousness about it, and dinner (the only meal served) is a stately rite that runs its leisurely course through two appetizers, soup, an entrée (which must be chosen when reservations are made), salad, dessert, and coffee, with plenty of crisp hot corn bread on the side.

*Omit one or two of the first three courses if the meal that follows seems too much.*

### CHICKEN LIVER AND CALIFORNIA WALNUT PÂTÉ

½ lb. fresh chicken livers
2 tbsp. melted butter
1 medium onion, chopped
salt, pepper, and paprika to taste
2 oz. dry Sherry
2 oz. Madeira
6 oz. California walnuts, chopped

¼ lb. sweet butter (room temperature)
¼ tsp. mace
1 pinch cayenne pepper
½ tsp. powdered thyme (optional)

Cut membranes and green spots from livers. Dice livers and place in broiler pan with melted butter and onion. Season lightly with salt and pepper and dust with paprika. Toss to coat livers with butter. Spread livers over pan bottom, leaving space between pieces. Broil close to high heat, turning with a spatula, until golden on all sides. Blend wines and pour half the wine mixture into a blender. With blender running, add walnuts, a few at a time, blending until smooth. Add livers and remaining wine and blend until all ingredients are thoroughly incorporated, scraping down sides of blender container with a rubber spatula when necessary. Add butter and blend well, then add mace, cayenne, and thyme and correct seasonings. Pour into a serving bowl and chill thoroughly. Serve on a crisp lettuce leaf and surround with thin slices of cucumber dusted liberally with fresh pepper. Serves 6.

## BUTTON MUSHROOMS WITH DILLED SOUR CREAM

1 lb. fresh unblemished button
  mushrooms
juice of ½ lemon
2 oz. butter

6 Buttered Toast Squares
Dilled Sour Cream
paprika to taste

Wash mushrooms under cold running water and dry with paper towels. Cut off stems and reserve for other uses. Pour lemon juice over mushrooms, turning mushrooms to coat them thoroughly. Heat butter in a pan, add mushrooms, and cook precisely 1 minute, tossing mushrooms continuously to coat them with butter. Place Buttered Toast Squares (recipe below) on serving plates. Arrange mushrooms on toast, blanket with Dilled Sour Cream (recipe below), and dust with paprika. Put under a hot broiler for less than 1 minute. Serves 6.

*Buttered Toast Squares*
Trim crusts from sliced white bread. Melt 6 oz. butter and brush on both sides of bread. Lay slices on cookie sheet and toast in a moderately hot oven until golden.

*Dilled Sour Cream*

Stir ½ cup snipped fresh dill (or 1 tsp. crushed dried dillweed) and 1 tbsp. onion juice into 1 pt. commercial sour cream, add salt and pepper to taste, and mix thoroughly.

## GOLDEN SQUASH SOUP WITH APPLES

| | |
|---|---|
| 1 2-lb. butternut squash | salt, freshly ground pepper, and |
| 2 McIntosh or Cortland apples | mace to taste |
| 4 cups Chicken Stock* | 1 cup heavy cream |
| 2 tbsp. lemon juice | 6 apple wedges (for garnish) |

Peel squash and cut into 1″ cubes. Peel, core, and quarter apples. Cook squash in stock about 10 minutes, until tender. Add apples, purée the mixture in a blender, and pour through a fine sieve. Heat squash mixture, add lemon juice, and season to taste. Stir in cream and heat thoroughly without boiling. Serve hot, garnished with apple wedges and accompanied by Herbed Bread Sticks. Serves 6.

*Herbed Bread Sticks*

Cut 4 slices whole wheat or soya bread into 4 sticks each, leaving crusts on. Melt ¼ lb. butter and add 2 tbsp. chopped parsley and 1 tbsp. chopped chives. Dip bread sticks in herbed butter, coating them thoroughly. Toast on a cookie sheet in a moderately hot oven until golden.

## BOURBON BEEF AND OYSTER POT

| | |
|---|---|
| 4 lbs. beef chuck or top or bottom round, cut into 1½″ cubes | 2 stalks celery, cut in 1″ lengths |
| 2 tbsp. lemon juice | 2 large potatoes, peeled and halved |
| salt and pepper to taste | 1 small bay leaf |
| 4 tbsp. vegetable oil | 1 garlic clove, pierced |
| 2 tbsp. butter | ¼ tsp. powdered thyme |
| 5 oz. bourbon | 2 tbsp. tomato sauce |
| 4 cups Beef Stock,* boiling | Tabasco and Worcestershire sauce |
| 2 medium onions | 3 doz. fresh shucked oysters with their liquor |
| 2 cloves | |
| 1 large carrot, cut in 1″ lengths | |

Dry meat thoroughly with paper towels, sprinkle with lemon juice, and let stand 15 minutes. Dust with salt and pepper. Sauté meat in oil and butter on all sides until golden brown. Pour 4 oz. of the bourbon over meat and flame. When flame subsides, place meat in a large stew pot or casserole attractive enough to take to the table. Pour boiling stock and 1 qt. boiling water over beef. Discard grease from sauté pan and deglaze with a little water, scraping all browned bits into meat pot. Stud onions with cloves and add all vegetables, herbs, and seasonings, except Tabasco and Worcestershire sauces, to meat. Bring to a brisk boil. Reduce heat, cover, and simmer 3 hours, or until meat is tender. Remove meat from pot, pour liquid and vegetables into blender, and blend until ingredients are puréed (if too thick, dilute with beef stock). Adjust seasoning and add Tabasco and Worcestershire to taste. Return meat and sauce to serving pot and heat until bubbling. Add oysters and their liquor and cook just until edges of oysters begin to curl. Warm remaining bourbon, pour over beef, and flame. Arrange a circle of toast points around serving pot and serve to 6–8, with grated horseradish on side.

### ORANGE-BEET SALAD

2 small heads Boston lettuce
6 California navel oranges
2 large beets, cooked, peeled, and shredded

1 cup French dressing
1 tbsp. mustard

Wash and refrigerate lettuce. Peel and section oranges. When lettuce is well drained, pull off leaves and arrange on a large serving platter. Spoon shredded beets onto center of platter and surround with concentric circles of orange sections. Beat 1 tbsp. of your favorite mustard into French dressing, spoon some of the mixture over beets, and serve remainder on side. Serves 6.

# WILD RICE AND RAISIN PUDDING

1 cup wild rice, washed
2½ cups water
½ cup seedless black raisins,
   washed
3 tbsp. clover honey
2 tbsp. butter

½ tsp. freshly grated nutmeg
pinch of salt
2 cups milk
2 eggs, lightly beaten
2 tbsp. brandy
½ pint heavy cream, whipped

Cook rice in 1½ cups of the water until tender, about 45 minutes, and toss with a fork to release steam. Cook raisins in remaining water until tender and all liquid has been absorbed. Add to rice and stir in honey, butter, nutmeg, and salt. Heat milk in top of double boiler, add rice mixture, and stir in beaten eggs. Cook without boiling until mixture thickens. Stir in brandy and, if desired, more honey and nutmeg. Serve warm or cold, topped with whipped cream. Serves 6.

# CHALET SUISSE

*6 East 48th Street*

Stucco walls adorned with Alpine crossbows, dark wooden beams, simple fabrics, and concerned, matronly waitresses in picturesque Swiss garb all combine to create an atmosphere notable for its *Gemüchtlichkeit.* A devoted clientele, made up in large part of German-speaking Swiss, testifies to the excellence of Chef Dietmar Schlueter's kitchen. Outstanding offerings include *Bündnerfleisch,* cold calf's brain vinaigrette, and *museau*

*de boeuf;* chicken *jurassienne,* sauerbraten, and butterflied trout in an herbed cream sauce.

## CHEESE AND ONION QUICHE

*The quiche, in its multifarious guises, has become the ubiquitous offering of suburban cocktail party hostesses in recent years. This shouldn't be held against it. This simple, hearty quiche from Chalet Suisse is one of the best. Serve it as a first course or with a tossed salad as a light lunch or late supper.*

| | | |
|---|---|---|
| 1 large onion, vertically sliced | | 1 unbaked 11" pie shell (in pan) |
| 1 tbsp. butter | | 4 beaten eggs |
| 9 oz. Gruyère cheese | shredded and mixed | 1 cup light cream |
| 9 oz. Swiss cheese | | 1 cup milk |
| | | salt and pepper to taste |

Sauté onion in butter until soft but not brown. Loosely and evenly pack half the cheese mixture into the pie shell and cover successively with onion and remaining cheese. Blend all other ingredients and pour into pie shell until ¾ full. Preheat oven to 400°F. and bake quiche 45 minutes. Serve immediately to 8.

## TOASTED FARINA POTAGE

| | | |
|---|---|---|
| 1 oz. butter | 59 | 1½ qts. heated Chicken Consommé* |
| ¾ cup farina | 60 | |
| 1 tbsp. flour | 61 | 2 oz. red wine (optional) |
| ½ onion, minced | 62 | salt and pepper to taste |

Melt butter, add raw farina, and toast over low flame, stirring, until brown. Mix in flour, add onion, and cook 1 minute longer. Add hot consommé and simmer 45 minutes. Add wine, if desired, season to taste, and serve. Serves 8 or more.

## VEAU À LA SUISSE

3 lbs. lean veal
1 oz. butter
1 oz. minced onion
1 cup dry white wine
1½ pts. heavy cream

¼ oz. cornstarch, diluted in a
  little water
1 cup Brown Gravy*
salt and pepper to taste

Cut veal up as you would French fried potatoes. Sauté meat in butter, turning to lightly brown it on all sides. Add onion and wine and cook over moderate heat until wine is almost completely evaporated. Add cream, bring to slow boil, and add diluted cornstarch. Add gravy and salt and pepper and simmer 3 more minutes. Serves 8 very generously and 12 adequately.

## CHALET SUISSE CHOCOLATE FONDUE

*Although many—some Swiss included—believe the chocolate fondue to have originated in Switzerland, it was actually invented by Konrad Egli, the restaurant's owner, and a collaborator at Chalet Suisse. It has been much imitated since, but here's the authentic recipe.*

2 3-oz. bars Toblerone
  chocolate
¼ cup heavy cream
1 tbsp. Kirschwasser, Grand
  Marnier, or cognac

16 or more sections mandarin
  orange
16 or more bite-sized pineapple
  chunks or wedges
8 or more small Profiteroles*

*Note   Other fruits may be added or substituted as desired.*

In the top of a double boiler, melt chocolate, stir in cream, and add liqueur. Arrange fruits and profiteroles on a serving dish. Present chocolate mixture in a chafing dish or warmer, with fruit dish and fondue forks within reach of the assembled company. The technique is simply to spear the goodies with the fork, dip them into the chocolate, and let nature take its course. The number of servings is contingent upon the decorum of the participants, but 6 wouldn't be unreasonable, Uncle Charlie's boardinghouse reach notwithstanding.

# Brussels Restaurant

*115 East 54th Street*

A memento of the New York World's Fair of 1939, where it was the jewel of the Belgian Pavilion, Brussels is a marvelous anachronism, a throwback to the Delmonican era. Victor, one of the few authentic sommeliers left on either side of the Atlantic in these crabbed times, still purrs his litany of the great vintages of Bordeaux and Burgundy for the delectation of a few patrons discriminating enough to know what he's burbling about; fresh *foie gras* is still accorded the reverence it deserves; and the venerable classics of *haute cuisine* are still prepared and presented as they were in the heyday of Auguste Escoffier (whose shade probably has been whirling like a dervish since the advent of *la cuisine minceur*). Physically, this is one of the most distinguished of the city's *grand luxe* establishments. A gravity appropriate to serious *gourmandise* prevails in the amply proportioned main dining room, where luxurious woods and an autumnal color scheme lend dignified warmth to the proceedings. And while the *patron,* Albert Giambelli, grouses in private about the cross that must be borne by defenders of the True Faith and threatens to chuck the whole business and open a simple *trattoria,* he continues to stock one of the nation's most awesome cellars with hand-blown bottles of 1830 Madeira, mid-nineteenth-century Port, and any other museum pieces he can get his hands on.

## CANAPÉ "SURPRISE"

16 oysters, shucked and drained
flour for dredging
1 egg, beaten
bread crumbs for dredging
oil for deep frying
16 thin rounds of French bread
(about 2″ in diameter), toasted

Dredge oysters in flour, shaking off excess, then dip in beaten egg and roll in bread crumbs. Fry in deep fat at 350°F. for 2 minutes, drain, and place an oyster on each toast round. Top canapés with Tangy Egg Sauce. Serves 4.

*Tangy Egg Sauce*

2 hard-boiled egg yolks
salt and pepper to taste
1 tbsp. vinegar
1 tbsp. onion ⎤
1 tsp. chives ⎟
1 tsp. shallots ⎟
1 tsp. garlic ⎟ chopped
1 tsp. fresh basil ⎟ fine
(optional) ⎟
2 tsp. capers ⎟
2 *cornichons* ⎦

2 oz. olive oil
½ cup mayonnaise
1 tsp. Dijon mustard
2 hard-boiled egg whites, chopped

In a mixing bowl, work the egg yolks, salt, and pepper into a smooth paste. Mix in all other ingredients except egg whites until thoroughly blended. Fold in egg whites.

## HOMARD AUX AROMATES

2  1½-lb. live lobsters
salt and freshly ground pepper
   to taste
2 oz. Clarified Butter*
*Mirepoix**

2 oz. Pernod
2 oz. cognac
8 oz. white wine
8 oz. Fish Stock*
8 oz. heavy cream

With a sharp knife and as much nerve as you can muster, halve lobsters lengthwise, reserving coral. Season lobsters with salt and pepper and sauté 6 minutes in very hot clarified butter. Add *mirepoix*, sprinkle with Pernod and cognac, and flame. When flame subsides, add wine and fish stock and boil 10 minutes. Remove lobsters from pan and legs from lobsters. Chop legs into ½" pieces, return to pan, and continue to cook until liquids are reduced to ⅓ their volume. Meanwhile, remove tail and claw meat from lobsters, leaving body and tail shells intact, and cut into small dice. Divide diced meat into 4 parts, pack loosely into 4 tail sections of shell, and keep warm. Add cream and reserved coral to boiling fish stock mixture, reduce heat, and cook 3–4 minutes, stirring gently. Strain resultant sauce through a chinois or several thicknesses of cheesecloth, pour into a sauceboat, and spoon sauce over lobsters, reserving some for use at table. Garnish lobsters lightly with julienne strips of briefly steamed carrots, celery, and turnips and serve at once on hot plates to 4.

## WATERZOOÏ DE VOLAILLE À LA GANTOISE

*This heartwarming dish, although not a product of haute cuisine, is served regularly at the Brussels and is one of the few Belgian specialties to be found in the city.*

1 stalk white celery, cut in
   julienne strips
3 leeks (white parts only)
2 medium carrots
1 medium onion, quartered
3 tbsp. plus ¼ lb. sweet butter
2 qts. Chicken Broth*

bouquet garni: thyme, bay leaf,
   parsley, tied in cheesecloth
1 4-lb. chicken, trussed
¾ cup heavy cream
juice of ½ lemon
3 egg yolks
chopped parsley for garnish

In a 5–6-qt. casserole simmer the vegetables gently in 3 tbsp.
butter for 4–5 minutes. Add chicken broth and bouquet garni,
cover, and cook over low heat for ½ hour. Add chicken and
continue cooking over low heat ½ hour longer. Remove chicken
and vegetables from pot and reserve. Bring pot to boil and
cook until liquids are reduced by ⅓. In another pot, melt ¼ lb.
butter and add reduced stock, cream, and lemon juice, beating
mixture with a wire whisk for 1 minute over medium heat.
Remove from heat, add egg yolks, and beat rapidly. Strain and
pour over quartered chicken and vegetables. Garnish with
parsley and serve at once in soup plates with boiled potatoes.
Serves 4.

## CHOCOLATE SOUFFLÉ

½ cup grated unsweetened
   chocolate
5 egg yolks, beaten

4 tbsp. *Crème Pâtissière**
5 egg whites
2 tbsp. sugar

Melt chocolate over low heat and mix it, with egg yolks, into
*crème pâtissière*. Beat egg whites until stiff and fold in sugar.
Very gently fold egg white mixture into chocolate mixture,
blending thoroughly. Butter and dust with sugar a 1½-qt. soufflé
dish. Shake out excess sugar and pour in soufflé mixture. Bake
15 minutes in a preheated 520°F. oven and serve immediately
to 4.

*234 West 44th Street*

There's no business like show business and no restaurant quite like this. Inextricably woven into the very fabric of the theater, Sardi's is an institution without which New York would be Dubuque. The atmosphere is as clubby today as it was when Vincent Sardi, Sr., opened the place as a haven for thespians in 1921. The walls are still decked with the famous theatrical caricatures. The stars still sweep in like comets on opening nights to sweat out the early reviews. Vincent Sardi, Jr., the unofficial mayor of 44th Street, is still as affable—and the deviled beef bones as good—as ever.

## STUFFED EGGS À LA RUSSE

9  hard-boiled eggs
3  tsp. chopped parsley
6  tbsp. mayonnaise
¾  tsp. mustard
3  tbsp. Russian dressing

3  tsp. caviar
1½ cups shredded lettuce
36  small pieces pimiento
18  sprigs parsley

Shell and halve eggs and scoop out yolks. In a bowl, mix yolks, chopped parlsey, mayonnaise, and mustard with a fork until creamy. Place mixture in a pastry bag and pipe into egg whites. Add a dab of Russian dressing to each egg half and top with caviar. Serve 3 egg halves per person on shredded lettuce. Decorate plates with pimientos and parsley. Serves 6.

## CREAM OF BROCCOLI SOUP

2  lbs. broccoli
8  cups Chicken Broth*
3  tbsp. butter
2  stalks celery, chopped
1  small onion, chopped
1  bay leaf

1  garlic clove, crushed
1  tsp. salt
⅛  tsp. white pepper
¼  cup flour
1  cup light cream, heated
croutons for garnish

Place cleaned, roughly chopped broccoli in a kettle with chicken broth, bring to boil, and simmer 20 minutes. Melt 2 tbsp. of the butter in a skillet, add celery, onion, bay leaf, garlic, salt, and pepper to butter, and sauté 10 minutes over moderate heat. Add flour and mix very well. Add contents of skillet to kettle, swilling out pan with some of the broth. Stir soup thoroughly and simmer 30 minutes. Cover kettle and leave in a preheated 350°F. oven for 30 minutes. Remove soup from oven and strain, pressing as much solid matter as possible through sieve. Add heated cream and remaining butter to liquid. Stir and season to taste. Serve topped with lightly toasted croutons, with a dry Sherry as an accompaniment. Serves 8 or more.

*Note*  *2 lbs. fresh asparagus can be substituted for broccoli.*

## DEVILED ROAST BEEF BONES

*A "leftover" lunch or supper dish that some devotees prefer to the original roast, this is best accompanied by a good Burgundy, preferably a Pommard.*

6 tsp. dry English mustard  
1½ cups water  
12 meaty beef bones from a cooked standing roast  

2¼ cups bread crumbs  
18 sprigs watercress  
12 tbsp. Deviled Sauce  

Blend mustard and water. Cover bones well, first with mustard mixture and then with bread crumbs. Arrange in a shallow baking pan and broil for about 7 minutes, or until browned and hot, turning occasionally. Garnish with watercress and serve with Deviled Sauce to 6.

### Deviled Sauce

½ cup dry Sherry  
¼ cup prepared Dijon mustard  

1¼ cups Brown Sauce*  

In a saucepan, heat Sherry over moderately high flame and allow to reduce for 10 minutes. Add mustard, stirring, and simmer 5 minutes. Add brown sauce, stir, and simmer 5 minutes longer. Serve hot.

# STRAWBERRIES WITH MARSALA

zest of $\frac{1}{2}$ lemon
1 qt. strawberries, washed and
   hulled

$\frac{1}{3}$ cup sugar
$\frac{3}{4}$ cup Marsala
$\frac{1}{2}$ cup dry white wine

Cut lemon zest into two strips and add to strawberries in a mixing bowl. Cover with sugar and shake well. Pour wines over berries and mix gently but evenly. Cover with a plate and allow to stand for 1 hour. Remove lemon zest and serve, preferably with Champagne. Serves 6–8.

**50 East 58th Street**

Uncompromisingly authentic north-Indian cuisine, served with great style in a palatial setting distinguished by a maharaja's ransom in rare inlaid woods, elaborately embellished tiles, rich fabrics, seductive scents, and exotic artifacts. The *tandoori* kitchen, sheathed in glass, is the theatrical focal point of the main dining room, and the lightly spiced food is delectable.

## MURGHI TIKKA

*Try this chicken brochette with fragrant saffron rice at your next alfresco dinner.*

1 2½–3-lb. chicken
1 cup yogurt
¼ tsp. turmeric
1 tsp. peeled and freshly grated
   gingerroot

1 garlic clove, finely minced
6 drops yellow food coloring
salt to taste

Pull skin off chicken and reserve, if desired, for soup. With a small sharp knife, cut meat from bones as cleanly and in as large sections as possible. Reserve bones for soup or stock. Cut meat into 2″ cubes. Blend remaining ingredients, add chicken cubes, and stir to coat them thoroughly. Cover and let stand several hours or overnight. Skewer chicken cubes on a rotating spit and broil over hot charcoal about 10 minutes, or until cooked through but moist inside. Serves 4–6.

*Note   If necessary, the brochette may be broiled directly on a grill. In that event, it should be turned frequently to cook evenly.*

# INDIAN SAFFRON RICE

½ onion, chopped
2 tbsp. butter
2 large cardamoms
2 small cardamoms
6–8 black peppercorns
2 cloves

1 cinnamon stick
2 cups rice
½ tsp. saffron threads
⅓ cup boiled peas
2 tbsp. freshly grated coconut

In a large pot, sauté onion in butter until lightly colored. Add 1 qt. water, bring to boil, and turn heat down as far as possible. Tie spices in muslin or double-thick cheesecloth and add, with washed rice, to pot. Bring to boil, add saffron, and stir well. Remove pot from heat and preheat oven to 300°F. Soak in cold water a clean cloth just large enough to cover pot, wring out thoroughly, and successively cover pot with cloth and lid. Place pot in preheated oven for 10 minutes, or until water has been absorbed by rice. Garnish rice with boiled peas, top with grated coconut, and serve piping hot. Serves 6 amply.

# JINGHA TARHI

*The restaurant's version of that old standby, shrimp curry.*

2¼ lbs. large shrimp
½ cup peanut or vegetable oil
1½ cups chopped onion
½ tsp. celery seed
1 tbsp. finely minced garlic
½ cup water
salt to taste
1 tsp. turmeric

2 tsp. ground coriander seed
1 tsp. ground cumin
2 tsp. paprika
½ cup yogurt
2 tbsp. fresh chopped coriander
    leaves
juice of ½ lemon

Shell and devein shrimp. Rinse, drain well, and set aside. Heat oil in a deep saucepan and add onion. Cook ten minutes, stirring often, until onion browns, then add celery seed, garlic, and half the water. Continue to cook about 3 minutes and add salt, turmeric, ground coriander, cumin, and paprika, stirring constantly. After 3 more minutes, add yogurt and remaining water.

Add shrimp 4 minutes later and cook 8–10 minutes, stirring often. Cover and cook 10 more minutes. Remove from heat, sprinkle with fresh coriander and lemon juice, and serve hot to 6 or more.

## BANANA RABRI

1 qt. milk
sugar to taste
1 pinch cardamom seed

1 tbsp. pistachio nutmeats
2 large bananas
rose water to taste

Bring milk to boil in a heavy-bottomed pot and allow to simmer until thick and creamy, stirring to dissolve any film that accumulates. Add sugar, cardamom seed, and pistachios, mix well, and set aside. Slice bananas into rounds, add the condensed milk mixture and toss, coating bananas well. Divide into portions, sprinkle with a little rose water, and serve, at room temperature, to 4.

# *Saito*

## *305 East 46th Street*

Spacious and somewhat austere, the largely black and gray
setting, punctuated here and there by a bamboo screen or a
bright green plant, has been designed to set off the visual appeal
of the food, which, to put it mildly, is spectacularly good. Chef
Kojima, who presides over the *sushi* bar, is a virtuoso with the
knife whose every dish is a tour de force. His colleagues, Mr.
Maeda and Mr. Sato, who are responsible for the *sashimi* and

*tempura,* respectively, are incomparable artists in their own right.

*Most Japanese appetizers are hardly more than tastes. If the two given here leave any trenchermen feeling somewhat hollow even after doing away with both of them, the seafood hotpot that follows should ameliorate any feelings of deprivation they may harbor.*

## SPINACH GOMA-AYE WITH SESAME SEEDS

5 large leaves of spinach with stems
1 tbsp. black or white sesame seeds

5 tbsp. *shoyu* sauce
2 tbsp. *sake*
½ tsp. sugar (optional)

Wash spinach thoroughly and cook in boiling water just until tender. Refresh in cold water, then press out as much moisture as possible while retaining contours of leaves. Cut into 1½″ squares and set aside. In a pan, stir sesame seeds over low heat until they start popping (2–3 minutes). Remove seeds from heat, spread on a flat surface, and crack them with the side of a cleaver or with the back of a heavy knife. In a small bowl, blend sesame seeds, *shoyu, sake,* and sugar. Carefully place spinach in another bowl, sprinkle sesame seed mixture over it, and toss lightly with chopsticks, taking care not to saturate spinach with sauce. Arrange spinach in small individual bowls and serve to 4.

## BEEF KAKUNI

½ lb. lean beef in 1″ cubes
water to cover meat
¾ cup *shoyu* sauce
2 tbsp. *sake*

2 tbsp. *mirin*
1 small piece fresh gingerroot, slivered

Place beef in a small pot and add water to cover. Bring to boil and cook meat through, skimming off any scum that rises to surface. Add all other ingredients and simmer over low heat until meat is tender. Serve meat with sauce in small individual bowls. Serves 4.

## SEAFOOD SUKIYAKI

*For this opulent dish, which should be cooked at table, you'll need an electric casserole, chafing dish, or similar contrivance. For a patio dinner, set a sturdy pot on a hibachi.*

2 live lobsters
8 1"-thick strips of filleted fish (see note)
8 clams (in shells)
8 stalks Chinese cabbage, cut in ¼" × 1½" strips
2 medium carrots, cut in thin 1" rectangles

8 *daikon* (white radish), peeled, cut in ¼" rounds, and parboiled
8 whole scallions, cut in 1½" lengths
4 mushrooms, sliced
10 cups *Dashi**
1 4" square *dashi kombu* (dried kelp)
salt and *shoyu* sauce to taste

*Note   Use firm-fleshed non-oily fish such as striped bass, red snapper, salmon, etc., and leave the skin on the fish.*

Split lobsters in half lengthwise with a cleaver or heavy knife. Handle carefully, so as not to lose *miso* (the green paste known in this country as tomalley). Discard gelatinous sacs from heads. Twist off claws and chop into serving pieces. Chop tail crosswise into 1" rounds. Cut fish into 1" cubes. Arrange lobster, fish, scrubbed clams, and vegetables attractively on a large serving platter.

In a medium-sized electric casserole or other pot suitable for table use, bring about 1 qt. *dashi,* with the *kombu* square, to boil and remove the *kombu.* Add lobster claws, legs, and heads (Watch that *miso!*), a few pieces of lobster tail, a few pieces of fish, and a few clams and skim off any foam that rises to surface. Add salt and *shoyu* sauce to taste (*shoyu* should darken broth moderately) and ladle out about ½ teacup of broth for each guest, to be sipped while seafoods cook.

As soon as clams open, allow guests to help themselves from the pot, ladling seafood and broth into individual bowls. Add more *dashi* and repeat procedure, reserving vegetables for the final go-round.

**Note**   *The pot should be watched carefully and replenished with* dashi *as it cooks down, to prevent excessive saltiness. Any* dashi *left over when fish and vegetables are consumed should be served with enough cooked rice to absorb the liquid.*

# The
# COACH
# HOUSE

*110 Waverly Place*

Restaurants, at least in this country, don't get much better than this. Housed in what was originally the carriage house of John Wanamaker, a nineteenth-century merchandising nabob, philanthropist, and member of Benjamin Harrison's cabinet, it's a warm, comfortable, uncommonly gracious operation with a long narrow dining room at street level and a second, more intimate dining area upstairs, in what was once the Wanamaker hayloft. Leon Lianides, a native of Corfu who opened the Greenwich Village landmark nearly thirty years ago, is a discerning art collector and has furnished his premises with the cream of his holdings, which range from early American folk art to contemporary abstractions. He is also a stickler for candor and simplicity, and the innate goodness of every dish prepared by his Cuban-born chef, Roul Santana, comes to the table undisguised by assertive sauces or culinary circumlocution of any kind. Seasonal ingredients of the highest quality are served as plainly as possible at the very peak of perfection, and such dishes as fresh spring asparagus, soft-shelled crabs *meunière,* and summer crab meat rolled in prosciutto are masterpieces of understated excellence. The black bean soup is legendary, the Kentucky spring lamb ambrosial, and even as prosaic a dish as chicken potpie takes on new dimensions at this incomparable establishment.

## FRESH SHRIMP MARINADE

20 medium shrimp
3 garlic cloves, crushed
1 large onion, sliced in fine
   rings
¾ cup light olive oil
1 tsp. sugar
½ cup wine vinegar

1½ cups tomato juice or white
   wine
½ tsp. dry mustard
2 tbsp. chopped parsley
2 tbsp. chopped fresh dill
salt and freshly ground pepper
   to taste

Cook shrimp in salted boiling water about 6 minutes, or until pink, and cool as quickly as possible under cold running water. Shell and devein shrimp. In a large ceramic or glass bowl combine shrimp and all other ingredients, mix well, and refrigerate overnight. Serve with marinade to 4.

# THE COACH HOUSE BLACK BEAN SOUP

3 lbs. beef bones
¾ lb. beef shin
3 lbs. ham shank (including
   bone and rind), cut up
3 cloves
¾ tsp. black peppercorns
¼ tsp. celery seed
2½ cups dried black beans
1 cup chopped onion

½ cup chopped celery
1 tsp. chopped garlic
¼ cup Sherry
1 tsp. salt
½ tsp. pepper
2 hard-boiled eggs, chopped
   fine
lemon slices dipped in chopped
   parsley

Make stock a day before use. In a large pot, place beef bones, beef shin, ham shank, 15 cups water, cloves, peppercorns, and celery seed. Bring to boil, reduce heat, and simmer, half-covered, 8–10 hours. Strain and reserve meats for other uses. Refrigerate stock. Soak beans in 10 cups water overnight in refrigerator. Next day, remove congealed fat from top of stock, reserving 2 tbsp. In a large pan, cook onion and celery in reserved fat until soft. Add drained beans, 2 cups water, 7 cups stock (if less stock has been yielded, add as much water as needed), and garlic. Simmer uncovered 2½ hours, stirring occasionally and adding water as needed to cover beans. Purée mixture coarsely with strainer, food mill, or blender. Heat, adding Sherry and salt and pepper to taste. Add chopped eggs to hot soup, mixing lightly. Top each serving with a thin round of lemon dipped in chopped parsley. Serves 10–12.

# SEAFOOD À LA MEDITERRANÉE

12 large shrimp
12 cherrystone clams,
   unopened
3 ½-lb. lobster tails
½ cup olive oil
4 garlic cloves, finely minced
¾ cup dry white wine
   (preferably Chablis)

2 cups canned plum tomatoes,
   drained
2 bay leaves
½ tsp. dried orégano
salt and pepper to taste
2 tbsp. finely chopped parsley

Without removing shells from shrimp, cut a slit down the center of each back with a sharp knife or scissors. Devein, wash, and dry shrimp. Scrub and dry clams. Wash and dry lobster tails and cut them, unshelled, into 1″ rounds. In a large deep skillet, heat olive oil, add garlic, and sauté over low heat 1 minute, until wilted but not brown. Add seafoods and cook 3 minutes, while wine heats in a separate pan. Pour wine over seafoods, increase heat, and simmer briskly 3 minutes. Stir in tomatoes and add bay leaves, orégano, and salt and pepper to taste. Reduce heat to moderate, cover pan, and continue cooking 10–12 minutes, or until clams open. Remove bay leaves, transfer contents of skillet to a heated serving dish, and sprinkle with parsley. Serve over steamed rice to 4.

## DAQUOISE

| | |
|---|---|
| 8 egg whites | $\frac{1}{2}$ lb. toasted blanched almonds, |
| 1 tsp. vanilla extract | finely ground |
| 1 cup + 3 tbsp. sugar | 1 tbsp. cornstarch |
| $\frac{1}{8}$ tsp. cream of tartar | confectioners' sugar |
| 1 pinch salt | |

Make a meringue mixture by beating egg whites until they form moist peaks, while gradually adding vanilla, 1 cup + 1 tbsp. sugar, cream of tartar, and salt. Mix ground almonds with remaining sugar, sieve cornstarch over this mixture, and lightly stir ingredients together. With a rubber spatula, thoroughly fold almond mixture into meringue. On a large sheet of baker's parchment, mark three 10″ circles. Cut out paper circles and place on a cookie sheet (use 2 smaller sheets if your oven won't accommodate 1 large enough). Fit a pastry bag with a plain No. 5 tube, fill with meringue mixture, and working outward from their centers cover each paper round with concentric circles of the meringue mixture. Bake meringues in a preheated oven at 250°F. for about 45 minutes, or until firm, dry, and sand-brown.

Cool on cake racks and remove paper. Spread Mocha Buttercream (recipe below) over each round of meringue, stack rounds one atop another, and spread perimeter with remaining buttercream. Sieve confectioners' sugar over top and refrigerate for 2 hours before serving. Serves 12.

### Mocha Buttercream

$\frac{2}{3}$ cup sugar
$\frac{1}{4}$ cup water
1 cup butter

2 tbsp. powdered instant coffee
6 egg yolks

In a heavy saucepan, boil together sugar and water until a candy thermometer registers 234°F., or the syrup spins a thin thread. In a bowl, cream butter with powdered coffee and keep cool. Beat egg yolks until thickened and to the egg yolks add the hot syrup in a continuous thin stream, beating constantly. When all syrup is incorporated, add creamed butter a little at a time and blend thoroughly. Refrigerate for 45 minutes before using.

*1458 First Avenue*

Don't be put off by an altogether unprepossessing storefront exterior. Owned and operated by Ramón San Martin (page 237), the restaurant combines traditional Spanish and Bauhaus design to uncommonly handsome effect. The sunken dining room, with its mirrored, plant-festooned central skylight and gleaming brass piping, is lapidary in its perfection and the food—mostly but not exclusively Spanish—is stylishly prepared and presented. Chef José Barcena's rib of beef with marrow sauce, Alaska king crab (prepared as the Galicians prepare their vaunted *xangurro*), and *zarzuela de mariscos* are all first-rate, but the restaurant's *angulas* are its real claim to greatness. These minute infant eels, jet-shipped fresh from Spain, are boiled in oil with sliced garlic and crumbled chili pepper, and eaten with a wooden fork from an earthenware casserole. Ambrosial.

*Of the world's major cuisines, the Spanish is least successfully exported. Alaska king crab is a pale substitute for the majestic* xangurro *of Galicia, but, taken on its own terms, Cafe San Martin's "Xangurro" is excellent. Prosciutto and melon would be an appropriate starter, particularly if you can convince yourself that the prosciutto is Serrano ham, which, alas, is unavailable in this country.*

### "XANGURRO"

| | | |
|---|---|---|
| 1 carrot | | 1 cup peeled, seeded, chopped, |
| 2 garlic cloves | chopped | and drained tomato |
| 2 shallots | fine | 2 cups Fish Stock* |
| 1 medium onion | | 1 lb. Alaska king crab meat, |
| 1 pinch crumbled hot red | | chopped fine |
| pepper | | $\frac{1}{2}$ cup heavy cream |
| 2 tbsp. olive oil | | salt and pepper to taste |
| 1 lobster head, chopped fine | | 1 tbsp. minced parsley |
| and forced through a sieve | | 4 large scallop shells |
| 2 tbsp. brandy | | 1 tbsp. bread crumbs |
| | | 1 tsp. melted butter |

Sauté carrot, garlic, shallots, onion, and red pepper in olive oil until lightly browned. Add lobster head (cleaned of sac), brandy, tomatoes, and fish stock. Simmer gently for 30 minutes, strain, and discard solids. In a saucepan, combine strained sauce with crab meat and cream. Cook over low heat, stirring, for about 10 minutes, or until mixture takes on a heavy consistency. Season with salt and pepper and stir in a little minced parsley. Divide mixture into 4 parts and fill a large scallop shell with each portion. Sprinkle with bread crumbs and parsley and drizzle tops with melted butter. Run shells under a hot broiler just long enough to glaze tops and serve immediately to 4.

## NARANJAS ALBUFERA

1 cup sugar
1 strip orange zest
1 strip lemon zest
4 tsp. butter
juice of 4 oranges
juice of 1 lemon

2 tbsp. Grand Marnier
2 tbsp. brandy
1 tbsp. orange zest, cut in
    julienne strips
4 large navel oranges

In a saucepan, caramelize the sugar with the 2 citrus zests by cooking over medium heat. Discard zests. Add butter and fruit juices, Grand Marnier, brandy, and julienne strips of orange peel and simmer until syrupy. Meanwhile, peel oranges, removing all traces of white membrane. Slice oranges and place in serving dish. When syrup is ready, pour it over orange slices, and chill well. Serves 4.

THE "*21*" CLUB

*21 West 52nd Street*

There is no viand so obscure, no wine so rare, no amenity so improbable that it can't be had, for a price, in this legendary rumpus room of the international elite. An institution, a landmark, a fourth-dimension ego trip, "21" is no more accessible to the "wrong" people today than it was when Jack Kriendler and Charlie Berns operated it, more or less clandestinely, as a Volstead-era speakeasy. (As one observer has noted,

"the simple act of being admitted seem[s] an enviable achieve-
ment.") A mind-boggling logistical operation requiring a staff
of three hundred, this is the quintessence and apotheosis of the
New York restaurant, and no amount of physical description
can convey anything of the almost palpable aura of *savoir faire*
that makes it unique among the restaurants of the world.

## MUSHROOMS A LA DAUM

2 cups sliced mushrooms
1 cup minced onion
1 cup Danish ham and/or
  cooked tongue, cut in
  julienne strips
salt and freshly ground pepper
  to taste

8 tbsp. (½ cup) sweet butter
¼ cup Brown Sauce*
1 tbsp. chopped parsley

In a mixing bowl, combine mushrooms, onion, meat, and
seasonings. Melt butter in a skillet and sauté mushroom mixture
over medium flame until mushrooms and onion are soft (about
5 minutes). Heat for 1 more minute, stirring in brown sauce.
Serve over toast or artichoke bottoms and garnish with parsley.
Serves 4.

## ESCALOPES DE VEAU CHARLEROI

8 tbsp. sweet butter
2 medium onions, chopped
1 doz. medium mushrooms,
  chopped
2 bay leaves
1 pinch rosemary
1 cup raw long-grain rice
3 cups water
salt and freshly ground pepper
  to taste

2 egg yolks, beaten
2 cups unsweetened heavy
  cream, whipped
½ cup grated Parmesan cheese
8 veal scallops, pounded (about
  3½″ diameter)
½ cup flour
½ cup Madeira
1 cup Brown Sauce*

Preheat oven to 350°F. In a deep flameproof casserole, melt 4 tbsp. of the butter and, over a low flame, sauté onions and mushrooms until soft but not brown. Add bay leaves and rosemary and cook another 15 minutes, keeping flame very low. Stirring constantly, add rice and cook briefly until coated with butter. Slowly stir in the water and season with salt and pepper. Bring mixture to boil, cover the casserole, and bake in oven about 25 minutes, or until rice is tender. After mixture has cooled, purée it in a food mill. Add egg yolks to purée, stirring well. Carefully fold in whipped cream and half the cheese. Put mixture in a pastry bag and set aside.

Lightly dredge the veal scallops in flour, shaking to remove excess. In a large skillet, melt the remaining butter and brown veal on both sides over medium flame, sautéing about 10 minutes in all. Arrange veal on an ovenproof serving dish and preheat broiler. Into the skillet in which veal was browned, pour the Madeira, stirring well. Boil over high flame for a few minutes, until liquids are reduced by about half. Mixing thoroughly with a whisk, slowly add brown sauce and simmer until warmed through. Set aside.

Squeeze mixture in pastry bag over veal to make a lattice pattern on each piece, then sprinkle veal with remaining cheese. Place veal under broiler until tops are golden brown. Pour Madeira sauce onto the serving dish around veal, or serve separately. Serves 4.

## CAFÉ DIABLE

*After all the foregoing richness, try this zingy coffee in lieu of dessert.*

| | | |
|---|---|---|
| peel of 1 lemon | removed in a | 2 cinnamon sticks |
| peel of 1 orange | single strip | 2 tbsp. sugar |
| 24 cloves | | 2 oz. brandy |
| | | 3 8-oz. cups espresso coffee |
| | | 2 oz. Kirschwasser |

Stud lemon and orange peels with cloves and place in a lined copper bowl with the cinnamon, sugar, and brandy. Flame mixture with a match, allow brandy to burn for a moment or two, and add hot espresso. Remove peels and cinnamon, add Kirschwasser, and serve immediately. Serves 4 with 6-oz. cups, 8 as demitasse.

# Dézaley

*54 East 58th Street*

If less really *is* more, this is a lot of restaurant. The premises are narrow, the acoustics are imperfect, and the setting is almost Spartan in its simplicity: unadorned buff-colored walls, dark wooden banquettes, a few mirrors—and that's about it. On the other hand, the service is congenial, the Swiss menu is imaginative, and the cooking is consistently superior. Moreover, there's a fine selection of unjustly neglected Swiss wines.

*Originated "somewhere between French-speaking Switzerland and New York City" by co-owners Hans Egg and Robert Keller, this cold fruit soup will hit the spot nicely on a hot summer evening.*

## SOUPE AUX ABRICOTS FROID

5 oz. dried apricots
¼ cinnamon stick
1 cup water
2 7-oz. bottles club soda

1 tbsp. lemon juice
confectioners' sugar to taste
2 tbsp. apricot brandy
4 mint leaves

In a covered saucepan, simmer apricots and cinnamon in the water for 15 minutes. Refrigerate until lukewarm, then remove cinnamon. Put apricots (which will have absorbed most of the cooking water) into a blender with 1 bottle soda and blend until smooth. Add more soda to achieve consistency desired, along with lemon juice and sugar to taste. Add apricot brandy, mix thoroughly, and refrigerate for several hours. Serve, garnished with mint leaves, to 4–6.

## MIROTON DE BOEUF

½ lb. sauerkraut
4 tbsp. vegetable oil
2 lbs. eye round of beef
salt and pepper to taste
2 tbsp. tomato paste
3 medium onions, sliced

1 tsp. paprika
1 garlic clove, crushed
1½ tbsp. flour
2 cups red wine
3 cups Beef Stock*
1 cup grated Swiss cheese

Soak sauerkraut in cold water for ½ hour before using. Heat oil in a large casserole and brown beef on all sides over high heat. Add salt, pepper, tomato paste, onions, paprika, and garlic, cover, and simmer 30 minutes. Sprinkle with flour and mix well. Add wine, beef stock, and drained sauerkraut. Cover and simmer 1½ hours, or until beef is tender. Remove beef, slice thinly, and place appropriate portions on individual oven-proof serving dishes. Cover beef with sauerkraut, sprinkle with cheese, and leave under hot broiler until cheese melts. Serve with parsleyed potatoes or buttered noodles. Serves 6.

## MOUSSE D'HIVER

2  3-oz. bars Toblerone white
   chocolate
⅓ cup milk

1  dash lemon juice
2  egg whites
1  cup heavy cream

In top of double boiler, break chocolate into small pieces and add milk. Melt slowly over hot water, stirring occasionally with a wooden spoon until smooth, and cool to room temperature. In a large bowl, beat lemon juice and egg whites until mixture stiffens. Using a rubber spatula, gently fold cooled chocolate into egg white mixture. Whip cream until it forms peaks and fold into chocolate mixture. Spoon into serving glasses and refrigerate at least 2 hours. Garnish as desired, with whipped cream, candied cherry halves, fan-shaped cookies, or the like. Serves 4.

## POTAGE BALOISE

*If guests have lingered late on a cold winter's evening, serve this specialty of Basel before sending them home. If there's any left over, try it next morning as a hangover remedy.*

4½ oz. flour
½ small onion, chopped fine
1  cup dry red wine
2⅔ cups Beef Stock*
2  cups cold water

1  bay leaf
salt and pepper to taste
grated Emmenthal cheese to
   taste

Place flour in a heavy pot and brown, stirring constantly, just until golden. In a separate pot, add chopped onion to wine and cook over high heat until wine is reduced by half. Add stock, bring to boil, and remove from heat. Mix cold water with browned flour until smooth and add to stock, together with bay leaf. Simmer, uncovered, 45 minutes. Remove bay leaf, add salt and pepper to taste, and top with freshly grated cheese. Serve in heavy mugs, with French bread and butter, to 4–6.

### 339 East 75th Street

In the years before the Communist take-over of Czechoslovakia, Jaroslav Vašata owned the largest restaurant in Middle Europe. Situated on Prague's Vaclavske Nemesti, it seated four thousand and was staffed by a crew of six hundred. Vašata's present restaurant, which has been in operation since 1952, is a somewhat more modest enterprise, but the caliber of the food is exceptionally high, particularly during the game season, when wild goose, duck, and venison are treated with all the respect they deserve. The atmosphere is unremarkable, but pleasant, bright, and tidy. Golden Zubrovka vodka, chilled to the point where it takes the breath away, makes a fine prelude to dinner here.

## TRIPE SOUP

1 lb. beef tripe
1 small onion, chopped
3 oz. butter or rendered pork fat
2½ oz. flour
1 tbsp. sweet paprika
1½ qts. Beef Stock*

1 pt. broth from smoked pork, ham, or tongue
salt and freshly ground pepper to taste
2 garlic cloves, crushed
2 tsp. dried marjoram

Cut tripe into ¼″ × 1½″ strips. Cover with water, bring to a simmer, and cook about 90 minutes, until soft. Drain, rinse under cold water, and set aside. In a heavy soup pot, sauté onion in butter or fat until golden. Add flour and paprika and cook over low heat 5 minutes, stirring constantly and taking care not to burn paprika. Pour heated beef and smoked meat stocks over mixture, stir well, and cook slowly, stirring often, for ½ hour, or until soup is creamy. (If too thick, dilute with more stock.) Add tripe and cook another 5 minutes, seasoning with pepper, garlic, and marjoram. Add salt to taste and serve very hot. Serves 8–10.

## BOILED BEEF WITH DILL SAUCE

4 lbs. rump or chuck pot roast (1 piece)
1 onion
1 carrot

1 stalk celery
1 parsley root
2 peppercorns

Wash meat and place in boiling salted water to cover generously. When water returns to boil, skim off scum and add vegetables and peppercorns. Cover and simmer until meat is tender (about 2 hours). Remove meat, drain, and keep warm. Strain cooking stock and reserve. Slice beef about ⅜″ thick and serve with Dill Sauce and Bread Dumplings (recipes below). Serves 10 or more.

### Dill Sauce

1½ qts. reserved stock

2 tbsp. flour  ⎫
½ cup cold water  ⎬ blended
 ⎭

1 tbsp. butter

1 tsp. sugar

1 cup sour cream  ⎫
½ cup evaporated  ⎬ blended
  milk  ⎭

juice of ½ lemon
½ cup chopped fresh dill
sugar and salt to taste

Bring stock to boil. Add flour mixture and beat well with a wire whisk. Add butter and 1 tsp. sugar and simmer at least ½ hour, stirring frequently. (If sauce doesn't thicken substantially after a few minutes, add more flour and water mixture, a bit at a time, until consistency of thick pancake batter is reached. If too thick, dilute with stock.) Before serving, add blended sour cream and evaporated milk, lemon juice, dill, salt, and sugar to taste. Serve warm.

### Bread Dumplings

1 lb. + 2 oz. flour
2 tsp. salt
½ pt. milk

¼ pt. cold water
4 eggs
1 lb. stale white bread, diced

Sift flour into a large mixing bowl and add salt. In another bowl, beat milk, water, and eggs together. Pour mixture slowly into flour while stirring with a wooden spoon. Beat dough until very smooth and fairly thick. Lightly stir in cubed bread and let stand ½ hour. Bring a large pot of water to boil and add salt. Divide dough into 2 or more parts, depending on size of pot, shape into loaves the diameter of Italian bread, and slip the loaves into the boiling water. Boil about 30 minutes, turning once with a wooden spoon. Cut drained dumplings into $\frac{1}{2}''$ slices with a sharp thin knife and serve hot.

*Note  Dumplings can be made ahead of time and steamed before serving.*

## QUICK JAM ROLL

5 tbsp. sugar

5 egg whites, beaten very stiff

5 tbsp. flour

4 egg yolks, beaten

1 small jar apricot jam mixed with 1 tbsp. rum

Beat 3 tbsp. of the sugar into the egg whites. Mix remaining sugar with flour and alternately fold this mixture and egg yolks into egg white mixture, adding a little at a time. Grease and flour a shallow rectangular pan or cookie sheet. Pour in batter, smooth surface with a rubber spatula, and bake in a preheated 450°F. oven about 5 minutes, or until cake is golden on top. Remove from pan with a broad metal spatula and place on sheet of wax paper. Spread with jam, roll up cake and, when cool, sprinkle with vanilla-flavored sugar. Serves 4–6.

# Nippon

*145 East 52nd Street*

Now a decade and a half old, this was the city's first uncompromisingly authentic Japanese restaurant and, with challengers to its supremacy proliferating apace, remains one of the best. The reasons aren't hard to find: Nobuyoshi Kuraoka, the owner, is the son of one of Japan's most respected restaurateurs, and Eijiro Tanaka, who supervises the kitchen, was personal chef to a Japanese prime minister before Kuraoka lured him to New

York. Everything on the premises, from structural materials down to the smallest serving utensil, was tailor-made in Japan for the establishment's exclusive use, and, while the finer points of the rather austere, Zen-inspired décor may be lost on most Americans, it requires nothing more than the normal complement of taste buds to appreciate the superiority of the food.

## SHRIMP TATSUTA-AGE

3 oz. *sake*
2 oz. soy sauce
1½ lbs. "25–30" shrimp (see note)

cornstarch for dredging
sesame or vegetable oil for frying

*Note  The designation "25–30" refers to the number of shrimp per pound.*

Blend *sake* and soy sauce in a small bowl. Shell and devein shrimp, dip them in sauce, and dredge them individually in cornstarch. Fill a large skillet with oil to about $\frac{7}{10}$ of its depth, heat until moderately hot, and drop in shrimp a few at a time, taking care not to let them touch one another. Fry 1–2 minutes, or until shrimp rise to surface. Remove with skimmer or slotted spoon and drain briefly on paper towels. Serve piping hot to 4.

## BATTER-FRIED PORK CUTLETS

1¼ lbs. pork fillet
flour for dredging
2 eggs, beaten
bread crumbs for dredging
vegetable oil for deep frying

8 leaves lettuce, shredded
4 slices lemon
½ tsp. Chinese mustard ⎫
⅓ cup *Tonkatsu* sauce ⎬ blended
                              ⎭

Cut pork fillet in slices ¼" thick. Successively dredge slices in flour, coat with beaten egg, and dredge in bread crumbs. Heat oil to 330°F. in a deep pan or fryer. Fry cutlets until well browned, drain on paper towels, and arrange on beds of shredded lettuce. Garnish with lemon slices and serve with blended dipping sauce on side. Serves 4–6.

# BEEF SHABU-SHABU

*Just as "hubba, hubba" was used by World War II G.I.'s to simulate animated conversation, "shabu-shabu" is supposed to be an onomato-poetic rendering of the sound of a boiling hot-pot. I've never heard boiling water say anything like "shabu-shabu," but water may boil with a different accent in Japan.*

four 2" × 4" pieces *kombu* (dried kelp), washed thoroughly in cold water
4 oz. *shirataki* (yam noodles), cooked and drained
10 oz. *udon* noodles, cooked and drained
1½ lbs. lean prime rib of beef, sliced very thin
1 lb. Chinese cabbage, cut in 1½" lengths

4 oz. watercress
1 medium onion, cut in ¼" slices
4 scallions, cut in 1½" lengths
4 mushrooms, cut in ⅛" slices
½ lb. fresh bean curd, cut in 1" cubes
*Gomadare* Sauce (recipe below)
*Ponzu* Sauce (recipe below)

**Gomadare Sauce** (all ingredients blended)

2 oz. sesame seed
2 oz. ground walnuts
2 tsp. *mirin*

3 oz. soy sauce
1 tsp. *sake*

**Ponzu Sauce** (all ingredients blended)

2 oz. soy sauce
2 oz. vinegar

juice of ¼ lemon

Fill a deep serving pot or casserole to ⅔ its capacity with water, add *kombu,* and bring to boil. Arrange noodles and all raw ingredients attractively on a large serving platter and bring to table. Transfer serving pot to table and keep as hot as possible over a Sterno heater or similar device, or, if dining outdoors, a well-stoked *hibachi.* Bring the two dipping sauces to table in individual serving dishes, furnish your guests with chopsticks, and, from here on in, they're on their own. The procedure is to pick up with the chopsticks whatever morsel takes one's fancy, swirl it in the boiling liquid until lightly cooked, and then dip it into the sauce of one's choice. Serves 4–6.

# OYSTER
## BAR·RESTAURANT
*Grand Central Station (lower level)*

For a major seaport situated a hundred miles or so from some of the world's richest fishing grounds, New York is pathetically underrepresented in the seafood department. Sad to say, the city's first-rate fish houses can be counted on the fins of one fluke, but the cavernous, tile-lined Oyster Bar remains a haven of refuge for fish fanciers in the midst of a veritable Sahara. The restaurant, which opened in 1913, in its heyday numbered

Diamond Jim Brady, Lillian Russell, Gentleman Jim Corbett, and Lillie Langtry among its habitués. (Diamond Jim always maintained he could distinguish a Wellfleet oyster from all others in a blind tasting, regularly put his money where his mouth was, always won his bets, and invariably left the ante— fifty dollars—as a tip for the waiter.) Over the years, as the single restaurant of note in the nation's greatest rail terminus, the Oyster Bar became famed from coast to coast for its shellfish stews and pan roasts. When it closed—the result of chaotic mismanagement—a few years ago, lamentations could be heard throughout the land. Reopened under the aegis of a restaurateur named Jerry Brody, it may be even better than ever today. The menu is exhaustive, the fish are luminously fresh, the desserts are absolutely outrageous.

## BAKED SHRIMP-STUFFED AVOCADO

2 large ripe avocados
2 tbsp. fresh lemon juice
1 tsp. salt
4 tbsp. ($\frac{1}{2}$ stick) butter
4 tbsp. flour
freshly ground white pepper to taste

1 cup light cream
$\frac{1}{4}$ cup thinly sliced celery, cooked
1 small pimiento, minced
$\frac{1}{2}$ lb. cooked shrimp, coarsely chopped
1 tbsp. cheddar cheese, grated

Preheat oven to 350°F. Halve and pit avocados, drizzle with lemon juice, and sprinkle with $\frac{1}{2}$ the salt. Melt butter in top of double boiler. Blend in flour, pepper, cream, and remaining salt and cook over boiling water, stirring constantly, until mixture thickens. Blend in celery, pimiento, and shrimp and fill avocado halves with mixture. Sprinkle with cheese (or, if you prefer, bread crumbs). Place avocados in a small baking dish and add $\frac{1}{2}''$ of water to dish. Bake 15 minutes and serve at once to 4.

# OYSTER STEW

*This recipe, for what is perhaps the best-known dish identified with a single restaurant in the United States, was a house secret for many years. It was made public when the Oyster Bar closed in 1974, presumably never to reopen.*

8 freshly shucked oysters
¼ cup oyster liquor
1 dash celery salt
1 tsp. Worcestershire sauce
1 oz. Sherry

1 cup half-and-half (milk and
    heavy cream)
2 tbsp. (¼ stick) butter
½ tsp. paprika

Bring water to boil in the lower half of a double boiler, leaving space for the top half to clear water. In the top half, place all ingredients except half-and-half, 1 tbsp. of the butter, and paprika; cook over boiling water, whisking constantly, for about 1 minute, until oysters just begin to curl at edges. Add half-and-half and continue to stir briskly until just on the point of boiling. Remove from heat at once, pour into a soup plate, and serve piping hot, topped with remaining butter and sprinkled with paprika. Serves 1.

## Variations

Shrimp (shelled and deveined) or shucked clams in the same quantity as oysters can be substituted, as can ¼ lb. fresh lobster meat, 10–12 bay scallops, or 14–15 freshly shucked mussels. I've found that a simple adaptation of the basic oyster stew produces a marvelous pasta sauce. To make it, substitute heavy cream for half-and-half and dry vermouth and a dash of cognac for Sherry and reduce liquids by ⅔ before adding oysters.

# SMELTS WITH CAPER SAUCE

⅓ cup flour
⅓ cup cornmeal
2 tsp. salt
1 pinch freshly ground black
    pepper
1 pinch paprika
2 lbs. smelts

½ cup light cream
1 cup corn oil
4 tbsp. (½ stick) butter
1 tsp. fresh lemon juice
1 tbsp. capers
1 tbsp. minced parsley

Thoroughly blend flour, cornmeal, salt, pepper, and paprika. Dip smelts in cream and roll in flour mixture until thoroughly coated. In a large heavy skillet, heat oil just until it sizzles when flicked with flour. Fry smelts 5 minutes on each side, or until nicely browned, turning with a slotted spoon. Meanwhile, melt butter in a small saucepan, add lemon juice, capers, and parsley, and blend. Remove smelts from oil with a slotted spoon and drain on paper towels. Arrange smelts on heated plates, pour sauce over them, and serve at once to 4.

## OYSTER BAR BISCUITS

6 cups flour      $\frac{1}{2}$ cup vegetable shortening
2 tbsp. baking powder      1 cup milk
1 tbsp. salt

Preheat oven to 375°F. In a large bowl, sift together flour, baking powder, and salt. Cut in shortening and mix until well blended. Add milk and knead until dough is soft and smooth. Roll out to $\frac{1}{2}''$ thickness on a lightly floured board and cut into $2\frac{1}{2}''$ circles with a floured cookie cutter. Cover a baking sheet with baker's parchment, place biscuits on it, and bake 15 minutes, or until golden brown. Yields about 20 biscuits.

## LEMON SHERBET

*Although the Oyster Bar is known and loved for its opulent pastries, this quick, light, and extremely refreshing sherbet would be my choice as the perfect conclusion to the foregoing meal.*

2 cups sugar      2 egg whites, beaten stiff
2 cups water      1 cup fresh lemon juice
1 pinch salt

In a small heavy saucepan, boil sugar, water, and salt 5 minutes. Pour mixture over egg whites in a thin stream, beating constantly. Stir in lemon juice, blending well. Pour into a container and leave in freezer about 1 hour, until partially frozen and slushy. Beat until smooth but not melted and return to freezer until firm enough to serve. Serves 4.

**Rusty's**

*1271 Third Avenue*

The Rusty in question is Rusty Staub, the formidable designated hitter for the Detroit Tigers and a chef of no mean accomplishment. His restaurant is small, tidy, and informal, with a decidedly eclectic bill of fare. Staub grew up in New Orleans and played three seasons of baseball in Montreal (where he was idolized as "Le Grand Orange"). Both experiences are reflected in the cuisine. Fish and shellfish get the big play here, with seafood gumbo, oysters Rockefeller, and shrimp à la Catalogne among the standout dishes, but the kitchen's veal and steaks shouldn't be overlooked either.

## RUSTY'S TORTELLINI

1 lb. chopped sirloin
¼ lb. butter
1 16-oz. can peeled tomatoes, crushed
salt, pepper, Tabasco, and Worcestershire sauce to taste
2 oz. white wine
1 tbsp. chopped garlic

⅔ lb. chicken livers, diced
½ lb. sliced mushrooms
1 tbsp. chopped parsley
1 tsp. thyme
1 tsp. orégano
1 chopped onion (optional)
1 lb. meat-filled *tortellini* (see note)

*Note* Tortellini (*ring-shaped pasta dumplings*) *are available at many Italian food shops. They can be made at home with a little manual dexterity, but a written description of the process, like a written description of the sex act, won't get the idea across satisfactorily.*

Sauté the beef in half the butter, separating it with a fork and browning it lightly. Add tomatoes, salt, pepper, Tabasco, Worcestershire, and wine, and simmer until liquids evaporate. In the remaining butter, sauté garlic until translucent. Add livers and mushrooms and sauté until they begin to take on color. Add remaining ingredients, except *tortellini,* and cook over moderate heat while *tortellini* cook in a separate pot of boiling salted water for 6–8 minutes, or until they have risen to the surface. Drain *tortellini,* pour sauce over it, and serve. Serves 6 as a starter, 4 as a main dish.

# STUFFED BREAST OF CHICKEN

4 whole chicken breasts,
  skinned and boned
salt and pepper to taste
¼ lb. garlic butter (see note)
4 slices moist cooked ham
4 slices Swiss cheese
4 slices Muenster cheese
flour for dredging

1 cup milk
2 eggs, beaten
bread crumbs for dredging
2 tbsp. cooking oil
4 tbsp. Bordelaise Sauce*
2 tsp. freshly grated Parmesan
  cheese
4 slices mozzarella cheese

*Note   For garlic butter, blanch 4 garlic cloves briefly in boiling water and then plunge into cold water. Dry, rub through a sieve, and knead well with ¼ lb. softened butter.*

Pound chicken breasts lightly between sheets of wax paper to flatten. Salt very lightly and pepper to taste. Center ¼ of the garlic butter on one side of each chicken breast. Successively layer same side of each breast with 1 slice each of ham, Swiss and Muenster cheese.

Preheat oven to 350°F. Fold unfilled sides of chicken breasts over filled sides and dredge in flour. Then dip them successively in milk and beaten egg, dredge in bread crumbs, and sauté in oil, turning, until crisp on both sides. Arrange in a baking pan and bake in oven for ½ hour. Pour 1 tbsp. bordelaise sauce over each portion and sprinkle with Parmesan cheese. Top each portion with a slice of mozzarella and leave under broiler until cheese melts and begins to brown. Serves 4.

# RUSTY'S BAKED APPLE

6 baking apples, cored
1 qt. maple syrup
3 oz. Sherry
3 oz. white wine
2 lemons, peeled, seeded, and
  crushed

1 cup orange juice
6–8 cinnamon sticks
2 oz. seedless raisins (optional)
2 oranges, peeled, seeded, and
  crushed

Combine all ingredients in a pot and let stand 8–12 hours. Bring pot to boil and turn off heat. Remove apples and arrange them in a deep-sided baking pan just large enough to accommodate them in a single layer. Pour syrup mixture over apples, place pan in a preheated 350°F. oven, and bake 15–20 minutes, until apples are soft. Remove cinnamon and serve apples individually in small bowls, with as much sauce as desired, to 6.

# Lüchow's

*110–112 East 14th Street*

Old August Lüchow (page 19), who drew his last seidel of Würzburger in the 1930s, would never recognize his once-fashionable neighborhood today, but his landmark restaurant is still much as he left it. The tall cast-iron scale on which Jim Brady and Lillian Russell kept track of their tonnage still stands in the vestibule, the Rhine Maidens still cavort on the walls of the Nibelungen Room, and the oompah band—its members a bit long in the tooth but still short in the pants—carries on as in days of yore. Life may or may not be a cabaret, but at Lüchow's it's a perpetual festival, be the excuse of the moment Bock beer, May wine, the Resurrection, the onset of summer, *Oktober,* Christmas, geese, or the arrival of the venison season. The cuisine is robust; the portions, enormous; the atmosphere, *gemütlich*; the history, palpable.

## PFIFFERLINGSALAT

| | |
|---|---|
| 1 lb. small button mushrooms | ½ tsp. chopped fresh thyme (or |
| 1 tbsp. salt | ½ tsp. dried thyme, crumbled) |
| 1 medium onion, chopped fine | 2 cups dry white wine |
| 1 garlic clove | 2 cups cider vinegar |
| ¼ cup chopped parsley | ½ cup olive oil |
| 2 bay leaves | juice of ½ lemon |
| 4 peppercorns, coarsely ground | |

Wash mushrooms thoroughly in cold water containing 1 tbsp. salt and drain. Blend all other ingredients and pour over mushrooms in an enameled saucepan. Bring to boil, reduce to simmer, and cook 8–10 minutes, or until mushrooms are tender. Let the mixture cool. Discard garlic and bay leaves. Keep covered in refrigerator before using. Serves 6.

## ST. HUBERTUS (OR WILDBRET) SUPPE

*A truly regal soup for the hunting season.*

| | |
|---|---|
| 1 shoulder of venison, boned | 2 onions, diced |
| salt and pepper to taste | 2 leeks, diced |
| flour for dredging | 2 sprigs parsley |
| 2 tbsp. butter | ½ tsp. dried thyme |
| 1 partridge, boned | 1 bay leaf |
| ¼ cup sausage meat | 2 cups water |
| 2 slices lean bacon | 12–18 toast triangles |
| 4 carrots, diced | 2½ cups Beef Stock* |

Cut venison in large cubes, season with salt, and dredge in flour. In a soup kettle or flameproof casserole, brown meat on all sides in butter. Add water to cover and cook 50 minutes over low heat. While venison cooks, rinse partridge and fill with sausage meat. Close openings tightly and skewer them with toothpicks.

Cut bacon in pieces and sauté gently in skillet until fat is rendered. Add partridge and vegetables and sauté over low heat, turning, until golden and tender. Add herbs and 2 cups water, cover, and simmer 10 minutes. Add contents of skillet to venison kettle, cover, and allow to boil gently 25 minutes. Skim surface, lower heat, and simmer 2 hours. Transfer venison cubes to a warm soup tureen and keep hot. Remove partridge from soup and stuffing from partridge. Chop or grind bird and mix with sausage stuffing, seasoning to taste. Spread mixture on toast triangles to be served with soup. Strain soup, add beef stock as needed, reheat, and add to meat in tureen. Serves 6.

## ROAST WATERTOWN GOOSE
## WITH STEWED APPLES

| | |
|---|---|
| 1 fattened young goose (about 12 lbs.) | 6 cups water |
| | 6 peppercorns |
| salt to taste | ¼ lb. butter |
| ½ onion, sliced | 2 tbsp. flour |

Have butcher remove wings from goose and reserve, with neck, giblets, liver, etc., for other uses. Wash goose inside and out, cover with cold water, and soak 15 minutes. Meanwhile preheat oven to 325°F. Drain goose, pat dry, and rub with salt inside and out. Place goose in baking pan with sliced onion and add 4 cups water and peppercorns. Roast goose 15–20 minutes per pound, basting frequently once water has evaporated. When done, transfer goose to a warm platter. Place roasting pan on range top, stir flour into rendered fat, and add 2 cups water. Stir and bring to boil. Continue boiling 2–3 minutes, until gravy is smooth and slightly thickened. Serve goose with gravy and Stewed Apples to 6.

*Stewed Apples*

2 lbs. apples, peeled and cored    ½ cup white wine
2 tbsp. butter    1 small piece lemon peel
½ cup sugar    1 tbsp. lemon juice
½ cup water

Cut apples in thick slices, sauté 2–3 minutes in butter over moderate heat, and sprinkle with the sugar. Add all other ingredients, cover, and cook slowly until tender. Serves 6.

## RASPBERRY BAVARIAN CREAM

1 10-oz. pkg. frozen raspberries    3–6 tbsp. sugar (to taste)
juice of 1 lemon    2 egg yolks
2 tbsp. gelatin    1¼ cups heavy cream
¼ cup milk    1 cup crushed ice

Thaw raspberries in a bowl with lemon juice. When thawed, drain ½ the accumulated juices into a saucepan and bring just to simmer. Pour hot juice into blender container, add gelatin and milk, and blend 1 minute at high speed. Add sugar, raspberries, and egg yolks and blend 5 seconds at high speed. Add cream and ice and blend until smooth. Pour into a mold and chill until set. Unmold and serve to 4–6.

# nirvana
## 30 Central Park South

A passage to India and a room with a view. The passage, as it turns out, is accomplished by means of an express elevator. The room is a wide-windowed penthouse dining alcove tented over with a colorful *shamiana,* or Hindu bridal canopy, and the view is a magnificent panoramic sweep that takes in all of Central Park and its environs. The restaurant's owner, Shamsher Wadud, who came to this country from Dacca, has combined what appears to be the contents of a sizable bazaar to create a shadowy, many-splendored cocoon swathed in rich appliqués and bedecked with all manner of ornamentation. A redolence of spices, incense, and roses fills the air, sitar music drones in the background, the atmosphere is romantic as pale hands beside the Shalimar, and the food—served forth in glittering crystal tureens—is excellent.

## SINGARA

*These vegetable turnovers can be made well in advance, frozen or refrigerated and reheated before serving.*

### Pastry

½ tsp. salt
3 tbsp. *Ghee**
1½ cups flour

½ cup water
vegetable oil for deep frying

In a mixing bowl, add salt and *ghee* to flour. Add water 1 tbsp. at a time, mixing, until a soft dough forms. Knead until smooth. Divide dough evenly into 18–22 portions. Roll between palms to form balls. Place dough balls on a large platter, cover with plastic wrap, and leave 30 minutes in a warm place. On a lightly floured board, roll dough balls out, forming thin circles about 3½″ in diameter. Cut circles in half and form halves into cones, moistening edges with water to seal. Hold cones in left hand and fill with 1 tbsp. Vegetable Filling (recipe below). Moisten edges of top of cone and seal carefully to form a triangle. Repeat until all cones are filled and sealed. Heat oil to 365°F. and deep-fry until crisp and golden brown. Serve hot with Tamarind Chutney (recipe below). Serve 3 per portion as an hors d'oeuvre.

### Vegetable Filling

¼ cup *Ghee**
1 cup vegetable oil
1 pinch cumin seed
1½ tsp. peeled and minced
    gingerroot
2 green chilies, seeded and
    chopped (optional)
¾ lb. fresh peas
1 medium potato, cut in small
    cubes
½ tsp. cayenne pepper
¼ tsp. turmeric

1 pinch sugar
½ tsp. salt
2½ tbsp. seedless raisins
¾ tsp. roasted ground coriander
    seed
1¼ tsp. roasted ground cumin
⅓ cup chopped blanched
    peanuts
⅘ tbsp. chopped fresh coconut
2½ tbsp. chopped fresh
    coriander leaves

Heat *ghee* and oil in a large skillet. Add cumin seeds, ginger, chilies, and peas and sauté 1 minute. Add potato, cayenne, turmeric, sugar, and salt and continue to cook for a few minutes over medium heat. Add raisins, cover, and simmer 8–10 minutes, until vegetables are tender. Remove cover and cook over low heat until all moisture is absorbed. Add ground roasted coriander and cumin. Stir in peanuts, coconut, and coriander leaves. Remove from heat and cool before filling pastry cones.

### Tamarind Chutney

4 oz. tamarind
1½–2 cups water
1¼ tbsp. peeled and finely
    minced gingerroot
⅔ tbsp. chopped coriander
    leaves

1¼ tsp. ground roasted cumin
½ tsp. cayenne pepper
2½ tbsp. lemon juice
½ cup brown sugar
¼ tsp. salt

Soak tamarind in warm water until soft, then drain. Combine all ingredients in blender container and blend until creamy. Refrigerate until ready to serve.

# PIAZI

*Another hot appetizer that can be served in combination with the foregoing* Singara, *this, too, can be accompanied by* Tamarind Chutney.

1 cup *besan* (chick-pea flour)
½ cup rice flour
½ tsp. baking powder
1 pinch cumin seed
1 pinch paprika
1 pinch turmeric
1 pinch sugar

½ tsp. crushed dried red chili
½ tsp. salt
1 cup water
1 tbsp. vegetable oil
8 large onions, cut in long strips
vegetable oil for deep frying

In a bowl, combine *besan,* rice flour, baking powder, cumin seed, paprika, turmeric, sugar, chili, and salt. Add enough water to make a smooth paste. Add 1 tbsp. oil and beat for 2 minutes. Mix onions in resultant batter. Heat oil to 375°F. With tongs or fork, drop 2" tangles of batter-coated onion in hot oil in batches of 4–5 pieces, taking care to keep tangles separated. Fry 5–6 minutes until golden brown on all sides and drain on paper towels. Serve hot. Servings: indeterminate, depending on size of meal. Caution: They're addictive.

# BHUNA FISH

¼ cup chopped onion
¼ tsp. turmeric
¼ tsp. cayenne pepper
¼ tsp. *garam masala* (see note)
1½ tsp. salt
1¼ tbsp. lemon juice
1½ lb. carp, whole and boned or cut into fillets (see note)
1 egg, lightly beaten
1½ cups bread crumbs

¼ cup vegetable oil
2 tbsp. *Ghee**
4 cardamoms, crushed
1 green chili, seeded
1 bay leaf
1 medium onion, thinly sliced
½ cup sour cream

*Note* Garam masala *is a combination of spices that can be found in any Indian specialty shop. If necessary, haddock or trout can be substituted for carp.*

Sauté onion in a little oil until soft and combine in a bowl with turmeric, cayenne, *garam masala,* salt, and lemon juice. Add fish and coat well with mixture. Cover and set aside for 1 hour. (If using whole fish, slit lengthwise on both sides before marinating.) Dip fish in beaten egg and dredge in bread crumbs. Heat remaining oil in a large skillet, add fish, and fry golden brown on all sides. Set fish aside on paper towels to drain. In a second skillet, heat *ghee,* add cardamoms, chili, bay leaf, and onion and sauté 2 minutes. Add fish marinade and cook gently until *garam masala* is absorbed. Add sour cream and stir. Return fish to sauce, cover and simmer gently for 5 minutes. Serve hot to 4–6.

## RAITA

*An immensely soothing between-course salad.*

1½ cups yogurt
¼ tsp. cayenne pepper
¼ tsp. paprika (optional)
½ tsp. salt
⅓ tsp. ground roasted cumin
1–2 green chilies, seeded and chopped (optional)

2½ tbsp. chopped coriander leaves
1 large cucumber, peeled, seeded, and finely chopped

Combine all ingredients except cucumber. Stir, blend well, and add cucumber to mixture. Chill and serve in a crystal bowl. Serves 4–6.

## KHEER

*This is an extremely seductive version of that usually humdrum old favorite, rice pudding.*

5 tbsp. *basmati* or long-grain rice
½ cup water
2 qts. milk

2½ tbsp. seedless raisins
1 pinch saffron, soaked in 1 tsp. milk

rose essence or rose water to
taste
1 qt. half-and-half (milk and
heavy cream)

1 cup sugar
$\frac{1}{4}$ cup mixed slivered almond
and pistachio nutmeats

Soak rice in $\frac{1}{2}$ cup water for $2\frac{1}{2}$ hours. Boil milk until reduced by $\frac{1}{2}$. Add drained rice and simmer, stirring occasionally, until very tender. Add half-and-half, bring to boil, add sugar, and cook, stirring, until thick and creamy. Add raisins, remove from heat, and cool. Add saffron-milk mixture and rose essence or rose water. Garnish with almonds and pistachios and serve to 8–10.

*The Concourse, 5 World Trade Center*

Another, and in many ways the most engaging, of Joe Baum's extravaganzas, this subterranean dining and drinking complex more or less subliminally harks back to the old Washington Market—New York's version of Les Halles—which once stood on the same site. Although the décor is sleekly contemporary, wood-walled booths recall the original market stalls, handsome lamppost finials summon up remembrance of shop signs past, and displays of crated eggs and produce testify to the superiority of ingredients hand-picked at the source of supply. Generosity is the watchword here, with substantial—and very good—hors d'oeuvres served without charge at dinner, and with all dishes heroically proportioned. The food is luminously fresh, stunningly presented, and prepared with real flair. In a final burst of hospitality, dinner guests are not only sent home with fresh double-yolk eggs for their next morning's breakfast but, more often than not, with anything else that can be carried away.

*This simple but delicious meal is ideally suited to alfresco dining. To duplicate the authentic Market Bar experience, the proceedings should get under way with a round or two of the restaurant's extraordinary bourbon sours. Here's the recipe, verbatim and straight from the horse's mouth:*

## MARKET BAR BOURBON SOUR

| | |
|---|---|
| 1½ tsp. honey | 1½ cups ice cubes |
| 1 oz. fresh lemon juice | ¼″ slice of orange |
| 2 oz. 100 proof bourbon | |

Stir honey, lemon juice, and bourbon together in a cocktail shaker until honey dissolves. Add ice, and shake like crazy. Pour into large rocks glass and garnish with ¼″ slice of orange. Cheers!

## CHARCOAL BROILED CALF'S LIVER

*Almost to a man, New York restaurateurs, regardless of their ethnic or religious orientation, agree that young kosher calf's liver has no equal. It is used exclusively at the Market Bar, and, if possible, should be used for this dish.*

| | |
|---|---|
| 1 2″-thick slice of center-cut calf's liver | kosher salt |
| | freshly ground black pepper |
| 1 cup olive oil | |

While a good hot fire builds up in the barbecue, remove membrane and as many veins as possible from liver. When fire is ready, oil barbecue grid thoroughly, repeating the process several times, if necessary, to prevent liver from sticking to the metal. Rub oil all over liver, sprinkle with salt and pepper, then sprinkle on more oil. Place liver on grid and move with spatula to make sure it doesn't stick. Position so that thickest part of liver is centered over fire. After 2 minutes, rotate liver 90 degrees. After 2 more minutes, turn liver over and broil 2 minutes. Rotate as before and broil 2 minutes longer. Slice and serve with Onion Crisps and Potatoes Fried in Their Jackets (recipes below). Serves 4.

## MARKET BAR ONION CRISPS

2 large onions, peeled          deep fat for frying
1 cup flour

### Batter

12 oz. light beer          1 tbsp. salt
1 cup sifted flour          1 tbsp. paprika

Cut onions into eighths, then halve each wedge. Drop onions into a large pot of boiling water and drain immediately into a colander. Tumble onion pieces in 1 cup flour, coating them liberally. Whisk together batter ingredients until frothy while frying oil heats to 350°F. Dip floured onion pieces in batter, allowing them to cling together in small clusters, and drop a few handfuls at a time into hot fat. Fry until puffed and golden brown. Remove with a skimmer, drain on paper towels, and repeat process until all onions are fried. Serve sprinkled with kosher salt, with malt vinegar on the side.

# POTATOES FRIED IN THEIR JACKETS

Small red Bliss potatoes in any      Deep fat for frying
    desired quantity

Quarter unpeeled potatoes and parboil in water for 20 minutes, or until almost done but still firm, and drain. Fry in oil at 350°F. until golden brown and crusty, about 7 minutes. Drain and salt to taste.

# FROZEN CHOCOLATE SOUFFLÉ WITH BURNT ALMOND SAUCE

8 oz. semisweet chocolate      ¼ cup superfine sugar
2 cups heavy cream              1½ tbsp. Sabra liqueur
3 egg yolks

Melt chocolate in double boiler and set aside to cool slightly. Whip and refrigerate cream. Beat egg yolks and sugar together until mixture is pale and thick and sugar has dissolved. Mix liqueur with a small scoop of whipped cream and with the melted chocolate. Add several more scoops of cream, folding them in quickly. Fold in egg mixture, then fold entire mixture into remaining whipped cream. Spoon or pipe resultant mixture into individual paper cups (about 5½ oz.). Sprinkle tops with shaved semisweet chocolate and freeze 3 hours, or until firm. Before serving, soften soufflés in refrigerator for ½ hour. Tear away cups and serve in individual dishes with Burnt Almond Sauce (recipe below). Serves 6–8.

*Burnt Almond Sauce*

¼ cup blanched almonds        1 cup *Crème Anglaise**
¼ cup superfine sugar

Preheat oven to 400°F. Place almonds and sugar in blender or processor and run machine for 2 minutes. Place mixture on a baking sheet and cook in oven, stirring from time to time, until pale golden. Stir into *crème anglaise.* Dribble over frozen chocolate soufflés.

*Hyo-Tan Nippon*

*119 East 59th Street*

The *hyotan* is a shmoo-shaped gourd that was used in seventh-century Japan as a *sake* bottle and worn beneath their clothing by ladies of the court, who warmed the wine against their bodies. Hyo-Tan Nippon is an offshoot of Nobuyoshi Kuraoka's Nippon restaurant and may be even better than the more formal parent establishment. The premises are notable for their hand-crafted appointments, which include distinctively glazed tile flooring and a central dining counter constructed of rare, beautifully finished cypress and shaped like—what else?—a *hyotan*. The service, rendered by kimono-clad lovelies, couldn't be better, and if there's a more appealing introduction to the ingestion of raw fish than Chef Kiyomitsu Nakamura's *fugu-zukuri*, I haven't encountered it. In Japan, hundreds of macho types risk their lives each year during the early run of the fugu, or tiger blowfish, a delicacy that can be lethally toxic if not prepared with the utmost care. At Hyo-Tan, fluke is substituted for the treacherous fugu. Served in pink-white curls that could pass for rose petals, it is absolutely exquisite. Don't overlook the imported Spanish eel spawn in garlicky soy sauce, either, the toothsome *negimayaki* (an original creation of the chef's), or the altogether magnificent lobster *sashimi,* a single dish served in two courses, one raw and one cooked.

### BEEF NEGIMA-YAKI

*These simple, bite-sized beef rolls are served as a first course at the restaurant. At home, I've found them to be a very popular cocktail accompaniment. Either way, four per person will do.*

| 1 bunch scallions, cut in 4″ lengths | 8 oz. soy sauce |  |
|---|---|---|
| 10 oz. very lean prime rib beef, cut in 8 thin slices | 3 oz. *sake* 10 oz. *mirin* | } blended |

Bunch 2 scallion lengths together and lay them lengthwise on a slice of beef. Roll beef tightly around scallions and press overlap against roll to prevent unraveling. Repeat until meat and scallions are used up. Preheat broiler, arrange beef rolls on a pan or broiler rack, and broil 6–7 minutes, turning once. Cut rolls in half and arrange on rimmed serving dishes. Pour blended soy sauce and wines over them and serve with lightly sautéed, salted, and peppered bean sprouts.

*Note   For use as a cocktail accompaniment, I marinate the beef rolls in the sauce, cut them in half, and skewer them with flat wooden picks before broiling them. This is a variation unsanctioned by the restaurant, but one that produces more manageable finger food. Semi-freezing the meat will facilitate slicing it to the desired thinness.*

## LOBSTER ONIGARA-YAKI

| 4 tbsp. *sake* | 4   1–1½-lb. live lobsters |
|---|---|
| 8 tsp. soy sauce | ½ tsp. powdered *sansho* pepper |
| 4 tsp. *mirin* | 8 sprigs parsley or coriander |

Preheat broiler to 450–500°F. Blend liquids and set aside. Split lobsters lengthwise without separating halves and twist off claws. Lay lobsters on their backs and make 2 or 3 crosswise incisions in tails to prevent curling. Cut claws apart at main joints and crack. (This doesn't quite do justice to Nobuyoshi Kuraoka's rich prose, which, in the original, reads, "Hit with back of knife and crash.") Flatten lobsters, brush with blended sauce, and broil (with claws) 15–20 minutes, depending on size, brushing them once more with sauce when half done. Arrange lobsters and claws on serving platters, pour remaining sauce over lobsters, and sprinkle bodies with *sansho* pepper. Garnish with parsley/coriander and serve to 4.

# BEEF SALAD

10 oz. shredded lettuce
10 oz. shredded carrot
10 oz. shredded green pepper
10 oz. thinly sliced onion
4 tsp. sesame oil
1¼ lb. prime rib of beef

4 tsp. vinegar
4 tsp. soy sauce
8 tsp. salad oil
⅓ tsp. garlic powder
⅓ tsp. white pepper
4 tsp. *sake*
1½ tsp. sesame seed

} blended

Toss vegetables with sesame oil and arrange in 4 serving bowls. Slice beef thinly to produce 16 slices. In a skillet, cook sliced beef to taste in blended sauce. Drain off and reserve sauce. Cover vegetables with 4 slices beef per serving and pour reserved sauce over salads. Sprinkle with sesame seed and garnish, if desired, with either chopped parsley or coriander. Serves 4.

# FONDA LOS MILAGROS

*70 East 55th Street*

Perhaps the most authentic of the city's Mexican restaurants, the "Inn of the Miracles" was opened in 1973 by Rafael ("Ralph") Gonzalez, a burly, affable native of the west-central state of Jalisco, who considered the mere launching of his venture improbable enough to justify its name. I'd hesitate to describe the cuisine as miraculous, but it is thoroughly gratifying, and the atmosphere—roughly plastered walls hung with paintings that range from innocuous to atrocious, alternately tiled and carpeted floors, comfortable captain's chairs, and a handsome fireplace that I've never seen in operation—is pleasing. Chef Manuel Olivan's *mole poblano* is excellent, and his *flautas de carne,* which properly are eaten with the fingers, couldn't be tastier.

## CHORIQUESO

A *simple but tasty appetizer similar to* nachos.

4 *chorizo* sausages, finely chopped
1 tbsp. water
3 wheat tortillas, about 7" in diameter

3 slices Muenster cheese, $\frac{1}{8}$" thick
2 pickled *jalapeño* peppers, cut in $\frac{1}{4}$" rounds

In a small skillet, lightly fry chopped sausages with water, using no grease. Drain and arrange meat on tortillas. Top each tortilla with a slice of cheese and broil until cheese melts. Cut each tortilla into 6 wedges and top each wedge with a slice of pepper. Serves 4.

## GUACHINANGO PUERTO BALLARTA

3 whole 1¼-lb. red snappers, cleaned
salt and pepper to taste
juice of 3 lemons
1 cup corn oil
6 garlic cloves
4 medium onions, sliced

5 cups water
2 pinches cumin
2 pinches orégano
4 tbsp. white vinegar
8 peppercorns
6 oz. white wine
5 bay leaves

Wash and dry fish and, with a sharp knife, slit each lengthwise on both sides, from just behind the gill almost to the base of the tail. (The incision should penetrate almost to the bone.) Season fish with salt and pepper, pour lemon juice over them, and let stand $\frac{1}{2}$ hour. Brown fish on both sides in $\frac{1}{2}$ the oil and set them aside. In the same oil, brown the garlic and reserve. Sauté onions in the same oil until transparent, then add the water to the pan. In a blender, mix reserved garlic, cumin, orégano, vinegar, peppercorns, and remaining $\frac{1}{2}$ cup oil until all solids disintegrate, then add to onions. Place fish in a pan and cover them with the sauce. Add wine, bay leaves, and salt and pepper to taste. Cover pan and cook 8 minutes over medium heat. Serve hot or cold with boiled potatoes. Serves 6.

*If you prefer chicken to fish, try . . .*

### POLLO ALMENDRADO

| | |
|---|---|
| 2 2$\frac{1}{4}$-lb. chickens | 3 oz. dry Sherry |
| 1 lb. fresh tomatoes | 1 medium onion, chopped |
| 3 oz. sliced blanched almonds | 4 garlic cloves, minced |
| 5 oz. lard | 1 qt. Chicken Broth* |
| 3 tbsp. flour | 1 pt. sour cream |
| salt and pepper to taste | 1 tbsp. chopped parsley |

Cut chickens into serving pieces. Broil and peel tomatoes. In a large heavy pot, brown almonds lightly in lard, remove them from fat, and reserve. Combine flour, salt, and pepper in a large paper bag. Add chicken pieces to bag and shake well. To the same pot used previously, add chicken and brown on all sides. Add wine, onion, and garlic and simmer gently. Meanwhile, in a blender, mix chicken broth, tomatoes, sour cream, almonds, and salt and pepper to taste until a smooth consistency is reached. Add this sauce to the pot, cover, and simmer gently 15 minutes, or until chicken is tender. Strain sauce, arrange chicken on a deep serving dish, and cover with sauce. Garnish with parsley sprigs and a few slivers of toasted almonds and serve immediately to 6.

# The Dardanelles

*86 University Place*

New York has its share of Middle Eastern restaurants, but few as good as Dardanelles, which, after some twenty years of operation, is something of a Greenwich Village institution. It's a roomy, comfortable sort of place, with low ceilings, well-spaced tables, and mellow golden lighting that suggests sunset over Istanbul, and you won't find a warmer welcome anywhere than the one accorded by Melik Ohanesian, the founder's genial son. The predominantly Armenian menu is more imaginative than most, and the cooking leaves nothing but more of the same to be desired.

## HARPOOT KEUFTA

*Stuffing meat balls with meat balls may seem an exercise in redundancy, but this dish—or close variants thereof—is celebrated throughout the Middle and Near East. This is the Armenian reading, as prepared by Chef Louise Dolbashian.*

### Step I: Filling

| | |
|---|---|
| 1½ lbs. ground fatty lamb | ½ tsp. black pepper |
| 2 large onions, chopped | 1 tbsp. allspice |
| 2 green peppers, chopped | 1 tsp. cinnamon |
| 2 tbsp. chopped parsley | 1 tbsp. chopped pine nuts |
| ¼ tsp. salt | (optional) |

Put meat in a large skillet, add 3 tbsp. water, and cook over medium heat, stirring frequently, for 15 minutes. Add onions, mixing thoroughly, and cook 5 minutes. Stir in green peppers, parsley, salt, and black pepper, mix well, and cook another 5 minutes. Blend in remaining ingredients and simmer over low heat until all non-fat liquids have evaporated. Cool and refrigerate in a covered bowl overnight. (Mixture can be prepared as long as 5 days in advance of use.)

### Step II: Outer Covering

| | |
|---|---|
| 1½ lbs. lean ground lamb (see note) | 1 cup very fine *bulgur* (cracked wheat) |
| 1¼ tbsp. salt | 1¼ cups cold water |
| pepper to taste | |

*Note   Lamb must be absolutely free of fat before it is ground.*

In a large bowl, mix meat, salt, pepper to taste, and $\frac{1}{2}$ the *bulgur,* adding water a little at a time, blending ingredients well and keeping the mixture quite moist. Dip hands in cold water to keep mixture from sticking to them and knead to a soft doughlike consistency, adding water as required and remaining *bulgur.* When dough is ready, form into walnut-size balls (keeping hands wet at all times). Indent meatballs deeply with thumb and work around inside wall with a finger to form a hollow ball. Stuff with refrigerated Filling (Step I), smooth outer layer over opening to seal, and smooth surface with wet fingers. (Chef Dolbashian: "The thinner the outer wall, the more successful your *keufta* will be.")

### Step III: Poaching

| | |
|---|---|
| 1$\frac{1}{2}$ qts Chicken Broth* or Beef Stock* | 1$\frac{1}{2}$ qts. water salt and pepper (see note) |

*Note* *Use very little salt, if any, since there is quite a lot in the outer walls of the* keufta.

In a pot, bring broth (or stock) and water to boil, seasoning very lightly. Drop in meatballs, a few at a time, and cook 5–8 minutes, until they rise to surface. Gently remove meatballs with a slotted spoon and set aside in a single layer. Repeat until all meatballs are poached and serve hot with broth or cold without broth.

*Note* *Portions will vary, depending on size of* keufta *and type of presentation (try them cold as hors d'oeuvres), but any surplus can be frozen and simmered unthawed in broth for 25 minutes when needed.*

### GATNABOUR

*Melik Ohanesian: "Armenian pastries appear in too many cookbooks. This rice pudding is very popular at the restaurant, and easy to make."*

¼ cup short-grain rice       ¼ cup sugar
1 qt. milk       1 tsp. vanilla extract (optional)
1 pinch salt       ground cinnamon

Place rice in a small deep dish, barely cover with lukewarm water, and let stand for 30 minutes. In a large saucepan, bring milk to boil and add contents of rice dish and salt. Stir well and simmer about 1 hour, or until rice is tender, stirring frequently. Add sugar and optional vanilla extract, stir well, and simmer 2 minutes longer. Remove from heat and allow to stand for about 5 minutes, then pour into individual dessert dishes. Cover with plastic wrap and chill well. Dust lightly with cinnamon before serving to 6.

*1 West 67th Street*

La Belle Epoque lives! A landmark since the years before the first World War, Café des Artistes closed briefly in 1975 but—to the immense relief of its habitués—was resurrected a few months later by the peripatetic George Lang, the noted *bec fin,* oenologist, author, raconteur, chef, calligrapher, violinist, and Hungarian, whose influence on restaurant design and management has been global in scope. Housed in one of three neighboring Beaux-Arts structures built as working digs for the city's more successful artists, the restaurant always has had an inimitable aura about it but was creaking noticeably before the Lang takeover. Today, it bubbles like Champagne—a bosky dell where Howard Chandler Christy's cotton-candy nymphs cavort winsomely amidst birch and alder, untrammelled by garments, untroubled by mosquitoes. As painters go, Christy was no great shakes. In Lang's vernal setting, however, his murals are delightful. So, for that matter, is just about everything about the restaurant, which retains the casual character of a neighborhood hangout while attracting knowledgeable diners from far and wide. The chef, André Guillou, is a Breton, but while the accent is French, the menu is an eclectic affair that reflects Lang's past tenure as resident genius of the Four Seasons.

## SNAILS WITH PROSCIUTTO

| | |
|---|---|
| 1 cup chopped onion | 6 doz. tinned snails, drained |
| 2 tbsp. butter | salt and pepper to taste |
| 1 tbsp. chopped garlic | chopped parsley for garnish |
| 5 thin slices prosciutto, cut in julienne strips | |

Cook onions in butter until soft but not brown. Add garlic and cook, stirring, 1 minute. Stir in prosciutto and then snails and cook briefly, stirring, just until flavors meld. Season to taste. Serve, sprinkled with parsley, with steamed rice and assorted fresh vegetables, cut in julienne strips and briefly steamed. Serves 6.

# SEAFOOD GAZPACHO 67th STREET STYLE

5 ripe tomatoes, peeled
1 pimiento
½ onion
3 garlic cloves, finely chopped
1 carrot
5 cups tomato juice
⅓ cup red-wine vinegar
salt and pepper to taste
white pepper to taste

Tabasco sauce to taste
2 tbsp. olive oil
4 oz. small shrimp, cooked and
  shelled
chopped cucumber ⎫
chopped scallions ⎬ for
chopped green     ⎬ garnish
  pepper          ⎪
chopped dill ⎭

Run vegetables (garnishes excepted) through meat grinder, blender, or processor to produce a rough-textured blend. Stir in tomato juice and vinegar. Season well, whip in olive oil, and chill. Add shrimp, adjust seasonings, and serve in cups or bowls with individual dishes of chopped vegetables on side. Serves 6 or more (any left over can be refrigerated for use as needed).

# GIN AND QUAIL CAFÉ DES ARTISTES

(based on a recipe by James Beard)

quail giblets, chopped
¼ lb. + 1 tbsp. butter
8 quail, split
flour for dredging
8–10 juniper berries, crushed
3½ oz. gin

2½ tbsp. sour cream
1⅓ tsp. lingonberries
salt and freshly ground black
  pepper
4 brioches (see note)

*Note  Brioches are available at any French bakery or may be made at home following directions in any standard French or bread cookbook.*

Sauté giblets in 1 tbsp. melted butter. Melt remaining butter in a large skillet. Meanwhile lightly dredge quail in flour. When butter is hot and bubbling, quickly brown quail on all sides. Add juniper berries and reduce heat. Cover and cook 5 minutes. Add gin, flame, and cook gently 5 minutes longer, basting birds with pan juices. Stir in sour cream and lingonberries, season to taste, and arrange quail on toasted slices of brioche. Top birds successively with any remaining sauce and sautéed giblets and serve to 4.


# HAZELNUT-MOCHA TORTE

$\frac{3}{4}$ cup hazelnuts
$\frac{1}{2}$ lb. unsweetened chocolate
$\frac{1}{2}$ lb. sweet butter
$\frac{1}{2}$ lb. sugar
6 egg whites
1 pinch salt

butter
flour
Mocha Filling (recipe below)
sweetened whipped cream
   (optional)

In a preheated oven, roast hazelnuts 10–15 minutes at 200°F. While they are still hot, peel nuts by rubbing them in a clean kitchen towel. In a processor, grind nuts to a fine floury texture. Increase oven heat to 375°F. Melt chocolate over boiling water and allow to cool. Whip $\frac{1}{2}$ lb. butter with sugar until foamy, then thoroughly beat in chocolate and hazelnut flour. Whip egg whites with salt until very stiff, then slowly and carefully fold into chocolate mixture. Butter a 12″ × 17″ baking pan well, sprinkle with flour, and pour in chocolate mixture. Bake 12–15 minutes. Cool and cut lengthwise into 3 equal sections. Spread Mocha Filling (recipe below) evenly over tops, stack torte in 3 layers, and spread remaining Mocha Filling over sides. Top with whipped cream, if desired, and serve to 8–10.

*Mocha Filling*

$\frac{1}{2}$ cup sugar
$\frac{1}{4}$ cup very strong espresso
   coffee
$\frac{1}{4}$ lb. semisweet chocolate,
   softened

$\frac{1}{3}$ lb. butter, softened
6 egg yolks

Cook sugar with coffee 3–4 minutes, until syrupy, and allow to cool. Blend in softened chocolate and butter. Add egg yolks one at a time, stirring constantly. Stir until mixture thickens and set aside to cool.

# Tandoor

*40 East 49th Street*

Thick carpeting, rich fabrics, sandalwood banquettes, hand-carved teak beams, pierced metal lamps, museum-quality Mogul paintings, fine Hindu reliefs, and rare brasses add up to one of the most distinguished settings in the city. The cuisine, for the most part, is north-Indian, which is to say, mildly spiced and suavely sauced. Chicken—either tandoor-roasted or stewed in one way or another—is the featured flesh, but the kitchen acquits itself admirably when lamb, beef, or fish is called for.

# ALOO BENGAN

*Try this savory vegetable dish as a first course at dinner or, by itself, as a light late supper.*

1 large potato, diced
2 tbsp. vegetable oil
1 medium onion, chopped
fresh coriander leaves to taste
peeled and minced fresh
  gingerroot to taste

turmeric to taste
Spanish paprika to taste
salt and pepper to taste
$\frac{1}{4}$ cup yogurt
$\frac{1}{2}$ cup heavy cream
1 medium eggplant, diced

In a large skillet, sauté potatoes in $\frac{1}{2}$ the oil until lightly browned. Remove potatoes from oil with a slotted spoon and set aside. Add onions to pan, and sauté until they take on color. Add coriander leaves and spices and cook 3–4 minutes, or until a pasty consistency is reached. Add yogurt and cream and cook 3–4 minutes longer. Meanwhile fry eggplant in remaining oil in another skillet. When eggplant is semi-tender, add it and potatoes to first pan and cook 3–5 minutes, or until tender. Serve piping hot to 2–4.

## SHRIMP MASALA

2 lbs. medium shrimp
1 cup water
3 oz. vegetable oil
1 lb. onions, chopped
2 tomatoes, cut in chunks
1 dash paprika
$\frac{1}{4}$ tsp. powdered ginger

$\frac{1}{4}$ tsp. turmeric
$\frac{1}{4}$ tsp. powdered coriander
$\frac{1}{4}$ tsp. cumin powder
$\frac{1}{4}$ tsp. ground cinnamon
2 whole cloves
salt and pepper to taste
2 oz. heavy cream

Boil shrimp in water just until pink; refresh under cold running water. Shell and devein and set aside. Heat oil in a large skillet and sauté onions until pale yellow. Add tomatoes and simmer 3–4 minutes, stirring often. Stir in all spices and cook 3–4 minutes, then stir in cream and cook until mixture begins to turn brown. Add shrimp and cook, stirring often, 3–4 minutes longer. Remove cloves and serve over boiled rice to 4.

# Landmark Tavern
### *626 Eleventh Avenue*

Years ago, the predominantly Irish neighborhood was known as Hell's Kitchen, and woe to the stranger who strayed onto the turf of its indigenous brigands. The Hudson Dusters, Tenth Avenue Gang, and their plunderous ilk are gone now, as is almost everyone else, and the district today is about as heavily populated—and as accessible—as the more remote fastnesses of Baluchistan. Don't be put off by any of the foregoing; the

Landmark Tavern would be worth the trip even were the street gangs still around to extend their quaint brand of hospitality to passing wayfarers.

Joe Carly's saloon opened in 1867, prospered through several subsequent generations of Carlys, was sold a century after its opening, foundered not long thereafter, and finally was gutted by fire. At this juncture, a young Ohioan named Dick Harvey acquired what was left of the place and set about to restore it. He made a little gem of it. Reopened as the Landmark Tavern in 1973, the restaurant occupies three floors of a small brick corner building that has been furnished much as it must have been by a century of Carlys, with period cash registers, radios, · telephones, and the like, all in good working order. What's more, the food (mostly Anglo-Irish, with a few French and more or less stateless offerings thrown in for good measure) is first-rate, stylishly presented, courteously served, and, happily, quite inexpensive.

## CURRIED TURKEY AND PINEAPPLE SALAD

*What to do with Thanksgiving leftovers? Here's what.*

| | |
|---|---|
| 1 lb. fresh pineapple | lettuce |
| 1½ lbs. boned roast turkey | hard-boiled egg wedges |
| ¾ oz. curry powder | black olives |
| 1 oz. fine sugar | tomato wedges |
| 3 tbsp. mayonnaise | chopped parsley |
| salt and pepper to taste | |

(hard-boiled egg wedges, black olives, tomato wedges, chopped parsley — for garnish)

Cut pineapple and turkey into 1″ cubes. Blend curry powder, sugar, and mayonnaise with salt and pepper to taste and toss pineapple and turkey cubes in the mixture until well coated. Refrigerate. When chilled, serve on beds of lettuce, and garnish with eggs, olives, tomato wedges, and parsley. Serves 4–6.

# SHEPHERD'S PIE

*Soy sauce in shepherd's pie? Well, the chef is named Lai Ki Lau.*

1 lb. ground lamb
1½ lbs. ground beef
½ lb. ground pork
1½ oz. Kikkoman soy sauce
1 green pepper, finely chopped
½ large onion, finely chopped
1 stalk celery, finely chopped

garlic powder to taste
salt and pepper to taste
1 large cooked potato, mashed
½ cup lightly cooked peas
1 lightly steamed carrot,
　 diagonally sliced

Brown meats together, stirring frequently. Drain off excess grease and add soy sauce, chopped vegetables, and garlic powder to meats. Season to taste and simmer gently 45 minutes, stirring occasionally. Pack mixture into round ovenproof serving dish. Pipe rosettes of mashed potato around edge of pie and cover center with peas and carrot slices. Broil until potatoes are lightly browned and serve to 4.

What Dick Harvey did for an old Irish saloon with the Landmark Tavern he has done again for a venerable (1889) German eating house with Harvey's Chelsea Restaurant. Once more, he has painstakingly restored a derelict period piece with understanding, tact, and style, and the result is one of the most attractive little establishments in the city. The massive mirror-backed bar, with its beautifully carved oak sash work, bowfront display cases, brassbound grandfather's clock, and gilded antique cash registers, is particularly noteworthy—indeed, it would be hard to miss—and visitors of a certain age will find a downstairs anteroom, done up like a Victorian parlor and furnished with a crank-operated Victrola, almost painfully affecting. As at the Landmark Tavern, the food is simple, straightforward, and enormously gratifying, with fish and chips, German mixed stew, and roast prime ribs outstanding.

## CLAM AND MUSHROOM BISQUE

6 cups clam broth
½ lb. fresh mushrooms, sliced
8 clams, shucked and minced
6 tbsp. butter
6 tbsp. flour

1 cup light cream
2 cups milk
salt and pepper to taste
1 tsp. chopped parsley

Heat clam broth, add mushrooms and minced clams, and simmer gently 45 minutes. In a heavy saucepan or top of double boiler, combine butter and flour and cook gently 8–10 minutes, without browning. Gradually add hot clam broth mixture to resultant *roux,* stirring constantly, until slightly thick and silken smooth. Simmer gently 20 minutes. Meanwhile, heat cream and milk together (do not boil). Stir mixture into thickened broth, add salt and pepper to taste, and serve, sprinkled with parsley, to 6–8.

## CHICKEN BREAST WILLIAMSBURG

6 whole boneless chicken
   breasts, with skin
6 apples, peeled, cored, and
   roughly chopped

2 oz. bread crumbs
6 oz. walnuts, chopped
2 tbsp. fine sugar
4 tbsp. melted butter

Preheat oven to 350°F. Place chicken breasts between sheets of wax paper and pound as thin as possible with a flat mallet or the side of a heavy cleaver, taking care to leave skins intact. Combine apples, bread crumbs, and walnuts. Dissolve sugar in butter, blend with apple mixture, and divide into 6 portions. Lay chicken breasts out, skin side down, and place 1 portion of apple mixture in center of 1 side of each breast. Fold unfilled sides over to cover and arrange chicken packets in a buttered baking dish. Bake, uncovered, 30 minutes and serve to 6 with wild rice and Raisin Sauce (recipe below).

### Raisin Sauce

| | |
|---|---|
| 1 pt. Chicken Stock* | 4 tsp. brown sugar |
| 4 oz. seedless raisins | 1 tsp. vinegar |
| ½ cup orange juice | 6 tsp. butter |
| 1 tbsp. lemon juice | 6 tsp. flour |

Heat chicken stock, add all ingredients except butter and flour, and simmer slowly until raisins soften. Combine butter and flour to make a *roux* and cook 8–10 minutes over low heat, without browning. Gradually add stock mixture to *roux* and continue to cook, stirring constantly, until sauce is slightly thickened and smooth.

## SKIP DILLON'S MOCHA ALMOND CHEESECAKE

*The eponymous author of this hedonistic little number is a former waiter at the restaurant who still prepares its cheesecakes.*

| | |
|---|---|
| ½ cup graham cracker crumbs | ⅓ cup double-strength espresso |
| ½ cup crushed blanched almonds | coffee |
| 4 tsp. melted butter | 2 eggs |
| 1 cup sugar | 1 cup sour cream |
| 24 oz. cream cheese | 1½ oz. almond extract |
| 8 oz. semisweet chocolate | ¼ cup shaved almonds |

Blend cracker crumbs, crushed almonds, and melted butter and press onto the bottom of a 10″ spring-form pan, adding butter if needed to obtain a malleable consistency. Butter sides of pan and dust with any remaining crumbs. Refrigerate. In a 2-qt. bowl, cream sugar and cream cheese together until fluffy and set aside. Melt chocolate over hot (*not* boiling) water, then add coffee, beat until smooth, and set aside. Add eggs and sour cream to cream cheese mixture and beat well. Slowly add chocolate and blend well, scraping bottom and sides of bowl to incorporate all ingredients. (Batter must be free of lumps.) Stir in almond extract, remove baking pan from refrigerator, and fill with batter. Bake 1–1½ hours in a preheated 325°F. oven, or until center of cheesecake puffs. Turn off oven but do not remove cheesecake for another ½ hour. After removing cake from oven, allow it to cool 15 minutes before removing sides of pan. Garnish with shaved almonds and chill well before serving. Serves 10.

# Havana East

*1352 First Avenue*

A slice of old Habana as it was back in the days before Fidel Castro was taken seriously. The courtly Mario Aguero is your host, the murals—some depicting architectural landmarks and others devoted to somewhat enigmatic idylls—are the handiwork of Aguero's talented wife, Cillia Lazo, and a profusion of tropical greenery contrasts happily with a good deal of exposed brick to create a most agreeable setting. The service here is exceptional, and the same can be said for the banana chips, a complementary house offering to which any number of regular patrons are incurably addicted.

## STUFFED GREEN PEPPERS CUBAN STYLE

1 lb. large shrimp
1 medium onion, chopped
½ tsp. minced garlic
½ cup tomato sauce
2 tbsp. olive oil
1 tbsp. dry white wine
3 cups cooked rice

2 eggs, beaten
1 tsp. salt
⅛ tsp. black pepper
6 medium green peppers
4 tbsp. grated cheese
8 tbsp. bread crumbs

Cook shrimp in boiling water 2–3 minutes, until firm. Drain, reserving cooking liquid, and refresh under cold running water. Shell and devein shrimp and chop them into fine dice. In a pan, mix shrimp, onion, garlic, tomato sauce, olive oil, wine, and cooked rice and simmer over medium heat, stirring constantly, 5 minutes. Turn heat down low and stir in beaten eggs, salt, and pepper. When thoroughly blended, remove mixture from heat and set aside. Remove and set aside pepper tops. Seed peppers, fill them with shrimp mixture, and pour 1 tbsp. reserved cooking liquid into each. Top fillings successively with grated cheese and bread crumbs, replace pepper caps, and arrange peppers in a baking dish after covering its bottom with ¼" of the cooking liquid. Sprinkle peppers with any remaining cheese and bread crumbs and bake 45 minutes in a preheated 375° oven. Serves 6.

## ROPA VIEJA

*Originally, this savory stew was made not with beef, but the meat of tough old goats, which was hung on clotheslines to dry in the air. Hence the name* Ropa Vieja, *or* Old Clothes.

| | |
|---|---|
| 3 lbs. flank steak | salt to taste |
| 2 medium onions, sliced | 1 oz. canned Spanish pimientos |
| 1 large green pepper, sliced | 2 large potatoes, diced and |
| 4 garlic cloves, mashed | fried |
| ½ cup olive oil | 1 cup canned baby |
| 1½ cups tomato sauce | peas |
| ½ cup white wine | 1 can white asparagus |
| 6 bay leaves | |

1 cup canned baby peas / 1 can white asparagus } see note

*Note  In this rare instance, canned goods are preferable to fresh vegetables.*

Simmer flank steak in water to cover 2 hours, until tender. Reserve cooking broth and pull the meat apart to produce thin, uniform shreds. Place shredded meat in a deep flameproof casserole and set aside. Place onions, green pepper, and garlic in a large skillet, add olive oil, and sauté 10 minutes over low heat. Add tomato sauce, wine, and bay leaves and cook 10 minutes longer. Add contents of skillet to beef casserole, pour in 1½ cups of the reserved beef broth, salt to taste, and cook over moderate heat 35 minutes, stirring occasionally to prevent sticking. At the last moment add Spanish pimientos, cut in thin strips, and serve over rice with a garnish of fried diced potatoes and heated peas and asparagus. Serves 8.

# *Appendix*

**Aspic** Classically, this jelly is made by concentrating clarified stock or consummé and allowing it to chill and set. For a natural aspic, calf's feet, veal knuckle, pork rind, and similar gelatinous substances should be included in the stock. For a quicker aspic, add dissolved gelatin to ordinary consommé. To clarify stock, stir beaten egg whites (about 1 per half gallon) into cool, thoroughly degreased stock and bring to a very slow simmer, stirring just until simmer is reached. Disturbing the pot as little as possible, move it partially off burner and rotate it by quarter-turns every five minutes. Strain through a colander lined with several thicknesses of cheesecloth.

**Béchamel Sauce** In a saucepan melt 1 tbsp. butter, blend in $1\frac{1}{2}$ tbsp. flour, and cook over low heat, stirring, about 2 minutes, until frothy but uncolored. Remove from heat, add 1 cup milk, heated to boiling (or 1 cup boiling White Stock), and beat thoroughly with a wire whisk. Bring to boil over moderately high heat and boil, stirring, 1 minute longer.

**Beef Broth** This is nothing more complicated than unclarified Beef Stock.

355

*Beef Consommé*   Reduce Beef Stock and clarify as for Aspic.

*Beef Stock*   Precise recipes for stocks abound, but most represent a foolish consistency that is best ignored. To put it somewhat unappetizingly, stocks are garbage soups and come off best when made with whatever comes to hand—leftover scraps of cooked and raw meat, poultry carcasses, giblets, necks, and the like. The key is to use plenty of bones and a roughly equivalent amount of meat. For about 3 qts. stock, figure about the same amount of meat and bones, a couple each of carrots, celery stalks, leeks, and onions (the last stuck with a whole clove at either end), a few whole garlic cloves, a handful of parsley sprigs, 2 or 3 bay leaves, a large pinch of thyme, and water to cover with a bit to spare. Bring the whole business to simmer over moderate heat, skim the surface of accumulated scum, and simmer very gently, partially covered, for at least 5 hours, adding boiling water to cover as needed. Strain stock and reserve meats for other uses (the vegetables, by this time, will be too far gone for anything but the compost heap). For beef stock, a predominance of beef and beef bones should be used, but fowl and other meats (lamb and significant amounts of pork excepted) can—and in my opinion should—be thrown in. For a rich, dark stock, brown ingredients before simmering.

*Bordelaise Sauce*   Boil down 1 cup red wine by $\frac{2}{3}$ with 1 tbsp. chopped shallot, a pinch of thyme, $\frac{1}{2}$ bay leaf, and a pinch of salt. Add 1 cup Demiglace and reduce by $\frac{1}{3}$. Remove from heat, swirl in 2 tbsp. butter, and strain through a fine sieve. Add 2 oz. poached (or stockpot salvaged) beef marrow, finely diced, and 2 tbsp. chopped parsley.

*Brown Gravy*   This is simply the pan stock from roast meat or fowl, cleared of its excess fat and bound with flour. To make it, pour off and reserve all but $\frac{1}{4}$ cup pan stock, add $\frac{1}{4}$ cup flour, and cook gently until browned. Gradually add reserved stock, stirring until thickened. Cook 5 minutes and season to taste.

*Brown Sauce*   For 1 cup, melt $1\frac{1}{2}$ tbsp. butter, add 3 tbsp. flour, and stir over low heat until brown. Gradually add 1 cup

Brown Veal Stock (see note), stirring constantly until thickened, and season to taste with salt and pepper.

*Note  Brown Veal Stock, made by browning meat, bones, and vegetables in the oven before simmering them, is preferable to plain White Stock. See Beef Stock.*

**Chicken Broth**  Unclarified Chicken Stock.

**Chicken Consommé**  Reduce Chicken Stock and clarify as for Aspic.

**Chicken Stock**  Prepare as for Beef Stock, using fowl.

**Choron Sauce**  In a saucepan, combine 1 tbsp. finely chopped shallot, 1 tbsp. tarragon, 1 tbsp. chopped chervil, 1 sprig thyme, and a small piece of bay leaf. Add $\frac{1}{4}$ cup each vinegar and white wine, and salt and pepper to taste. Bring to boil and reduce by $\frac{2}{3}$. Cool mixture and add 2 egg yolks and a few drops of water. Beat constantly over very low heat until yolks begin to thicken, then gradually whisk in $\frac{1}{4}$ lb. butter. Add cayenne pepper to taste and a few drops of lemon juice if desired. Strain sauce and add tomato paste at a ratio of $1\frac{1}{2}$ tbsp. per cup of sauce.

**Clarified Butter**  Cut desired amount of butter in pieces and melt over moderate heat. Skim off surface foam and strain through several thicknesses of cheesecloth, leaving as much milky residue in pan as possible.

**Court Bouillon**  Gently simmer $\frac{1}{2}$ cup finely chopped onion in $\frac{3}{4}$ cup olive oil until soft but not brown. Add $\frac{3}{4}$ cup each white wine and water and the juice of 1 lemon. Add 1 unpeeled garlic clove, crushed, and a bouquet garni (classically, this should include parsley root, fresh thyme, fresh fennel, sweet pimientos, and coriander seeds, but dried thyme, fennel seed, and parsley leaf will do in a pinch). Season to taste with salt and pepper, boil 15 minutes, and strain.

**Crayfish Butter**  Over low heat, cook in butter the shells and trimmings of crayfish, a small carrot, diced as finely as possible, a small onion, finely diced, and half as much celery as onion, also finely diced. Season with salt, powdered thyme, and crumbled bay leaf and cook slowly until vegetables are quite tender. Remove crayfish detritus to a mortar, pound it as fine as possible, and then pound it some more. Blend with an equal amount of softened butter. Melt mixture over boiling water and strain through a cloth into a chilled bowl, wringing as much butter as possible into bowl. Refrigerate until set.

*Crème Anglaise*   For 2 cups, gradually add ½ cup sugar to 4 egg yolks, beating constantly until mixture forms a ribbon. In a very thin stream, add 1¾ cups boiling milk, beating vigorously. In a heavy-bottomed saucepan, cook mixture gently over moderate heat, stirring slowly but thoroughly, until thick enough to coat spoon lightly. Remove from heat and beat 2 minutes longer, adding 1 tsp. vanilla extract.

*Crème Fraîche*   Using 1 tsp. buttermilk for each cup of heavy cream needed, heat mixture until lukewarm and let stand at room temperature 10–12 hours, loosely covered. Stir well, cover tightly, and refrigerate until needed.

*Crème Pâtissière*   In a thick-bottomed pan, thoroughly blend ½ cup sifted flour, ¾ cup sugar, a mere hint of salt, 4 whole eggs, and 1 tbsp. butter. Add 2 cups boiling milk and 1 tsp. vanilla extract, stir thoroughly, and bring to boil, stirring constantly and cooking a few minutes longer. Pour mixture into a bowl and allow to cool, stirring occasionally.

*Crêpes*   For 1 dozen crêpes, beat vigorously or machine-blend 1 cup milk, 1 cup water, 4 eggs, and a pinch of salt until well incorporated. Successively add 2 cups sifted flour and 4 tbsp. melted butter, beating until a light creamlike consistency is reached. Refrigerate 2 hours or more and cook in a lightly greased 6"–7" pan, heated until just smoking. The trick here is to use no more batter than absolutely necessary, pouring it onto the center of the pan, which is immediately tilted this way and that to spread batter thinly over the bottom. Cook about 1 minute, or until holes left by air bubbles are firm around edges. Then jiggle pan to loosen crêpes, turn, and brown flip side 30 seconds. Crêpes can be made well in advance of need and refrigerated or even frozen.

*Dashi* To make this basic Japanese soup stock, bring 2½ qts. water to boil over high heat and drop in a 3″ × 3″ square of *kombu* (dried kelp). When water returns to boil, remove *kombu*. Stir in 1 cup flaked *katsuobushi* (dried bonito) and turn off heat. Let stock rest undisturbed until fish flakes sink to bottom. Skim off surface scum and strain stock through a fine sieve or double-thick cheesecloth. (*Kombu* and *katsuobushi* can be found in any Japanese food shop, of which there are probably dozens in Tuscumbia, Alabama; Turkey, Texas; and Woods Cross, Utah.)

*Demiglace* This, one of the basic or "mother" sauces of French cuisine, is a complex, time-consuming affair best made in large batches and frozen for use as needed. Start by making an Espagnole Sauce as follows:

Blend 4 qts. warmed Brown Veal Stock (note, page 357) with ¾ brown *roux* (made by slowly cooking together 3 parts Clarified Butter and 2 parts flour until brown, taking care not to burn flour) and bring to boil over high heat. Reduce heat and make a *mirepoix* of 1 medium carrot, 1 medium onion, and 4 slices lean bacon, all diced and sautéed together. Discard rendered bacon fat, deglaze pan with ½ cup white wine, and simmer 2–3 minutes with 1 sprig thyme and ½ bay leaf. Add *mirepoix* to thickened stock and cook gently 2½ hours, skimming often. Strain sauce into a large bowl through a fine sieve, squeezing vegetables to extract juices. Return sauce to pot, add 3½ cups stock, and cook slowly 2½ hours longer, skimming as before. Again strain sauce, stir until well cooled, and refrigerate overnight. Next day, add 1 qt. stock and 1 pt. tomato purée, stir well, and cook 1 hour over low heat, skimming often. Strain through cloth and remove all traces of surface grease. So much for the Espagnole Sauce and the better part of your labors.

Now, add 4 parts clarified brown stock to 2½ parts Espagnole Sauce, toss in any mushroom peelings that happen to be lying around (this, in the highly unlikely event that there are none, isn't essential), and cook down the whole business by ⅔. Remove from heat, stir in Madeira (1 part wine to 26 parts combined Espagnole Sauce and stock *before* reduction), and strain through cloth. *Voila!* And aren't you glad you asked?

***Fish Stock***   For about 1 qt., place in a large saucepan 4 lbs. fish heads (minus gills), bones, trimmings, and/or whatever shellfish debris you have on hand. Add a few parsley stems (sans leaves), 2 sliced onions, 2 tsp. lemon juice, $1\frac{3}{4}$ cups white wine, and a pinch of salt. Bring to simmer, skim, and simmer 25–30 minutes. Strain through cloth and refrigerate or freeze until needed.

***Ghee***   This is simply Clarified Butter.

***Glace de Viande***   According to an eighteenth-century French cookbook, the proper ingredients for this meat extract are a quarter of beef, a whole calf, 2 sheep, and 2 dozen geriatric fowl. Lacking a pot—or ark—large enough to accommodate this menagerie, reduce clarified meat stock by boiling it several times, skimming between boilings, until it takes on a syrup-like consistency thick enough to coat a spoon. *Glace de Viande* freezes well and can be cut with ease immediately after removal from the freezer.

***Lobster Butter***   Proceed as for Crayfish Butter, using lobster shells and trimmings.

***Mirepoix***   Cook 2 small carrots, $\frac{1}{2}$ cup onions, and $\frac{1}{4}$ cup celery, all diced extremely fine, in butter with salt, powdered thyme, and bay leaf, until very tender.

***Nantua Sauce***   Reduce by half $\frac{1}{2}$ cup béchamel sauce (milk or White Stock thickened with a *roux* of cooked flour and butter) to which $\frac{1}{2}$ cup cream and $\frac{1}{2}$ cup crayfish (or shrimp) cooking liquid have been added. Swirl in 3 tbsp. Crayfish Butter, a pinch of cayenne pepper, and a squirt of brandy, then strain.

***Pesto***   No two aficionados agree on the proper composition of this uncooked green sauce. I get excellent results by filling a food processor loosely with clean fresh basil leaves, adding about 2 oz. each of aged Parmesan and pecorino cheese, 2 garlic cloves, 2 oz. pine nuts, 1 cup good olive oil, and a suggestion of salt. The texture should be well on the unfinished side of a purée. *Pesto* will keep for months if stored, covered, in a cool place under $\frac{3}{4}''$ or so of olive oil, but, if so storing it, don't add cheese until sauce is to be used, to prevent discoloration.

*Port Aspic*   Prepared as is plain Aspic, with the addition of enough Port wine to imbue it with a rich coloration.

*Profiteroles*   Bring to boil $1\frac{1}{2}$ cups water, $4\frac{1}{2}$ oz. butter, and $1\frac{1}{2}$ tsp. salt. Remove from heat and add $1\frac{1}{2}$ cups flour, all at once. Cook over moderate heat, beating constantly, until mixture comes away from sides of pan. Remove from heat and, one by one, break 6 large eggs into mixture, beating well after each addition. Preheat oven to 425°F. and fill pastry bag with profiterole mixture. Squeeze mixture onto a baking sheet in small mounds about the size of quail eggs, brush tops lightly with water-diluted beaten egg, and bake 20 minutes, or until well puffed and brown. Remove from oven and pierce on 2 sides to let steam escape. Turn off heat and return to oven to dry, leaving door ajar. Remove after 10–15 minutes and cool on a well-ventilated rack.

*Puff Pastry*   On a pastry board, heap up $3\frac{3}{4}$ cups flour, make a well in the center, and put in $1\frac{1}{2}$ tsp. salt and $1\frac{1}{4}$ cups water. Mix and knead until smooth and elastic. Shape dough into a ball and set aside $\frac{1}{2}$ hour or more, covered with cloth. On a lightly floured surface, roll out dough into a level 8″ × 8″ square. Place 1 lb. butter in center and fold dough over to completely envelop butter. Refrigerate 10–20 minutes. On a lightly floured board, roll out dough in a rectangle about 8″ × 24″ and fold resultant sheet into thirds to make a 3-layer 8″ × 8″ square. Refrigerate 10–15 minutes and roll out at right angle from first rolling, again to form an 8″ × 24″ rectangle. Fold again into thirds, refrigerate and repeat process step-by-step 4 more times, giving dough 6 turns in all.

**Red Wine Sauce**  Prepare as for Bordelaise Sauce, omitting marrow and parsley.

**Veal Stock**  Prepare as for Beef Stock, using a preponderance of veal and veal bones. Knuckles, calf's foot, and the cartilaginous rib ends from the breast will produce a particularly rich, viscous stock.

**Velouté Sauce**  Add 5½ parts White Stock compatible to the main ingredient of the dish (i.e., don't gussy up beef with a fish-flavored sauce) to 1 part light blond *roux* (2 parts butter to 3 parts flour, cooked together). Bring just to boil, stirring, lower heat, and cook very slowly 1½ hours, skimming top as necessary. Strain through a fine sieve or cheesecloth and stir until cold.

**White Stock**  This is simply a stock—usually chicken or veal—made without first browning the meat, bones, and vegetables.

**White Wine Sauce**  Measure 1 part dry white wine and 2 parts Velouté Sauce. Boil wine until reduced sufficiently as not to overly dilute velouté sauce. Add reduced wine to sauce, simmer 2–3 minutes, and stir in a little butter just before serving.

# L'Addition

Heartfelt thanks are due, first of all, to my collaborators, the chefs and restaurateurs who not only contributed their recipes, but gave unstintingly of their time, knowledge, and patience, often suffering stupid questions with saintly forbearance and always offering warm encouragement where rebuffs would have been understandable. I am also deeply indebted to Bruce Lee, whose grace under pressure gave this project the impetus it needed. My thanks, too, to Donald Aspinwall Allan, who was instrumental in making a food writer of me, and to Jane Montant and Gail Zweigenthal, who patiently endured my on-the-job training. Acknowledgment is also due Derek Morgan, who provided valuable research material, Zanne E. Zakroff, who frequently ferreted out information I was too lazy to go after myself, and Barbara Poses Kafka, Mary McCoy, Douglas Gon, Richard Auleta, and Gene Schoor, who were kind enough to do some of my legwork for me. Above all, I am grateful to Nancy Kelly, for her invaluable counsel, her constant encouragement, her sensitive editing of the manuscript, and for sharing some five thousand meals without losing her figure.

J.J.

# Selected Bibliography

*The American Heritage Cookbook and Illustrated History of American Eating and Drinking,* by the American Heritage Editors and Helen McCully Associates; The American Heritage Publishing Company, New York, 1969.

*The Big Spenders,* by Lucius Beebe; Doubleday and Company, New York, 1966.

*Chinese Cuisine,* by Huang Su Huei, translated by Nina Simonds; Wei-Chuan Publishing Co., Taiwan.

*Cooks, Gluttons, and Gourmets,* by Betty Wason; Doubleday and Company, New York, 1962.

*Curtain Up at Sardi's,* by Vincent Sardi, Jr., and Helen Bryson; Random House, New York, 1957.

*Delmonico's: A Century of Splendor,* by Lately Thomas; Houghton Mifflin Company, Boston, 1967.

*Dictionary of Gastronomy,* by André L. Simon and Robin Howe; McGraw-Hill Book Company, New York, 1970.

*The Escoffier Cook Book,* by A. Escoffier; Crown Publishers, New York, 1941.

*Feeding the Lions, An Algonquin Cookbook,* by Frank Case; The Greystone Press, New York, 1942.

*The Food Book,* by James Trager; Avon Books, New York, 1970.

*Food in History,* by Reay Tannahill; Stein and Day, New York, 1973.

*History of the City of New York,* by Mrs. Martha Lamb and Mrs. Burton Harrison; The A. S. Barnes Company, New York, 1877.

*The Improper Bohemians,* by Allen Churchill; E. P. Dutton & Company, New York, 1959.

*Incredible New York,* by Lloyd Morris; Random House, New York, 1951.

*Kettner's Book of the Table,* by E. S. Dallas; Centaur Press Ltd., London, 1968.

*Larousse Gastronomique;* Crown Publishers, New York, 1961.

*Lights and Shadows of New York Life* (facsimile edition), by James D. McCabe, Jr.; Farrar, Straus and Giroux, New York, 1970.

*Lüchow's German Cookbook,* by Jan Mitchell; Doubleday and Company, New York, 1952.

*New York: Not So Little and Not So Old,* by Sarah M. Lockwood; Doubleday, Page & Company, New York, 1926.

*Once Upon a City,* by Grace M. Mayer; The Macmillan Company, New York, 1958.

*On the Town in New York,* by Michael and Ariane Batterberry; Charles Scribner's Sons, New York, 1973.

*The Philosopher in the Kitchen (La Physiologie du goût),* by Jean-Anthelme Brillat-Savarin, translated by Anne Drayton; Penguin Books, Middlesex, England, 1970.

*The Plaza: Its Life and Times,* by Eve Brown; Meredith Press, New York, 1967.

*Recollections of an Old New Yorker,* by Frederick Van Wyck; Liveright, Inc., New York, 1932.

*Tales of a Wayward Inn,* by Frank Case; Frederick A. Stokes Co., New York, 1938.

"That Was New York," by Robert Shaplen; *The New Yorker,* Nov. 10 and Nov. 17, 1956.

*The Upper Crust,* by Allen Churchill; Prentice-Hall, Inc., Englewood Cliffs, N.J., 1970.

# *Index*